THE COMMON LAW LIBRARY

JACKSON & POWELL

ON

PROFESSIONAL NEGLIGENCE

g733a

LONDON
SWEET & MAXWELL
2005

Published in 2005 by
Sweet & Maxwell Limited of 100 Avenue Road,
London NW3 3PF
Computerset by
J&L Composition, Filey, North Yorkshire
Printed and bound in Great Britain by Athenaeum Press,
Gateshead

No natural forests were destroyed to make this product. Only farmed
timber was used and replanted.

A catalogue record for this book is available from the British Library

ISBN Main Work 0–421–82600–2

ISBN Supplement 0–421–861–606

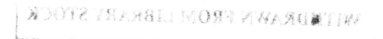

HOW TO USE THIS SUPPLEMENT

This is the Third Supplement to the Fifth Edition of
Jackson and Powell on Professional Negligence, and has been
compiled according to the structure of the main volume.

At the beginning of each chapter of this Supplement the mini
table of contents from the main volume has been included.
Where a heading in this table of contents has been marked with the
symbol ■, the material under the heading had been added to or
amended, and should be referred to. Where a heading is marked with
the symbol □, the material under that heading was added to or
amended in the First Supplement but has not been updated further in
this Supplement.

Within each chapter, updating information is referenced to the
relevant paragraph in the main volume.

TABLE OF CASES

TABLE OF STATUTES

TABLE OF STATUTORY INSTRUMENTS

CHAPTER 2

DUTIES AND OBLIGATIONS

3. TORTIOUS LIABILITY

(b) *Theoretical basis for the duty of care*

(v) *The exclusive approach*

2–042   The actual decision in *X (minors) v. Bedfordshire C.C.* [1995] 2 A.C. 633 in relation to the claims by children is no longer good law: see *D v. East Berkshire Community NHS Trust* [2003] EWCA Civ 1151; [2004] 2 W.L.R. 59 at [83]. This is a consequence of the enactment of the Human Rights Act 1998.

(vii) *The co-existence of difference approaches*

2–053   Add to NOTE 52: See also *Attorney-General v. Carter* [2003] 2 N.Z.L.R. 160 at [30] *per* Tipping J. (giving the judgment of the New Zealand Court of Appeal):

> "The outcome of a duty of care issue should not depend on what analytical method is employed. The ultimate enquiry is whether it is fair, just and reasonable to require the defendant to take reasonable care to avoid causing the plaintiff loss or damage of the kind for which compensation is being sought."

In *Kyrris v. Oldham* [2003] EWCA Civ 1506; [2004] 1 BCLC 305 the same result was reached whether by adopting the three-stage test of *Caparo Industries plc v. Dickman* [1990] 2 A.C. 605 or the assumption of responsibility approach of *Henderson v. Merrett Syndicates Ltd.* [1995] 2 A.C. 145.

(viii) *Commonwealth approaches to duty of care issues*

2–055   Add to NOTE 55: See also *Wellington District Law Society v. Price Waterhouse* [2002] 2 N.Z.L.R. 767 at [42] in the judgment of the Court of Appeal where the approach to novel claims in New Zealand was helpfully summarised. The Court quoted from the speech of Lord Pearson in *Dorset Yacht Co. Ltd v. Home Office* [1970] A.C. 1004 at 1052 and drew attention to the relevance of the kind of damage from which it was being alleged there was a duty to protect the claimant when considering whether a duty was owed. Another helpful overview of current position in New Zealand can be found in paragraphs [22]–[32] of the judgment of Tipping J. in *Attorney-General v. Carter* [2003] 2 N.Z.L.R. 160.

Add new paragraph **2–062A**:

2–062A   In *Cooper v. Hobart* (2001) 206 D.L.R. (4th) 193 the Supreme Court of Canada gave an authoritative re-statement of the *Anns* test as it is applied in Canada. The first stage involves two questions: (1) Was the harm that occurred the reasonably foreseeable consequence of the defendant's act? (2) Are there reasons, notwithstanding the proximity between the parties established in the first part of the test, that tort liability should not be recognised here? The first part focuses primarily on the specific relationship between the parties. At the second stage of the test wider policy considerations fall to be considered, such as "the effect of recognising a duty of care on other legal obligations, the legal system and society more generally". This is very similar in effect to the threefold test laid down by the House of Lords in *Smith v. Eric S. Bush* [1990] 1 A.C. 831 and *Caparo Industries plc v. Dickman* [1990] 2 A.C. 605 (see paragraphs 2–030—2–035). The Supreme Court of Canada explained that proximity was generally used to characterise the type of relationship in which a duty of care may arise and that such relationships were usually identified by categories. The factors needed to satisfy the requirement of proximity are, however, "diverse and depend on the circumstances of the case. One searches in vain for a single unifying characteristic". The present position in Canada is that a modified *Anns* test is applied, but with explicit recognition of the limited value of producing a clear definition of what will constitute proximity. The decision in *Cooper v. Hobart* is discussed by Neyers, "Distilling Duty: The Supreme Court of Canada Amends Anns", (2002) 118 L.Q.R. 221.

Add to NOTE 85: See Witting, "The Three-stage Test Abandoned in Australia—or Not", (2002) 118 L.Q.R. 214 for a discussion of recent Australian authority.　　**2–065**

Add new paragraph **2–065A**:

In *Sullivan v. Moody* [2001] HCA 59; (2001) 183 A.L.R. 404 the High Court of Australia held that medical practitioners and others investigating allegations of child abuse did not owe a duty of care in tort to the relations of the children. They also held that the threefold test did not apply in Australia. (See also *Graham Barclay Oysters Pty Ltd v. Ryan* [2002] HCA 54, *per* Kirby J. at [229]–[244]; Kirby J. remains an advocate of the *Caparo* threefold test.) It is now clear that "proximity" has ceased to be the test in Australia.　　**2–065A**

(ix) *Analysis*

Add to NOTE 3: For further criticisms of "proximity" as a source of practical guidance see *Sullivan v. Moody* [2001] HCA 59; (2001) 183 A.L.R. 403 at [48].　　**2–069**

Add new NOTE 11A at the end of (2): See *Hamilton v. Papakura District Council* [2002] UKPC 9; [2002] 3 N.Z.L.R. 308 at [37]–[39]. There is no single, fixed standard of reasonable foreseeability. It is linked to the damage which might be foreseen. The more serious the damage, the lesser the degree of likelihood of its occurrence that is needed: see *Jolley v. Sutton London Borough Council* [2000] 1 W.L.R. 1082, at 1091 *per* Lord Hoffmann and *Attorney-General of the British Virgin Islands v. Hartwell* [2004] UKPC 4; [2004] 1 W.L.R. 1273 at [21] per Lord Nicholls.　　**2–071**

Add to NOTE 16: However, care is needed when adopting this approach: the High Court of Australia disagreed with the result of Lord Steyn's poll: see *Catanach v. Melchior* [2003] HCA 38. See also *Graham Barclay Oysters Pty Ltd v. Ryan* [2002] HCA 54, *per* Gleeson C.J. at [6]: "At the centre of the law of negligence is the concept of reasonableness."

Add to NOTE 18: The comments of La Forrest J. were repeated by the Supreme Court of Canada in *Cooper v. Hobart* (2001) 206 D.L.R. (4th) 193　　**2–072** at [35]. In *Sullivan v. Moody* [2001] HCA 59; (2001) 183 A.L.R. 403 the High Court of Australia also expressed reservations about the "fair, just and reasonable" element of the three-stage test, saying at [49]:

> "The question as to what is fair, and just and reasonable is capable of being misunderstood as an invitation to formulate policy rather than to search for principle. The concept of policy, in this context, is often ill-defined. There are policies at work in the law which can be identified and applied to novel problems, but the law of tort develops by reference to principles, which must be capable of general application, not discretionary decision-making in individual cases."

The Court went on to quote from the speech of Lord Diplock in *Dorset Yacht Co. Ltd. v. Home Office* [1970] A.C. 1004.

Add to NOTE 20: See also *Attorney-General v. Carter* [2003] 2 N.Z.L.R. 160 at [26] *per* Tipping J., giving the judgment of the New Zealand Court of Appeal.

2–078   Add to NOTE 50: See also the comments of Tipping J. giving the judgment of New Zealand Court of Appeal in *Attorney-General v. Carter* [2003] 2 N.Z.L.R. 160 at [23] for a defence of the expression "deemed assumption of responsibility".

(c) Particular situations

(i) Public and local authorities: duty of care and statute

2–080   The actual decision in *X (minors) v. Bedforshire C.C.* [1995] 2 A.C. 633 in relation to the claims by children is no longer good law: see *D v. East Berkshire Community NHS Trust* [2003] EWCA Civ 1151; [2004] 2 W.L.R. 59 at [83]. This is a consequence of the enactment of the Human Rights Act 1998.

2–083   Add: This distinction may have arisen because different considerations apply to claims based on alleged common law duties said to arise solely from the existence of some broad public law duty and cases in which public authorities have chosen to enter into relationships or to accept responsibilities which give rise to a common law duty of care: see the speech of Lord Hoffmann in *Gorringe v. Calderdale M.B.C.* [2004] UKHL 15; [2004] 1 W.L.R. 1057, at [38].

2–084   Add to NOTE 72: However, in *Tomlinson v. Congleton Borough Council* [2003] UKHL 43; [2003] 3 W.L.R. 705 the House of Lords did address the question of liability under section 1(3) of the Occupiers' Liability Act 1984 by weighing up various policy considerations, including to a limited extent the cost of taking measures to reduce or eliminate a perceived risk (see paragraphs [34]–[50] of the speech of Lord Hoffmann, with whom Lords Nicholls, Hobhouse and, to an extent, Scott agreed).

Add to NOTE 73: See also *Graham Barclay Oysters Pty Ltd v. Ryan* [2002] HCA 54, *per* Gleeson C.J. at [6]:

"Citizens blame governments for many kinds of misfortune. When they do so, the kind of responsibility they attribute, expressly or by implication, may be different in quality from the kind of responsibility attributed to a citizen who is said to be under a legal liability to pay damages in compensation for injury. Subject to any insurance arrangements that may apply, people who sue governments are seeking compensation from public funds. They are claiming against a body politic or other entity whose primary responsibilities are to the public. And, in the case of an action in negligence against a government of the Commonwealth or a State or Territory, they are inviting the judicial arm of government to pass judgment upon the reasonableness of the conduct of the legislative or executive arms of government; conduct that may involve action or inaction on political grounds. Decisions as to raising revenue, and setting priorities in the allocation of public funds between competing claims on scarce resources, are essentially political. So are decisions about the extent of government regulation of private and commercial behaviour that is proper. At the centre of the law of negligence is the concept of reasonableness. When courts are invited to pass judgment on the reasonableness of governmental action or inaction, they may be confronted by issues that are inappropriate for judicial resolution, and that, in a representative democracy, are ordinarily decided through the political process. Especially is this so when criticism is addressed to legislative action or inaction. Many citizens may believe that, in various matters, there should be more extensive government regulation. Others may be of a different view, for any one of a number of reasons, perhaps including cost. Courts have long recognised the inappropriateness of judicial resolution of complaints about the reasonableness of governmental conduct where such complaints are political in nature."

Add new NOTE 79A: For an alternative approach see the judgment of McHugh J. in *Crimmins v. Stevedoring Industry Finance Committee* (1999) 200 C.L.R. 1, at [39]–[40].

Add to NOTE 97: The Supreme Court of Canada dismissed an appeal in **2–086** *Cooper v. Hobart* (2001) 206 D.L.R. (4th) 193. See also *Attorney-General v. Carter* [2003] 2 N.Z.L.R. 160 where the New Zealand Court of Appeal struck out claims against shipping regulators, following *Yuen Kun Yeu v. Attorney General of Hong Kong* [1988] A.C. 175, *Fleming v. Securities Commission* [1995] 2 N.Z.L.R. 514 and *Cooper v. Hobart* (2001) 206 D.L.R. (4th) 193.

(ii) *Directors and employees*

Add to NOTE 11: See also *Partco Group Ltd. v. Wragg* [2002] EWCA Civ **2–090** 594, [2002] 2 BCLC 323 (Leveson J. and Court of Appeal) (arguable case that company directors had assumed personal responsibility for statements made during friendly takeover) at 330e–333a (paragraphs [14]–[18] of the judgment of Leveson J.) and 359g–360c (paragraph [39] of the judgment of Potter L.J., with whom the other members of the Court of Appeal agreed).

Add to NOTE 13: For trenchant criticism of this aspect of the decision in **2–091** *Standard Chartered Bank v. Pakistan National Shipping Corp.* [2000] 1 Lloyd's Rep. 218, see the judgment of Toulson J. in *Noel v. Poland* [2002] 2 BCLC 645. The decision of the Court of Appeal has since been reversed on this point: *Standard Chartered Bank v. Pakistan Shipping Corpn (Nos 2 and 4)* [2002] UKHL 43; [2003] 1 A.C. 959.

(iv) *Immunity*

2–097   Add to NOTE 34: Advocates retain immunity in Scotland: *Wright v. Paton Farrell* [2003] P.N.L.R. 20 (T.G. Coutts Q.C., sitting as a temporary judge in the Outer House).

(e) *Liability to third parties*

2–114   Add: This approach to duty of care was applied by the Court of Appeal in *Dean v. Allin & Watts (a firm)* [2001] EWCA Civ 758; [2001] P.N.L.R. 39. The defendant solicitors had been retained to give effect to a loan transaction, it being intended by their borrower clients and by the lender (who was not their client) that the loan would be secured. They negligently failed to arrange the intended security and, when the borrowers were unable to repay the loan, were held to have owed a duty of care to the lender on the basis of assumption of responsibility. As with the will cases, by the time the problem came to light, it was too late to make good the earlier failure.

4. THE STANDARD OF SKILL AND CARE

(a) *The meaning of reasonable skill and care*

2–117   Add to NOTE 93: This decision was applied to solicitors by the Court of Appeal in *Patel v. Daybells (a firm)* [2001] EWCA Civ 1229; [2002] P.N.L.R. 6. It was held:

> "If a practice in the profession exposes clients or patients to a foreseeable and avoidable risk, the practice may not be capable of being defended on rational grounds, and in those circumstances the fact that it is commonly (or even universally) followed will not exclude liability for negligence."

5. FIDUCIARY OBLIGATIONS

(a) *The nature of fiduciary obligations*

2–127   Add to NOTE 28: See also *Worwood v. Leisure Park Services Ltd.* [2002] 1 BCLC 249 (Park J.).

2–128   Add at the end of the paragraph: Nor should fiduciary duties by superimposed on common law duties "simply to improve the nature or extent of the remedy": *Nornberg v. Wynrib* [1992] 2 S.C.R. 226, *per* Sopinka J. at 272, quoted with approval in *Pilmer v. Duke Group Ltd* [2001] 2 BCLC 773 at 733c–d.

2–129   Add to NOTE 34: In *Brandeis (Brokers) Ltd. v. Black* [2001] 2 All E.R. (Comm) 980 at 991e–g Toulson J. adopted the definition of fiduciary given by Professor Finn in *Commercial Aspects of Trust and Fiduciary Relations* (1992) at page 9: "A person will be a fiduciary in his relationships with another when and insofar as that other is entitled to expect that he will act in that other's interest or (as in a partnership) in their joint interests, to the exclusion of their several interests."

Add to NOTE 36: See also the judgment of Mummery LJ in *Peskin v.* **2–130** *Anderson* [2001] 1 BCLC 372 at 379 (paragraphs [32]–[34]).

Add to NOTE 38: See also *Brandeis (Brokers) Ltd v. Black* [2001] 2 All E.R. (Comm) 980 at [40] *per* Toulson J.: "Fiduciaries are not all required, like the victims of Procrustes, to lie on a bed of the same length." Toulson J. then referred to the speech of Lord Browne-Wilkinson in *Henderson v. Merrett Syndicates Ltd* [1995] 2 A.C. 145, at 206.

Add new NOTE 38A at the end of the first sentence: So, while usually a company director owes a fiduciary duty to the company to promote its interests, each case must be looked at on its facts. In *Plus Group Ltd. v. Pyye* [2002] EWCA Civ 370; [2002] 2 BCLC 201 the company had ceased to pay the director and had excluded him from its management. The Court of Appeal held that he was not in breach of fiduciary duty when he set up his own company in the same area of business. Brooke L.J., with whom Jonathan Parker J. agreed, said at [75]:

"the facts and circumstances of each case must be carefully examined to see whether a fiduciary relationship exists in relation to the matter of which complaint is made".

Add to NOTE 46: In *Longstaff v. Birtles* [2001] Lloyd's Rep. P.N. 826 the **2–131** Court of Appeal held that the fiduciary obligations of a solicitor retained by a client on a proposed purchase of a hotel business extended to a proposed investment by the client in a different hotel business owned by a partnership of which the solicitor was a partner. This decision is at best borderline. The solicitor's retainer was to act on the proposed purchase and not, it would seem, a more general retainer to advise as to how the client should invest in the hotel business.

Add to NOTE 49: This passage from the judgment of Mason J. has been fol- **2–132** lowed at first instance in the English courts: see *Global Container Lines Ltd. v. Bonyard Shipping Co.* [1998] 1 Lloyd's Rep. 528 (Rix J.) and *Land Rover Group Ltd. v. UPF (UK) Ltd. (in administrative receivership)* [2003] 2 BCLC 232 (HH Judge Norris Q.C., sitting as a judge of the High Court). In the same way a fiduciary duty cannot modify the terms of a contract, it cannot alter the operation of a statute. Parliament, not equity is sovereign: see *Tito v. Waddell (No.2)* [1977] Ch. 106, at 139, followed in *Cubillo v. Commonwealth of Australia* [2001] FCA 1213; (2001) 183 A.L.R. 249, at [465].

(b) *Dealing with the principal*

Add: In all such cases, liability of the fiduciary does not depend upon **2–134** whether the fiduciary was actually acting in bad faith or not (as required, for example, to establish a claim for breach of fiduciary duty against a solicitor who is acting for both borrower and lender) see *Bristol & West Building Society v. Mothew* [1998] Ch. 1 at 18D–E *per* Millett L.J. and *Johnson v. (1)*

EBS Pensioner Trustees Ltd. (2) O'Shea [2002] Lloyd's Rep. P.N. 308, at paragraphs 37–39 of the judgment of Mummery L.J., with whom the other members of the Court of Appeal agreed.

2–137   Add to NOTE 67: The fiduciary is required to disclose all material information (which does not involve considering the actual causative effect of the non-disclosure): see *Johnson v. (1) EBS Pensioner Trustees Ltd (2) O'Shea* [2002] Lloyd's Rep. P.N. 308: see paragraph 55 of the judgment of Mummery L.J.

2–140   Add to NOTE 80: As Lord Upjohn, the same judge expressed similar views in his speech in *Boardman v. Phipps* [1967] 2 A.C. 721, at 756:

> "The phrase 'possibly may conflict' requires consideration. In my view it means that the reasonable man looking at the relevant facts and circumstances of the particular case would think that there was a real sensible possibility of conflict; not that you could imagine some situation arising which might, in some conceivable possibility in events not comtemplated as real sensible possibilities by any reasonable person, result in conflict."

See also *Bhullar v. Bhullar* [2003] EWCA Civ 241; [2003] 2 BCLC 241 at [30] *per* Jonathan Parker L.J.

Add new NOTE 80A: See also *Pilmer v. Duke Group Ltd* [2001] 2 BCLC 773 at [78], where the statement by Mason J. in *Hospital Products Ltd v. United States Surgical Corp.* (1984) 156 C.L.R. 41 that the fiduciary is precluded from pursing a gain in circumstances in which there is "a conflict or a real or substantial possibility of a conflict" between the interests of the fiduciary and the person to whom the duty is owed was cited by McHugh, Gummow, Hayne and Callinan JJ. with approval. Mason J. (and McHugh, Gummow, Hayne and Callinan JJ.) went on to quote with approval a statement by Judge Learned Hand in *Phelan v. Middle States Oil Corp.* (1955) 220 F (2d) 593 at 602–603:

> "[If] the doctrine be inexorably applied and without regard to the particular circumstances of the situation, every transaction will be condemned once it is shown that the fiduciary had such a hope or expectation, however unlikely to be realized it may be, and however trifling an inducement it will be, if it is realized . . . We have found no decisions that have applied this rule inflexibly to every occasion in which the fiduciary has been shown to have had a personal interest that might in fact have conflicted with his loyalty. On the contrary in a number of situations courts have held that the rule does not apply, not only when the putative interest, though in itself strong enough to be an inducement, was too remote, but also when, though not too remote, it was too feeble an inducement in determining motive."

(c) *Unauthorised profits and diversion of opportunities*

2–141   Add: The principle was recently summarised by the Court of Appeal in *DEG-Deutsche Investitions and Entwicklungsgesellschaft mbH v. Koshy (No 3)* [2003] EWCA Civ 1048 at [44]–[45] by reference to the judgment of Rich, Dixon and Evatt JJ. in the High Court of Australia in *Furs Ltd. v. Tomkies* (1936) 54 C.L.R. 583 at 592 and the decision of the House of Lords in *Regal (Hastings) Ltd v. Gulliver* [1967] A.C. 134.

Add to NOTE 84: A fiduciary who resigns from the position which gave rise to his fiduciary obligations and then exploits for himself an opportunity of which he learnt from his fiduciary position will be liable to account for the profits he makes, as will a company which he forms in order to exploit the opportunity: *CMS Dolphin Ltd. v. Simonet* [2001] 2 BCLC 704 (Lawrence Collins J.). In any particular case, what matters is whether the opportunity was one which the fiduciary was under a duty to refer to the beneficiary. If he was so that there was a real conflict of interest, then he will be accountable: *Bhullar v. Bhullar* [2003] EWCA Civ 241; [2003] 2 BCLC 241.

(d) *Undue Influence*

(i) *The classes of undue influence*

Add: ***Royal Bank of Scotland plc v. Etridge (No.2)***: The existing para- **2–142** graphs 2–142 and 2–146 set out the law as it was generally understood before the decision of the House of Lords in *Royal Bank of Scotland plc v. Etridge (No.2)* [2001] UKHL 44; [2002] 2 A.C. 773 (noted in (2002) 118 L.Q.R. 337; applied by the Privy Council in *R. v. Her Majesty's Attorney-General for England and Wales* [2003] UKPC 22). While the decision was mainly concerned with the relationship between banks and other lenders and guarantor spouses, it is important for understanding undue influence more generally. The paragraphs now need to be restated as set out in paragraphs 2–143 to 2–146 below.

Add: **Undue Influence:** Gifts, deeds and other transactions may be set aside **2–143** if procured by undue influence of one person over another. Equity provides relief for undue influence where the common law principle of duress might not. It extends to more subtle, less overt pressure or improper persuasion. In every case the question is whether the intention to enter the transaction or to confer the benefit was produced by the improper exercise of another's influence. No more precise definition of the circumstances in which equity will intervene is possible, because of the varied circumstances in which influence may arise and be improperly exercised: see the speech of Lord Nicholls in *Royal Bank of Scotland plc v. Etridge (No.2)* [2001] UKHL 44; [2002] 2 A.C. 773, at [7].

Add: **Presumptions and classes:** Once it is appreciated that undue influence **2–144** must be proved in each case, the true significance of the "presumptions" and "classes" referred to in the earlier cases can be seen. So, where the person seeking relief establishes both that he was in a relationship of trust and confidence with another, such as to give the other influence over him, and that the transaction is not one readily explained—as would be, for example, a moderate Christmas present by a client to a solicitor—then the evidential burden falls on the other to show that the transaction was not produced by the improper or undue exercise of his influence. The person seeking relief has done all that is needed to establish his entitlement to relief. If the other party does not adduce evidence to show that the transaction was entered otherwise than under his undue influence it will be set aside: see *Royal Bank of Scotland plc v. Etridge (No.2)* [2001] UKHL 44; [2002] 2 A.C. 773, *per* Lord Nicholls at [13]–[20] and *per* Lord Scott at [151]–[161].

2–145 Add: Certain relationships are expected to have given one person influence over another. Examples are given in paragraph 2–144 of the existing text. If the party seeking to set aside a transaction or gift proves such a relationship then there is a further presumption that the other party was in a position to influence him. However, although this presumption is irrebuttable (*Royal Bank of Scotland plc v. Etridge (No.2)* [2001] UKHL 44; [2002] 2 A.C. 773, *per* Lord Nicholls at [18]), it remains open to the party alleged to have exercised his influence unduly to show that the transaction was in fact entered free from that presumed influence. So a solicitor who enters a transaction with a corporate client may find it relatively easy to show that the client was acting of its own free, informed will and so uphold the transaction (as in *Westlemetton (Vic) Pty Ltd v. Archer* [1982] V.R. 305). Where the relationship is not one which is presumed to give one party influence over another, the specific relationship will have to be proved if the evidential presumption is to be established. This is addressed in paragraph 2–145 of the original text. It is important to bear in mind that it is not just the relationship but also a transaction which, as Lord Nicholls said in *Royal Bank of Scotland plc v. Etridge (No.2)* [2001] UKHL 44; [2002] 2 A.C. 773 at [13] "cannot be accounted for by the ordinary motives of ordinary persons in that relationship" which must be proved. It is preferable not to use the expression "manifest disadvantage" (which came from the speech of Lord Scarman in *National Westminster Bank plc v. Morgan* [1985] A.C. 686, at 703–707). The relevant circumstances were better described (*Allcard v. Skinner* (1887) 36 Ch.D. 145) by Lindley L.J. in the context of gifts. He said at page 185:

> "But if the gift is so large as not to be reasonably accounted for on the ground of friendship, relationship, charity or some other ordinary motives on which ordinary men act, the burden is upon the donee to support the gift."

(ii) *Rebutting the presumption*

2–146 Add: **Rebutting the presumption:** Once it is appreciated that the presumption is evidential, it is clear that there is no defined way in which it can be rebutted. It is for the person seeking to uphold a transaction or gift to prove that it was not procured by the improper exercise of his influence. The evidence needed to rebut the presumption will depend on how strongly the presumption has been established. In *Powell v. Powell* [1900] 1 Ch. 243 the presumption was extremely strong: it was proved that strong moral pressure had been applied on a girl only just of age by her stepmother. In such an extreme case, proof of independent advice might not be enough. However, in a more usual case, proof of independent advice will rebut the presumption. In the words of Fletcher Moulton L.J. in *Re Coomber, Coomber v. Coomber* [1911] 1 Ch. 723, at 730:

> "All that is necessary is that some independent person, free from any taint of the relationship, or of the consideration of interest which would affect the act, should put clearly before the person what are the nature and the consequences of the act. It is for adult persons of competent mind to decide whether they will do an act, and I do not think that independent and competent advice means independent and competent approval. It simply means that the advice shall be removed entirely from

the suspected atmosphere; and that from the clear language of an independent mind, they should know what they are doing."

This passage was quoted with approval by Lord Nicholls in *Royal Bank of Scotland plc v. Etridge (No.2)* [2001] UKHL 44; [2002] 2 A.C. 773 at [60].

6. CONFIDENTIALITY

(c) *Elements of the cause of action*

Add to NOTE 50: See also *Australian Broadcasting Corporation v. Lenah*   **2–157**
Game Meats Pty Ltd [2001] HCA 63; (2001) 185 A.L.R. 1 at [53].

Add at the end of the paragraph:

"The obligation of confidentiality 'extends to matter which a reasonable person would understand to be intended to be secret, or to be available to a limited group to which that person does not belong'": *per* Gleeson C.J. in *Australian Broadcasting Corporation v. Lenah Game Meats Pty Ltd* [2001] HCA 63; (2001) 185 A.L.R. 1, at [36].

Add to NOTE 62: The earlier authorities on confidentiality and the press now   **2–161**
need to be read subject to Article 10 of the Convention for the Protection of Human Rights and Fundamental Freedoms, which requires interference with the freedom of the press to be justified: see *A v. B* [2002] EWCA Civ 337; [2003] Q.B. 195 and *Campbell v. MGN Ltd.* [2004] UKHL 22; [2004] 2 W.L.R. 1232.

Add to NOTE 65: More recent examples are helpfully collected in the judgment of Gray J. in *Jockey Club v. Buffham* [2002] EWHC 1866 (Q.B.); [2003] Q.B. 462 at paragraphs [46]–[51]. Having set out the authorities, Gray J. held that the public interest in horse racing justified use by the BBC of otherwise confidential information.

Add to NOTE 67: The recent decision of the Court of Appeal in *H (a healthcare worker) v. Associated Newspapers Limited* [2002] EWCA Civ 195, [2002] Lloyd's Rep. Med. 210 illustrates the fine balance that has to be struck between confidentiality (in particular the information imparted in confidence by a healthcare worker to his employer that he was HIV positive) and the public interest and freedom of the press. A solicitor who knows from confidential information obtained from his client that his client might lack mental capacity might be justified in making an application to the Court of Protection, but not disclosure of that information to another solicitor retained by the client on another matter: *Marsh v. Sofaer* [2003] EWHC 3334 (Ch); [2004] P.N.L.R. 24 (Morritt V.-C.).

(d) *The continuing duty to former clients*

Add to NOTE 78: In *Longstaff v. Birtles* [2001] Lloyd's Rep. P.N. 826,   **2–164**
Mummery L.J., with whom the other members of the Court of Appeal agreed, said that a solicitor's fiduciary duty to tell a client to obtain

independent advice before dealing with him could extend beyond the termination of the retainer if the trust and confidence engendered by that retainer remained. While this may be the case in relation to the specific subject matter of the retainer and while questions of undue influence might arise in relation to a transaction entered after the termination of the retainer, as a wider statement of the law this must be doubted. In particular the authorities cited above were not cited in *Longstaff*.

2–166   Add to NOTE 81: For a less favourable view of Chinese walls see the judgment of Bryson J. in *D & J Constructions Pty Ltd v. Head* (1987) 9 N.S.W.L.R. 118, at 122–123 quoted by Clarke L.J. in *Koch Shipping Inc. v. Richards Butler (a firm)* [2002] EWCA Civ 1280; [2003] P.N.L.R. 11 at [31].

2–167   Add to the end of the paragraph: The number of those who are in possession of the confidential information may also be relevant. The risk of disclosure is very different if only one, experienced professional is involved, rather than members of a large team. In the former case, personal undertakings may suffice to render the risk of disclosure fanciful. The recent decision of the Court of Appeal in *Koch Shipping Inc. v. Richards Butler (a firm)* [2002] EWCA Civ 1280; [2003] P.N.L.R. 11 illustrates this. Holding that there was no real risk of disclosure Tuckey L.J. said at paragraph [52]:

> "In these days of professional and client mobility it is of course important that client confidentiality should be preserved. Each case must depend upon its own facts. But I think there is a danger inherent in the intensity of the adversarial process of courts being persuaded that a risk exists when, if one stands back a little, that risk is no more than fanciful or theoretical. I advocate a robust view with this in mind, so as to ensure that the line is sensibly drawn."

For a recent Canadian decision on similar facts see *Freyn v. Bank of Montreal* (2002) 224 D.L.R. (4th) 337 (New Brunswick Court of Appeal).

Add new NOTE 83: See also *Ball v. Druces & Attlee (a firm)* [2002] P.N.L.R. 23, where Burton J. granted an interim injunction restraining a firm of solicitors from acting for a defendant when they had earlier acted for the claimant and another individual in relation to the subject matter of the current action.

CHAPTER 3

REMEDIES

1. DAMAGES

3–001 Add to NOTE 2: In New Zealand exemplary damages may be awarded in exceptional cases of negligence: see *A v. Bottrill* [2002] UKPC 44; [2003] 1 A.C. 449. *Farley v. Skinner* is now reported at [2002] 2 A.C. 732.

3–002 Add to NOTE 8a: *Aneco Reinsurance Underwriting Ltd v. Johnson Higgins* is now reported at [2002] 1 Lloyd's Rep. 157. The distinction between "information" and "advice" is better seen as a way of expressing two related questions, namely (i) what is the scope of the duty and (ii) what is the prospective harm, or kind of harm, from which the person to whom the duty is owed falls to be protected? (see *Equitable Life Assurance Company v. Ernst & Young* [2003] EWCA Civ 1114, at [105]). The advice/information distinction is helpful in some cases, but in others the professional's duties will be more complex and a wider inquiry will be appropriate. In determining the scope of a professional's duty, the acts of his client had the professional acted with appropriate skill and care should be considered. For example, if the client would have sought further information with a view to adopting a particular course of action, then that decision and loss resulting from failure to take it, might fall within the scope of the original duty: *Equitable Life Assurance Company v. Ernst & Young* [2003] EWCA Civ 1114 at [129].

3–005   Add to NOTE 19: However, this aspect of the decision in *Smith v. National Health Service Litigation Authority* [2001] Lloyd's Rep. Med. 90 has been held by Burnton J. to have been reached *per incuriam*: see *Hardaker v. Newcastle Health Authority and Chief Constable of Northumbria* [2001] Lloyd's Rep. Med. 512.

2. LOSS OF REMUNERATION

3–007   Add to NOTE 25: The same also applies in a case of non-performance as in *Adrian Alan Ltd. v. Fuglers* [2002] EWCA Civ 1655; [2003] P.N.L.R. 14.

3. EQUITABLE REMEDIES

(a) *Rescission*

3–010   Add to NOTE 37: See also *Dunbar Bank plc v. Nadeem* [1998] 3 All E.R. 876 at 884H–J *per* Millett L.J., applied in *Johnson v. (1) EBS Pensioner Trustees Ltd (2) O'Shea* [2002] Lloyd's Rep. P.N. 308. In the latter case it was held that rescission is a discretionary remedy. While this is true, it is the usual remedy unless it is not possible to undo the transaction for both parties.

(b) *Equitable compensation*

(i) *Compensation for loss caused by breach of fiduciary obligation*

3–011   Add: Equitable compensation may also be awarded when rescission of a transaction entered after a fiduciary has failed to make proper disclosure is no longer possible: *Meara v. Fox* [2002] P.N.L.R. 93, at paragraph 49 per Pomfrey J, citing *Moody v. Cox & Hatt* [1917] 2 Ch. 71. Equitable compensation is discussed by Congalen in *"Equitable Compensation for Breach of Fiduciary Dealing Rules"* (2003) 119 L.Q.R. 246.

3–013   Add to NOTE 49: See also *Johnson v. (1) EBS Pensioner Trustees Ltd. (2) O'Shea* [2002] Lloyd's Rep. P.N. 308, at paragraph 55 of the judgment of Mummery L.J. See also *DEG-Deutsche Investitions-und-Entwicklungsge-sellschaft mbH v. Koshy (No 3)* [2003] EWCA Civ 1048 at [144]–[147] where the Court of Appeal considered the dictum of Lord Thankerton in *Brick-enden v. London Loan & Savings Co* [1934] 3 D.L.R. 465, at 469 and explained that it applied to claims to rescind transactions entered into in breach of fiduciary duty, but not to claims for equitable compensation, where causation had to be established.

Add: The remedy is compensatory, not punitive, so that, as recently held by **3–014** the New South Wales Court of Appeal in *Harris v. Digital Pulse Pty Ltd.* [2003] N.S.W.C.A. 10 there is no power to make an exemplary award.

Add to Note 54: See also *Youyang Pty. Ltd. v. Minter Ellison Morris Fletcher* [2003] HCA 15 where the trustee's liability to repay in full moneys paid away in breach of trust was not reduced by subsequent events.

CHAPTER 4

CONTRIBUTION BETWEEN DEFENDANTS

3. LIABILITY OF THE PERSON CLAIMING CONTRIBUTION

(a) *Basis of liability*

Add: The decision of the Court of Appeal in *Dubai Aluminium Co. Ltd. v. Salaam* [2001] Q.B. 113 has been reversed by the House of Lords on the issue of vicarious liability: [2002] UKHL 48; [2002] 3 W.L.R. 1913. It was held that whether a partner was acting in the ordinary course of the business of his firm was "a question of law, based on primary facts, rather than a simple question of fact" (see paragraph [24] of the speech of Lord Nicholls with whom Lords Slynn, Hutton and Hobhouse agreed; Lord Millett considered that it was "a factual conclusion based on an assessment of the primary facts": see paragraph [112] of his speech; he then went on to conclude that the conclusion that the partner was so acting was "legally open to the trial judge had the case proceeded to trial": paragraph [131]).

4–005

Delete the second sentence after the quote from section 6(1) and replace with the following: However, it is not so widely drafted as to enable a claim to be made between defendants where the claimant has a claim against one for professional negligence and against the other for restitution in respect of the same matter: see *Royal Brompton Hospital National Health Service Trust v. Hammond* [2002] UKHL 14; [2002] 1 W.L.R. 1397 at [33] *per* Lord Steyn, with whom the other members of the House of Lords agreed, disapproving this aspect of the decision of the Court of Appeal in *Friends' Provident Life Office v. Hillier Parker May & Rowden* [1997] Q.B. 85. Lord Steyn accepted the criticisms made in *Goff & Jones, The Law of Restitution*, 5th ed., at page 396: a claim in restitution is not for "damage suffered" by the claimant, but in respect of the unjust enrich-ment of the defendant. It is not a claim for compensation and so does not fall within section 1(1). However, at [26] Lord Steyn also stated that the

4–006

1978 Act was intended to extend the reach of the contribution principle to a wider range of cases than before.

Add at the end of the paragraph: Obviously the person against contribution is claimed must be liable to the person to whom the person claiming contribution is or may be liable. So, where no claim would lie by an employer under a building contract against the building contractor because of the contractual provisions as to insurance, architects and engineers sued by the employer could not claim contribution from the building contractor: see the decision of the House of Lords in *Co-operative Retail Services Ltd. v. Taylor Young Partnership Ltd and others (Carillion Construction Ltd and another, Part 20 Defendants)* [2002] UKHL 17; [2002] 1 W.L.R. 1419 and the decision of the High Court of Australia in *Alexander v. Perpetual Trustees WA Ltd.* [2004] HCA 7.

Add to NOTE 14: See further *Hampton v. Minns* [2002] 1 W.L.R. 1, where Kevin Garnett Q.C., sitting as a deputy High Court judge, held that the Civil Liability (Contribution) Act 1978 did not apply to a claim in debt, including a claim against a guarantor of a debtor.

(b) Meaning of "the same damage"

4–008   Add: The decision of the Court of Appeal in *Royal Brompton Hospital National Health Service Trust v. Hammond* [2000] Lloyd's Rep. P.N. 643 has been upheld by the House of Lords, [2002] UKHL 14; [2002] 1 W.L.R. 1397. By the time the case was heard in the House of Lords the decision of the Alberta Court of Appeal in *Wallace v. Litwiniuk* (2001) 92 Alta.L.R. (3d) 249 had been reached on the facts used by Stuart-Smith L.J. in his example and with the result he had indicated. The House of Lords approved this decision. The decision of the House of Lords was followed by the Court of Appeal in Northern Ireland in *Dingles Building (NI) Ltd v. Brooks* [2003] P.N.L.R. 8. It was held that the damage which formed the subject of a claim by the claimant company for breach of warranty of authority against a sole trustee who purported to contract on behalf of his fellow trustees was not the same as that suffered by reason of any negligent failure of the claimant company's solicitors to advise that the other trustees be asked to sign the contract. The damage for which the solicitors might be liable was the loss of the chance to obtain those signatures, whereas the sole trustee was liable for the damage suffered by reason of his lack of authority.

4–009   Add to NOTE 22: *Eastgate Group Ltd. v. Lindsey Mordern Group Inc.* is now reported at [2002] 1 W.L.R. 642.

Add new paragraph **4–009A**:

4–009A   The test suggested in *Howkins & Harrison v. Tyler* [2001] Lloyd's Rep. P.N. 1 was considered by the House of Lords in *Royal Brompton Hospital National Health Service Trust v. Hammond* [2002] UKHL 14; [2002] 1 W.L.R. 1397. Lord Steyn, with whom the other members of the House of Lords agreed, said at [28] that the *Howkins & Harrison* test might render questions of contribution unnecessarily complex if it were regarded as a threshold and that it was best regarded as "a practical test to be used in considering the very statutory question whether two claims under consideration are for 'the same damage'." However, he said that the safest course was to apply the statutory test. At [6] Lord Bingham, with whom the other members of the House of Lords agreed, said:

> "When any claim for contribution falls to be decided the following questions in my opinion arise. (1) What damage has A suffered? (2) Is B liable to A in respect of that damage? (3) Is C also liable to A in respect of that damage or some of it? . . . I do not think it matters greatly whether, in phrasing these questions, on speaks (as the 1978 Act does) of 'damage', or of 'loss' or 'harm', provided it is borne in mind that 'damage' does not mean 'damages' (as pointed out by Roch L.J. in *Birse Construction Ltd v. Haiste Ltd* [1996] 1 W.L.R. 675, 682) and that B's right to contribution by C depends on the damage, loss or harm for which B is liable to A corresponding (even if in part only) with the damage, loss or harm for which C is liable to A."

(See also *Alexander v. Perpetual Trustee WA Ltd.* [2004] HCA 7.) Deciding whether B and C are both liable to A for the same damage can raise difficult questions of causation and, in particular, as to whether the subsequent negligence of C has broken the chain of causation in relation to B's earlier negligence. The decision of Davies J. in *Luke v. Kingsley Smith & Co. (a firm)* [2003] EWHC 1559 (QB); [2004] P.N.L.R. 12 contains a helpful discussion.

4. THE CLAIM

(c) *Basis of assessment of contribution*

Add: The decision of the Court of Appeal in *Dubai Aluminium Co. Ltd v.*   **4–012**
Salaam [2001] Q.B. 113 has been reversed by the House of Lords on the issue of vicarious liability: [2002] UKHL 48; [2002] 3 W.L.R. 1913. The House of Lords held that the assessment of contribution should be on the basis that the party claiming contribution was liable, but should take account of the receipt of the proceeds of the original fraud by those against whom contribution was sought. In deciding the issue of vicarious liability they were faced with the difficulty that the material was limited to the pleaded allegations, which were assumed to be correct.

Add: Where the party claiming contribution has settled the original claim   **4–013**
on a costs-inclusive basis, then he is able to recover a contribution towards the whole sum paid in settlement. He is also able to recover sums paid in respect of the injured party's costs under section 51 (3) of the Supreme Court Act 1981. (See *BICC Ltd. v. Cumbrian Industrial Ltd.* [2001] EWCA Civ 1621; [2002] Lloyd's Rep. P.N. 526 at [114]–[123], *per* Henry L.J. giving the judgment of the Court of Appeal.)

Add to NOTE 34: Thus in considering the respective responsibilities of the   **4–014**
parties, a judge is entitled to take into account not only factual responsibility in the causative sense, but also;

> "moral responsibility in the sense of culpability and organisational responsibility in the sense of where in the hierarchy of decision-making and in the organisational structure leading to the damage the contributing party was located".

(See *BICC Ltd v. Cumbrian Industrial Ltd* [2001] EWCA Civ 1621; [2002] Lloyd's Rep. P.N. 526 at [106]–[108], *per* Henry L.J. giving the judgment of the Court of Appeal.) However, it is not possible to proceed upon assumptions as to the existence and breach of a duty for the purposes of making an apportionment. The actual duty and breach need to be found: *Amaca Pty. Ltd. v. The State of New South Wales* [2003] HCA 44.

(d) *The time for bringing a claim for contribution*

4–015 Add: Where an agreement is later embodied in a consent order, time will run from when the agreement was made and not from the date of the order: *Knight v. Rochdale Healthcare NHS Trust* [2003] EWHC 1831 (QB); [2004] 1 W.L.R. 371 (Crane J.).

CHAPTER 5

DEFENCES

1. Exclusion or Restriction of Liability

(b) *Exclusion of Liability to Third Parties*

Add to Note 34: The equivalent passage in the fourth edition of this work **5–007** was approved by Lord Eassie in *The Governor and Company of the Bank of Scotland v. Fuller Peiser* [2002] P.N.L.R. 13.

5–008   Add to NOTE 37: A disclaimer of liability by a valuer was held to be reasonable in a commercial context in *The Governor and Company of the Bank of Scotland v. Fuller Peiser* [2002] P.N.L.R. 13.

2. LIMITATION IN CONTRACT AND TORT

(a) *The Limitation Period*

5–013   Add: A claim for failure to diagnose dyslexia is a claim for personal injuries: *Adams v. Bracknell Forest Borough Council* [2004] UKHL 29; [2004] 3 W.L.R. 89.

(b) *Date when Cause of Action in Contract Accrues*

5–014   Add new NOTE 65A: In *Morfoot v. W F Smith & Co.* [2001] Lloyd's Rep. P.N. 658, H.H. Judge Havelock-Allan Q.C., sitting as an additional judge of the High Court, applied the reasoning of the Court of Appeal in *Bell v. Peter Browne & Co.* [1990] 2 Q.B. 495 when considering whether a failure to obtain a deed of release was a continuing breach of contract. He held that it was not.

(c) *Date when Cause of Action in Tort Accrues*

(i) *Claims against architects and engineers*

Add new paragraph **5–034A**:

5–034A   **Inadequate or incorrect specification**: Where an architect or engineer negligently specifies inappropriate materials or equipment, damage is not suffered until the materials or equipment are delivered. Until then, the client has not suffered any quantifiable loss or damage: see *Proctor & Gamble (Health and Beauty Care) Ltd. v. Carrier Holdings Ltd.* [2003] Building L.R. 255 (Forbes J.). The distinction, if any, between this decision and those summarised in paragraphs 5–040, 5–046 and 5–047 in the main work is hard to identify.

(iii) *Claims against solicitors*

5–040   Add to NOTE 66: See also *McCarroll v. Statham Gill Davis* [2002] EWHC 2558 (Q.B.); [2003] P.N.L.R. 19 (Gray J.): damage suffered when contract entered on unfavourable terms and not later, when band member was expelled without compensation as permitted by those terms (decision upheld on appeal: [2003] EWCA Civ 425; [2003] P.N.L.R. 509).

5–043   Add: In the light of the later decisions of the Court of Appeal in *Khan v. R.M. Falvey* [2002] EWCA Civ 400; [2002] P.N.L.R. 28 and *Hatton v. Chafes (a firm)* [2003] EWCA Civ 341; [2003] P.N.L.R. 24 the decision in *Hopkins v. MacKenzie* (1995) 6 Med.L.R. 26 is of only very limited application, if it can be said to have survived at all. The first decision, *Khan*, was another case against a solicitor following the striking out of earlier litigation for want of prosecution. The losses suffered included sums paid to the defendant more than six years before the action commenced, so the claims were statute barred in any event. However, the Court of Appeal took the opportunity to reconsider the decision in *Hopkins v. MacKenzie* in the light of the decision of the House of Lords in *Nykredit Mortgage Bank plc v. Edward Erdman Group Ltd. (No.2)* [1997] 1 W.L.R. 1627 (see paragraph 5–036). They held that where it was inevitable or there was a serious risk that an action would be struck out, actionable damage was suffered even if the action was not struck out until some time later. This decision is to be welcomed. It is wrong to consider when the claimant first suffered actionable damage solely by reference to the way that the claimant pleads his loss. *Hopkins v. MacKenzie* was always hard to reconcile with other authorities and the effect of *Khan* is to bring limitation in this area back into line with other areas. This was confirmed by the decision in *Hatton* which followed *Khan* and held, on the facts, that the underlying action had been bound to be struck out more than six years before the proceedings against the solicitors were issued. The Court of Appeal left open the question whether it would have sufficed if it was either more probable than not that the earlier action would have been struck out or whether there was a real (as opposed to a minimal or fanciful) risk that it would have been struck out more than six years before the issue of the later proceedings. The same result was reached on slightly different facts in *Polley v. Warner Goodman & Street (a firm)* [2003] EWCA Civ 1013; [2003] P.N.L.R. 40 (order extending validity of writ bound to be set aside so that time did not start to run only when it was in fact set aside).

(v) *Claims against financial advisers*

Add: The same approach applies in relation to claims against accountants **5–048** for allegedly negligent reports under section 36 of the Solicitors' Act 1974: *Law Society v. Sephton & Co. (a firm)* [2004] EWHC 544 (Ch); [2004] P.N.L.R. 27 (Michael Briggs Q.C., sitting as a deputy High Court judge).

(d) *Effect of the Latent Damage Act 1986*

Add to NOTE 5: In *McKillen v. Russell* [2002] P.N.L.R. 29 the Court of **5–050** Appeal in Northern Ireland, considering the Northern Irish equivalent of section 14A, held that where the claimant had learnt of some damage (in this case that his surveyor had failed to detect one problem with his house), time began to run in respect of his claim, even though there was further damage of which he was not then aware. Similar views were expressed by Lord Woolf L.C.J. in *Babicki v. Rowlands (a firm)* [2002] Lloyd's Rep. P.N. 122.

Add: Nor does section 14A apply to claims under the Defective Premises **5–053** Act 1972: *Payne v. John Setchell Ltd.* [2002] P.N.L.R. 7 (H.H. Judge Humphrey Lloyd Q.C.).

Add: The decision of the Court of Appeal in *Hallam-Eames v. Merrett* **5–054** (now also reported at [2001] Lloyd's Rep. PN 178 was followed by the Court of Appeal in *Haward v. Fawcetts (a firm)* [2004] EWCA Civ 240; [2004] P.N.L.R. 658. Where a claimant does not know whether the relevant losses were attributable to some act or omission of the defendant or to some other cause, then he will not have the knowledge required for time to run under section 14A. The judgment of Jonathan Walker L.J. in *Haward* contains a full discussion of earlier decisions under sections 14 and 14A of the Limitation Act 1980.

5–055   Add to NOTE 31: *Fennon v. Anthony Hodari & Co (a firm)* [2001] Lloyd's Rep. P.N. 183 was followed by Nelson J. in *Bowie v. Southorns* [2002] EWHC 1389 (Q.B.); [2003] P.N.L.R. 7. In the latter case the claimant did not know that the solicitor who had failed to explain to her the meaning and effect of a guarantee owed her a legal duty to do so, but did know that he had not done so. Time ran against her on the basis of actual knowledge. She did not have constructive knowledge by reason of having instructed lawyers to act for her in defence to a possession claim, having taken all reasonable steps to obtain legal advice (see section 14 A (10)). See also *Swansea Building Society v. Bradford & Bingley (t/a BBG Surveyors)* [2003] P.N.L.R. 38 (H.H. Judge Tyzack Q.C. sitting as a deputy High Court judge) where the claimant was held to have acquired constructive knowledge once it received advice to obtain further specialist reports.

(e) *Special Rules re Personal Injury and Death*

(i) *Primary limitation periods*

5–057   Add to NOTE 45: See also *Rowbottom v. Royal Masonic Hospital* [2002] EWCA Civ 87, [2002] Lloyd's Rep. Med. 173, a borderline case.

5–060   Add to NOTE 51: However, in *Babicki v. Rowlands (a firm)* [2002] Lloyd's Rep. P.N. 121 Lord Woolf L.C.J., with whom Simon Brown and Buxton L.JJ. agreed, said that, while Brooke L.J.'s judgment in *Spargo v. North Essex District Health Authority* [1997] 8 Med.L.R. 125 provided "some very helpful guidance", on the facts of *Babicki* it was better to turn to the words of the statute (section 14A, rather than section 14) rather than to seek to place a gloss on them.

5–062   Add: The test of what knowledge a person might reasonably have been expected to have acquired under section 14(3) is essentially objective: what would a reasonable person who had suffered the injury have done? Any special characteristics of a particular claimant can be taken into account under section 33 of the Limitation Act 1980: see *Adams v. Bracknell Forest Borough Council* [2004] UKHL 4; [2004] 3 WLR 89. Thus on the facts of *Adams* the claimant should reasonably have sought professional advice more than three years before proceedings were commenced and so could not rely on section 14 of the Limitation Act 1980.

(f) *Fraud or Concealment*

5–070   Add to NOTE 89: See also *Cave v. Robinson Jarvis & Rolfe (a firm)* [2002] UKHL 18; [2003] 1 A.C. 384 at [58] *per* Lord Scott (but see the approach of Lord Millett in the same case at [19]–[23]: three other members of the House of Lords, agreed with Lord Scott, only two with Lord Millett).

Add: However, as held by the Court of Appeal in *Ezekiel v. Lehrer* [2002]   **5–071**
Lloyd's Rep. P.N. 260, once a claimant is aware of the relevant facts, a subsequent attempt to conceal them from him did not allow the claimant to invoke section 32. The genie is not deemed to have been put back in the bottle.

Add to NOTE 92: The "statement of claim" test was also applied by Gray J.   **5–072**
in *McCarroll v. Statham Gill Davis* [2002] EWHC 2558 (Q.B.); [2003] P.N.L.R. 19. His decision was upheld on appeal: [2003] EWCA Civ 425; [2003] P.N.L.R. 25. The reason why a defendant deliberately concealed a fact relevant to the right of action is irrelevant; what matters is whether he did so deliberately: see *Williams v. Fanshaw Porter Hazelhurst (a firm)* [2004] EWCA Civ 157; [2004] P.N.L.R. 29.

Add to NOTE 93: See also *Leeds & Holbeck Building Society v. Arthur &*   **5–073**
Cole (a firm) [2002] P.N.L.R. 4.

Replace NOTE 95 with the following: In paragraph 50 of the judgment in *Biggs v. Sotnicks (a firm)* [2002] Lloyd's Rep. P.N. 331, Arden L.J., with whom Robert Walker and Aldous L.JJ. agreed, described this as "the classic statement of what section 32(1) requires". In the same case Robert Walker and Aldous L.J. declined to adopt a qualification of this passage of the judgment of Millett L.J. suggested by Crane J. in *UCB Home Loans v. Carr* [2000] Lloyd's Rep. P.N. 754. On the facts of the case it was held that the claimant had sufficient knowledge more than six years before the issue of proceedings and so was out of time. The claimant's suggestion that time did not run until he received a copy of the defendant's solicitor's file was rejected: with reasonable diligence it would have been obtained more than six years before proceedings began. For another case where it was held that time began to run before the claimant had sight of the defendant's working papers see the decision of Michael Briggs Q.C., sitting as a deputy High Court judge, in *Law Society v. Sephton & Co. (a firm)* [2004] EWHC 544 (Ch); [2004] P.N.L.R. 27.

Add: The decision in *Liverpool Roman Catholic Archdiocese Inc. v. Gold-*   **5–074**
berg [2001] 1 All E.R. 182 was overruled by the House of Lords in *Cave v. Robison Jarvis & Rolf (a firm)* [2002] UKHL 18; [2003] 1 A.C. 384. Paragraph 5–074 should therefore be deleted.

Replace the existing text with the following: **Section 32 (2): "Deliberate**   **5–075**
commission of a breach of duty": The recent decision of the House of Lords in *Cave v. Robison Jarvis & Rolf (a firm)* [2002] UKHL 18; [2003] 1 A.C. 384 has confirmed the understanding of this provision which was generally held before the decision of the Court of Appeal in *Brocklesby v. Armitage & Guests (Note)* [2001] 1 W.L.R. 599 CA, discussed in paragraph 5–075 in the main work and now overruled on this point. Lord Millett, with whom Lord Mackay and Lord Hobhouse agreed, said at [25]:

"In my opinion, section 32 deprives a defendant of a limitation defence in two situations: (i) where he takes active steps to conceal his own breach of duty after he has become aware of it; and (ii) where he is guilty of deliberate wrongdoing and conceals or fails to disclose it in circumstances where it is unlikely to be discovered for some time. But it does not deprive a defendant of a limitation defence where he is charged with negligence if, being unaware of his error or that he has failed to take proper care, there has been nothing for him to disclose."

Lord Scott, with whom Lord Slynn, Lord Mackay and Lord Hobhouse agreed, said at [58]:

"The relevant words in section 32 (2) are 'deliberate commission of a breach of duty . . . amounts to deliberate concealment of the facts involved in that breach of duty'. These are clear words of English. 'Deliberate commission of a breach of duty' is to be contrasted with a commission of a breach of duty which is not deliberate, a breach of duty which is inadvertent, accidental unintended—there are a number of adjectives that can be chosen for the purpose of the contrast, and it does not matter which is chosen. Each would exclude a breach of duty that the actor was not aware he was committing."

He went on to explain at [60] that under subsection (2):

"The claimant need not concentrate on the allegedly concealed facts but can instead concentrate on the commission of the breach of duty. If the claimant can show that the defendant knew he was committing a breach of duty, or intended to commit a breach of duty—I can discern no difference between the two formulations; each would constitute, in my opinion, a deliberate commission of the breach—then, if the circumstances are such that the claimant is unlikely to discover for some time that the breach of duty has been committed, the facts involved in the breach are taken to have been deliberately concealed for subsection (1)(b) purposes."

This decision is clear and requires no elaboration.

5–076   This paragraph is now superseded by the decision of the House of Lords in *Cave v. Robison Jarvis & Rolf (a firm)* [2002] UKHL 18; [2003] 1 A.C. 384: see paragraph 5–075 above.

5–077   This paragraph is now superseded by the decision of the House of Lords in *Cave v. Robinson Jarvis & Rolf (a firm)* [2002] UKHL 18; [2003] 1 A.C. 384: see paragraph 5–075 above.

3. LIMITATION IN EQUITY

(a) *Express application of the Limitation Act 1980*

5–082   Add new NOTE 14A: A claim against a company director who has acquired and disposed of the company's property is a claim against him as a trustee and falls within section 21(1)(b): *JJ Harrison (Properties Ltd) v. Harrison* [2002] 1 BCLC 162 (Court of Appeal). However, a claim against a company director for an account of secret or unauthorised profits does not, because there was no pre-existing fiduciary responsibility for the relevant property (*i.e.* the profits): see *DEG-Deutsche Investitions-und-Entwicklungsgesellschaft mbH v. Koshy and Others (No.3)* [2003] EWCA Civ 1048 at [119].

Add to NOTE 18: The same distinction can be drawn in relation to   **5–084**
claims for breach of fiduciary duty: see *DEG-Deutsche Investitions-und-*
Entwicklungsgesellschaft mbH v. Koshy and Others (No 3) [2003] EWCA
Civ 1048 at [89]. In that decision the Court of Appeal took the opportunity to review recent Court of Appeal authority in this area (see
[71]–[111]). Thus claims against fiduciaries who were in a fiduciary relationship before the claim arose (rather than against those whose fiduciary
obligation only arises by reason of their wrongful acts) fall within section
21 of the Limitation Act 1980 and will be subject to a six-year time limit
unless they are either for a fraudulent breach or for the recovery of property held on trust. Section 21 would not apply to claims against the second
type of fiduciary, but some other limitation period might be applied by
analogy (see paragraphs 5–088—5–095 of the main text). The Court of
Appeal disapproved the decision of Sir Robert McGarry V.-C. in *Tito v.*
Waddell [1977] Ch. 107 at 248–251 that the liability of a fiduciary to
account for profits for breach of the self-dealing rule and the fair-dealing
rule did not fall within section 21 and the decision of Harman J. in an earlier stage of the litigation before the Court of Appeal that the claim was
simply one for an account and so not barred by the Limitation Act 1980
(*Gwembe Valley Development Co Ltd. v. Koshy* [1998] 2 BCLC 613). At
[111] the Court of Appeal summarised the application of the Limitation
Act 1980 to claims against fiduciaries as follows:

"The starting assumption should be that a six year limitation period will apply—
under one or other provision of the Act, applied directly or by analogy—unless it
is specifically excluded by the Act or established case-law. Personal claims against
fiduciaries will normally be subject to limits by analogy with claims in tort or contract (1980 Act s 2, 5; see *Seguros*). By contrast, claims for breach of fiduciary duty,
in the special sense explained in *Mothew*, will normally be covered by section 21.
The six-year time-limit under section 21(3) will apply, directly or by analogy, unless
excluded by subsection 21(1)(a) (fraud) or (b) (Class 1 trust)."

(b) *Application of the Limitation Act 1980 by Analogy*

Add to NOTE 52: See also *Leeds & Holbeck Building Society v. Arthur &*   **5–095**
Cole (a firm) [2002] P.N.L.R. 4 where Morland J. held that section 5 of the
Limitation Act 1980 applied by analogy to a claim for breach of fiduciary
duty. In *Meara v. Fox* [2002] P.N.L.R. 5, Pumfrey J. would have applied a six-
year period of limitation to a claim for breach of fiduciary duty provided that
to do so would not cause injustice which could not be avoided by application
of other provisions of the Limitation Act, such as section 32. It is doubtful,
however, whether all breaches of fiduciary duty can be said to be analogous
to claims for breach of contract.

Add new paragraph **5–095A**:

Where a period of limitation is now prescribed, but was not before July 1,   **5–095A**
1940, then section 36 of the Limitation Act 1980 does not apply and that
period will not be applied by analogy. An example is the two-year limitation
for bringing a claim for contribution under the Civil Liability (Contribution)
Act 1978: see the decision of Kevin Garnett Q.C., sitting as a deputy High
Court judge in *Hampton v. Minns* [2002] 1 W.L.R. 1.

4. Other Equitable Defences: Laches and Acquiescence

(a) *Laches*

5–099   Add to Note 65: Applied in the recent decision of the Supreme Court of Canada in *Wewakym Indian Band v. The Queen* (2002) 220 D.L.R. (4th) 1.

5. Contributory Negligence

(a) *Contributory negligence and contract*

5–116   Add Note: In *Standard Chartered Bank v. Pakistan National Shipping Corpn (Nos 2 and 4)* [2002] UKHL 43; [2003] 1 A.C. 959, the House of Lords held that a defence of contributory negligence only arose under the Law Reform (Contributory Negligence) Act 1945 in cases in which it would have provided a complete defence of contributory negligence before that Act came into force. The claim in that case was in deceit, so that the position in contract was not decided.

(c) *Methods by which plaintiffs might seek to circumvent a plea of contributory negligence*

5–119   Add to Note 30: See now *Standard Chartered Bank v. Pakistan National Shipping Corpn (Nos 2 and 4)* [2002] UKHL 43; [2003] 1 A.C. 959.

CHAPTER 6

LITIGATION

1. GROUP ACTIONS

(d) *Costs*

Add to NOTE 26: Further guidance on costs can be found in the cases **6–005** referred to in the *White Book* at paragraph 19.0.10. See also *Sayers v. Merck SmithKline Beecham plc* [2002] 1 W.L.R. 2274, CA.

2. EXPERT EVIDENCE

(b) *Cases where expert evidence is not required*

Add to NOTE 39: See also *Linden Homes South East Ltd. v. LBH Wembley* **6–010** *Ltd.* [2002] EWHC 3115 (TCC), (2003) 87 Con.L.R. 180 (finding of negligence by construction professionals in face of evidence of defendant's expert witness because there was not evidence of two respectable but differing bodies of opinion, merely of differing views as between the two individual experts).

Add: For a detailed discussion of the role of expert evidence in professional **6–011** negligence claims, particularly claims against construction professionals, see paragraphs 16–25 of the judgment of Judge Lloyd Q.C. in *Royal Brompton Hospital NHS Trust v. Hammond* [2002] EWHC 2037 (TCC), (2003) 88 Con.L.R. 1. The judge commented that expert evidence may be needed to assist court to assess the evidence, for example, by indicating which factors or technical considerations would influence the judgment of a professional person, in cases where the negligence alleged is not a failure to follow an established professional practice. Otherwise, in such cases, expert evidence is not indispensable. The issue of breach of duty may be determined as a matter of common sense. Alternatively, the court may itself possess the necessary expertise to assess the evidence; the Technology and Construction Court has such expertise in disputes arising in the construction industry and in other areas of commerce. Even so, expert evidence may remain desirable in order to satisfy the court that its decision on the required standard of care is in line with the expectations and understanding of the profession. The judge also pointed out that, since the role of the expert witness under the Civil Procedure Rules is to assist the court rather than to make a case for the expert's instructing party, it is not necessary for a party which alleges negligence to adduce supporting expert evidence, provided that in a case where such evidence is necessary or desirable it is available from an expert called by another party.

(d) *Relevance and admissibility of expert evidence*

(ii) *The appropriate questions*

6–015   Add to NOTE 52: See also *Stephen Donald Architects Ltd. v. Christopher King*, [2003] EWHC 1867 (TCC), (2003) 94 Cov. L. R. 1. Judge Seymour Q.C. (evidence of defendant's expert architect unhelpful because he did not address the question whether any reasonably competent architect would have prepared a different design in response to the client's brief).

(iv) *Impartiality*

6–018   Add: Where there is a close pre-existing professional or personal relationship between the defendant and an expert whom he wishes to give evidence on his behalf, the test for admissibility of the expert's evidence flows from the principle that justice must be seen to be done. In *Liverpool Roman Catholic Archdiocesan Trust v. Goldberg (No.3)* [2001] 1 W.L.R. 2337, Evans-Lombe J. held that the test is whether a reasonable observer might think that the relationship between the expert and the party calling him is capable of affecting the views of the expert so as to make them unduly favourable to that party. If so, the evidence will not be admitted. It is not necessary, for the evidence to be excluded, to show that the relationship *has* so affected the expert's views. (In that case, the defendant tax barrister was not permitted to adduce the expert evidence of a colleague in his chambers, with whom the defendant had a close personal and professional relationship of long-standing.) Furthermore, in expressing his opinion of the defendant's performance, an expert must not be deterred by the fact that the defendant is held in high esteem by the members of their common profession. In *Hubbard v. Lambeth Southwark & Lewisham Health Authority* [2001] EWCA Civ 1455, [2002] Lloyd's Rep. Med. 8, the Court of Appeal held that the court should generally order experts of like disciplines to engage in without prejudice discussions in order to narrow the issues in a case once their reports have been exchanged. Good reason was required before such an order would not be made. The claimants' experts' reluctance to subject the competence of a colleague to critical discussion because he was a well-known and highly respected practitioner was not good reason.

(e) *The single joint expert*

Add to NOTE 62: In practice, an order that evidence shall be given by a sin- **6–019**
gle joint expert may be refused until the issues in the case have been clarified
by the service of a defence: see *Simms v. Birmingham Health Authority* [2001]
Lloyd's Rep. Med. 382. *In Coopers Payen Ltd. v. Southampton Container Ter-
minal Ltd.* [2003] EWCA Civ 1223; [2004] 1 Lloyd's Rep. 331, the Court of
Appeal provided guidance upon how the court should approach the evidence
of a single joint expert. While it will be a rare case in which the court will
disregard the evidence of a single joint expert, it was necessary for the judge
to evaluate that evidence in the light of all the evidence in the case (see the
judgment of Clarke L.J. at paragraphs [41]–[43]).

Add to NOTE 63: Similarly, discussion between one party and a jointly
instructed expert will not be permitted unless the other party is present or
gives its consent to such discussion taking place in its absence. In *Peet v. Mid-
Kent Healthcare Trust (Practice Note)* [2001] EWCA Civ 1703, [2002] 1
W.L.R. 210, the Court of Appeal held that for a party to test the evidence of
a jointly instructed expert by means of an unilateral discussion was inconsistent with the structure and overriding objective of the Civil Procedure Rules
on joint experts and would never be permitted against the wishes of the other
party. In an earlier decision to like effect, the judge pointed out that if a party
wished to test the evidence of a joint expert, it should use the procedure for
submission of written questions to the expert which is set out in CPR 35.6:
Smith v. Stephens [2001] C.I.L.L. 1802.

NOTE 66: Replace the reference with the following: [2001] Lloyd's Rep. **6–020**
Med. 347, CA.

Add: In *Layland v. Fairview New Homes plc* [2002] EWHC 1350 (Ch),
[2003] B.L.R. 20, it was held that a claimant could resist summary judgment
if it showed a realistic prospect of successfully challenging a single joint
expert's evidence by either submissions or cross-examination. But it is clear
that the parties do not enjoy an unfettered right to challenge the evidence of
a joint expert by cross-examining him at trial. In *Peet v. Mid-Kent Healthcare
Trust (Practice Note)* [2001] EWCA Civ 1703, [2002] 1 W.L.R. 210, Lord
Woolf C.J. explained that, normally, the evidence of a joint expert should be
contained in his written report so that he would not be required to give oral
evidence at trial and the parties would not be entitled to cross-examine him.
Those remarks were *obiter* in *Peet* but Lord Woolf's approach was adopted
and applied by the Court of Appeal in the later case of *Popek v. National
Westminster Bank plc* [2002] EWCA Civ 42, [2002] C.P.L.R. 370. There, the
trial judge's decision to strike out the claimant's case as hopeless in the light
of the joint expert's report was upheld, notwithstanding that the claimant
had not had the opportunity to put his version of the facts to the expert by
way of cross-examination. Cross-examination of a joint expert was not to be
the norm. The claimant should have tested the expert's evidence in advance
of trial by submitting written questions to him in accordance with the procedure set out in CPR 35.6.

HUMAN RIGHTS AND PROFESSIONALS

1. INTRODUCTION

Add: For an analysis of the impact of the HRA in its early years of oper-   **7–001**
ation, particularly in relation to sections 3 and 4 HRA, see "Two Years of the
Human Rights Act", Kier Starmer Q.C. [2003] 1 EHRLR 14.

Add to NOTE 2: *Marcic* is reported at [2002] 2 W.L.R. 1000, [2001] 4 All E.R. 326, TCC. On appeal, the Court of Appeal agreed that the defendant's failure to repair sewers resulting in flooding to the claimant's home constituted a breach of Article 8 and Article 1 of Protocol No. 1 but held that a common law remedy in nuisance did exist and that damages at common law would constitute "just satisfaction" for the purposes of an action under s.7(1) of the HRA: *Marcic v. Thames Water Utilities* [2002] 2 W.L.R. 932; [2002] 2 All E.R. 55, CA. However, the case was appealed to the House of Lords [2003] UKHL 66; [2004] 2 A.C. 42; [2003] 3 W.L.R. 1603; [2004] 1 All E.R. 135 who reversed the Court of Appeal's decision. Their Lordships held that Mr Marcic could have no claim in nuisance or under the Human Rights Act 1998 as both would be inconsistent with the statutory scheme for sewerage under the Water Industry Act 1991. That Act created its own enforcement procedure, and one of its important purposes was to prevent householders from launching proceedings in respect of failures to build sufficient sewers. Because the Water Industry Act created a reasonable and fair system for balancing competing interests, regulated by a statutory regulator whose decisions were subject to judicial review, the House of Lords found the statutory scheme to be Convention-compliant. See also *Dennis v. Ministry of Defence* [2003] EWHC 793 (Q.B.), *The Times*, May 6, 2003, (2003) 19 EG 118 which held that a public interest defence to an action for nuisance should not be allowed to succeed where a human rights claim on the same facts would also succeed.

Add to NOTE 3: But note the retreat from the *Douglas* Article 8 analysis in the context of privacy and confidentiality in *A v. B* [2002] 2 All E.R. 545, CA where the Court applied a traditional balancing approach based on the law of confidence. A similar approach was followed in *D v. L* [2003] EWCA Civ 1169, CA with recognition that different factual situations would produce different balancing exercises. In *Wainwright v Home Office* [2003] UKHL 53; [2003] 3 W.L.R. 1137; [2003] 4 All E.R. 969 the House of Lords held that English law recognises no general tort of "invasion of privacy". However, in *Campbell v MGN Ltd.* [2004] UKHL 22; [2004] 2 W.L.R. 1232; [2004] 2 All E.R. 995 the House recognised that, while it does not create any new cause of action between private persons, the Human Rights Act does oblige the court, as a public authority, to act compatibly with Convention rights. This has spurred the development of protection for various aspects of privacy, including through the vehicle of the action for breach of confidence. Echoing Lord Woolf C.J. in *A v. B* [2002] EWCA Civ 337; [2002] All E.R. 545, their Lordships acknowledged that the courts have moulded the cause of action of breach of confidence so that the values enshrined in both Articles 8 and 10 of the Convention are now part of that cause of action, giving it new breadth and strength.

2. RELEVANT CONVENTION RIGHTS

(b) *Article 8*

Add new paragraph **7–031A**:

7–013A   There is still uncertainty as to the degree of the HRA's horizontal effect, and the matter has yet to be conclusively resolved. However, recent cases such as *Campbell v. MGN Ltd* [2004] UKHL 22; [2004] 2 All E.R. 995 perhaps evidence a preference on the part of the courts to adopt some form of indirect horizontality rather than full horizontality (for example through modifying the existing law of confidence to protect privacy interests rather than relying directly on Article 8). This apparent preference may partly be due to the fact that full horizontality, with the result that Article 8 could be invoked directly in any case, cuts across section 6 of the HRA which imposes Convention obligations on public bodies only.

3. NEGLIGENCE AND DUTY OF CARE

(d) *Tort or Convention?*

Add to NOTE 61: In *Hamilton Jones v. David & Snape (a firm)* [2003] EWHC   **7–027**
3147 (Ch); [2004] 1 All E.R. 657 the claimant sought damages for mental distress from the defendant firm of solicitors for failing to re-register her children with the passport agency so that their father would not remove them from the country. The claimant's children were subsequently removed to Tunisia by their father. Rather than raising any argument based on Article 8 in parallel with his arguments based on negligence and breach of contract, counsel for the claimant expressly disclaimed any right to damages on the basis of Article 8 or other Convention provision. However, this concession was probably based on the fact that Convention rights cannot be invoked directly against a defendant who is not a public body rather than being based on any perception that damages under the Human Rights Act would be harder to obtain or of a lower order than at common law. In *R. (on the application of KB) v. Mental Health Review Tribunal* [2003] EWHC 193 (Admin); [2004] Q.B. 936; [2003] 2 All E.R. 209 the Court considered the appropriate measure of damages for frustration and distress, deprivation of liberty, and damage to mental health in respect of a breach of Article 5(4) of the Convention. Stanley Burnton J. found that the European Court of Human Rights tended to award global sums on an equitable basis, with no breakdown between different items of damages. The judge held that English courts must be free to depart from Strasbourg in order to award adequate compensation in United Kingdom terms. He stated that there was no justification for an award of damages being lower under the HRA than for a comparable tort. While there was no comparable tort or other wrong under purely English law in the case before him, Stanley Burnton J. held that damages should, so far as possible, reflect the English level of damages. The judge noted that Parliament had provided, in section 8(3) of the HRA, that an award of damages should be made "where necessary". This meant in effect that in some circumstances an award of damages beyond a finding of breach would be unnecessary to afford "just satisfaction". He also noted that the award of exemplary damages was expressly prohibited by section 9(3) HRA.

Add new heading (f) and new paragraph **7–029A**:

(f) *Further developments since Z and T.P.*

Since *Z*, there have been several European Court cases in the same vein.   **7–029A**
Lam v. United Kingdom App. No. 41671/98, July 5, 2001 concerned the failure by domestic courts to find that a duty of care existed in negligence in

respect of the manner in which a local authority failed to exercise its enforcement functions to put an end to a statutory nuisance because it was not fair, just and reasonable to impose one. The courts had assumed for the purposes of a strike-out application that it might be possible on the facts to establish foreseeability of harm and proximity. The applicants complained that the domestic courts invoked public policy considerations in order to bestow an immunity on the local authority for its wrongful acts and omissions with the result that they were denied access to a court in breach of Article 6(1). The Court dismissed the complaint as manifestly ill-founded. Accordingly, it is clear that there is no longer any breach of Article 6(1) by striking out a case at an interlocutory stage solely on the basis that there is no duty of care because it is not fair, just and reasonable to impose one. In the social care context, see also *D.P. and J.C. v. United Kingdom* (2003) 36 E.H.R.R. 14 following the *Z* and *T.P. & K.M.* approach to Articles 6(1) and 13 and *E v. United Kingdom* (2003) 36 E.H.R.R. 31 [2003] 1 F.L.R. 348 on Article 13.

In *Reid v. United Kingdom* Application No. 33221/96, June 26, 2001, the European Court of Human Rights held that the applicant's inability to sue the Crown Prosecution Service for negligence in assessing whether there was sufficient evidence against him for a prosecution resulted from principles governing the substantive cause of action and not from an immunity. In *Patel v. United Kingdom* App. No. 38199/97 February 19, 2002, the European Court of Human Rights declared inadmissible a complaint that the applicant had been denied access to a court under Article 6(1). The applicant had brought a claim for negligence against his former counsel in earlier criminal proceedings. Part of the claim was struck out on the ground of advocates' immunity and the rest of the claim was stayed. The action was discontinued in 2001 with no order as to costs. The European Court held that there was no restriction on the applicant's access to court under Article 6(1) since his stayed High Court action would have permitted him to apply to amend the statement of claim to cover the barrister's alleged negligent conduct in court which was no longer covered by immunity following the House of Lords decision in *Arthur J.S. Hall v. Simons* [2000] 3 W.L.R. 543, HL.

Domestic cases include *Walters v. North Glamorgan National Health Service Trust* [2002] Lloyd's Rep. Med. 227, QBD, in which Mr Justice Thomas held that the inability of the applicant to sue for damages for "nervous shock" as a result of a pathological grief reaction following the death of her son whilst in the Trust's care flowed from the applicable principles governing the substantive right of action, not from any immunity. In *Re A Debtor No. SD 38 of 2001 Miller v. Law Society* [2002] 4 All E.R. 312; (2003) P.N.L.R. 4; *The Times*, June 3, 2002, Ch. D., Geoffrey Vos Q.C. held that a solicitor was confined to the statutory rights of appeal to the High Court under the Solicitors Act 1974 regarding the conduct of an investigation of his affairs under the Solicitors Accounting Rules 1991 before any intervention. It was not contrary to Article 6(1) that a solicitor could not bring a claim against the Law Society for breach of a private law duty of care arising from its conduct of the investigation. In *D. & others v. East Berkshire Community Health NHS Trust, Dewsbury Health Care NHS Trust & Kirklees Metropolitan Council; Oldham NHS Trust & Dr Blumenthal* [2003] EWCA Civ 1151, [2003] 4 All ER 796, *The Times*, August 22, 2003, the Court of Appeal dismissed appeals by parents from the dismissal of their damages claims against local and health authorities for psychiatric harm arising from false allegations made against them by child welfare professionals. An attempt by the claimants to resurrect *Osman* failed. The Court held that the judgments appealed against did not violate Article 6 by reference to *Z* and *T.P. & K.M.* and found that it was not difficult to draw a line between procedural and substantive limitations in the area in question which was concerned with the application of a fundamental principle of the law of negligence. However, it also held that factual enquiries, including the conduct of the individuals involved, were required where a claim alleged a breach of Article 3 in circumstances such as *Z*, and Article 8 based on the removal of a child from a parent without justification, and the decision in *X v. Bedfordshire* [1995] 2 A.C. 633 was contrary to the HRA in relation to the position of a child since it was no longer legitimate to rule that, as a matter of law, no common law duty was owed to a child in relation to the investigation of suspected child abuse and the initiation and pursuit of care proceedings. Whether the imposition of a duty of care was fair, just and reasonable had to be determined on the facts of each case. There were strong public policy reasons for concluding that no common law duty of care was owed to parents in relation to childcare decisions. On consideration of whether suspicion of child abuse justified proceedings to remove a child from the parents, a common law duty of care could be owed to a child but not to the parents.

4. IMMUNITIES

Add: However, in *Trevor Rush McCafferty Wright v. Paton Farrell & ors*, **7–030** (2003) P.N.L.R. 410; L.T.L. August 29, 2002, Ct. Sess.(Scot), the Outer House of the Court of Session held that advocates' immunity from suit in respect of their conduct in court of criminal proceedings did not of itself give rise to a violation of Article 6(1).

Add at end: In *Benjamin Gray v. Laurie Avadis* [2003] EWHC 1830, *The Times Law Reports* August 19, 2003, Tugendhat J. found that letters sent to the Office for the Supervision of Solicitors in connection with a complaint it was investigating attracted absolute privilege and that the consequent immunity from suit was compatible with Article 6.

Add to NOTE 69: The extent of existing immunities would appear to be generally compatible with Article 6. In *Taylor v. United Kingdom* (Application no. 49589/99, June 10, 2003 ECtHR) the applicant solicitor had been prevented from pursuing a libel action against the Serious Fraud Office by reason of witness immunity attaching to certain documents. Following his unsuccessful appeal to the House of Lords against the High Court's decision to strike out his claim, the applicant alleged a breach of Article 6 before the European Court of Human Rights. Referring to *Z v. United Kingdom* (*supra* at NOTE 41), the Court stated that whilst Article 6 applied to the proceedings brought by the applicant, it did not guarantee any particular content for his civil rights. The Court held that the immunity from suit was necessary to encourage freedom of speech and communication in the judicial process, such that the limitation it imposed on the applicant's access to court was proportionate and compatible with the spirit of Article 6(1). Similarly, in a domestic case, *Heath v. Commissioner of Police for the Metropolis* [2004] EWCA Civ 943; *The Times*, July 22, 2004, the appellant argued that the application of the absolute immunity rule to her claim for unlawful sex discrimination in relation to alleged conduct by members of a disciplinary board in the conduct of a quasi-judicial proceeding violated her right to a fair hearing under Article 6(1) because it denied her access to the Employment Tribunal. The Court of Appeal stated that the appellant's right of access to the Employment Tribunal under Article 6(1) was not absolute. It was confined to overcoming procedural bars and immunities, as distinguished from rules as to substantive rights or the lack of them. The Court held that the immunity operated as a substantive bar to the appellant's claim so as not to engage Article 6(1). However, if that conclusion was wrong and the immunity operated as a procedural bar so as to engage Article 6(1), the Court held that the immunity was for a legitimate purpose and was necessary and proportionate in the public interest for the protection of the integrity of the judicial system. See also *D v. East Berkshire Community Health NHS Trust* [2003] EWCA Civ 1151, [2003] 4 All E.R. 796 CA where the Court of Appeal held that the judge had erred in finding that witness immunity precluded liability in circumstances where it was not clear that the circumstances fell within the scope of the immunity.

5. LAWYERS

(a) *Wasted costs orders*

7–032   Add: In *Medcalf v. Mardell* [2002] 3 W.L.R. 172; [2002] 3 All E.R. 721, HL, the House of Lords held that it was unfair to make wasted costs orders against leading and junior counsel who had put their signatures to allegations of fraud and other impropriety in a draft notice of appeal where legal professional privilege prevented them from adducing evidence as to whether they had reasonably credible material before them to justify making the allegations. Despite *B v. United Kingdom* cited above, the House of Lords was prepared to assume that Article 6(1) was relevant to the wasted costs jurisdiction. The House of Lords fortified their conclusion that it is unfair and contrary to the appearance of justice to condemn wasted costs respondents unheard by reference to Strasbourg case-law relying on *De Haes & Gijsels v. Belgium* (1997) 25 E.H.R.R. 1, where the European Court found an infringement of Article 6(1) in circumstances where two journalists were prevented from putting evidence before a court in proceedings brought by judges whom they had roundly criticised for their handling of a case. Lord Hobhouse at paragraph 60 of the judgment appeared to suggest that legal professional privilege may not be absolute by reference to the Convention. He stated:

> "The need of a lawyer to be able to ask a court to look at privileged material when a lawyer's conduct is in question may not be so intractable . . . It may be that, as in the context of Article 6 and 8 of the European Convention on Human Rights, the privilege may not always be absolute and a balancing exercise may sometimes be necessary."

This approach of balancing competing rights, inherent in the Convention, is potentially inconsistent with *R v. Derby Magistrates ex p. B* [1996] 1 A.C. 487, HL in which the House of Lords held that legal professional privilege was absolute and trumped all other competing interests. It may be that Lord Hobhouse's dictum will provide some encouragement for a future attack on the absolutist approach to privilege in *ex p. B*.

(b) *Lawyer/client confidentiality and the Convention*

Add: In *Three Rivers District Council & Bank of Credit & Commerce Inter-* **7–035**
national SA (In Liquidation) v. Governor & Company of the Bank of England
[2003] 3 W.L.R. 667, CA, the Court of Appeal held that material prepared by
Bank of England employees for the Bingham inquiry into the collapse of
BCCI was not covered by legal advice privilege since the dominant purpose
of such material was to put relevant factual material before the inquiry, not
to obtain legal advice. At first instance [2002] EWHC 2039 (Comm), Tomlinson J. held that Article 8 was not relevant as any incursion into privacy that
might be involved was necessary for the protection of the rights and freedoms
of the parties to the litigation, except in specific instances where, for example,
the parties agreed to preserve the anonymity of an informant. In *R (on the
application of Millar Gardner Solicitors) v. Minshull Street Crown Court*
[2002] EWHC 2079 (Admin), the Divisional Court held that a warrant to
obtain telephone contact details held at a solicitors' office in documents
including the office diary was lawful since these details were not subject to
legal professional privilege. Whilst Article 8 was engaged, it was justified as
necessary in a democratic society for the prevention of crime and protection
of others. In *R. (on the application of Howe) v. South Durham Magistrates
Court* [2004] EWHC 362 (Admin); *The Times*, February 26, 2004, the
claimant was prosecuted in 2003 for driving whilst disqualified. The question
whether or not he had been disqualified was in issue. In 2000 a person of the
same name had been disqualified but the claimant did not admit to being that
person. The claimant's solicitor had acted for the person disqualified in 2000,
and the Crown Prosecution Service issued a summons compelling the solicitor to give evidence as to whether the claimant was a person against whom a
disqualification order had been made. The claimant sought to judicially
review the issue of the summons, submitting that it infringed legal professional privilege and that it breached his rights under Article 6 of the Convention as it breached his privilege against self-incrimination and deprived
him of his solicitor of choice. The Divisional Court held that the summons
did not infringe legal professional privilege as the solicitor was only required
to identify whether the claimant was the person disqualified from driving in
2000 and not to reveal what was told to him by his client. The Court also held
that the summons did not breach Article 6. A solicitor acting for a client was
not *de facto* the client, so that calling a solicitor to give evidence against his
own client was not equivalent to calling a defendant to incriminate himself.
The solicitor would not be called in his capacity as the claimant's solicitor but
as a person present in court at the relevant time. The claimant's right to a
solicitor of choice was not absolute and could be overridden in the interests
of justice. However, the Court did say, *obiter*, that such a summons should be
used only as a last resort where no other means was available to identify
whether an individual had been disqualified from driving.

Add new paragraph **7–035A**:

The HRA has been invoked in relation to applications for disclosure of **7–035A**
documents in a lawyer's possession not involving issues of privilege. In *Bodle
v. Coutts & Co.* unreported, July 17, 2003, Ch.D, the claimant was seeking an
order that Coutts & Co.'s solicitors be restrained from acting for the bank in

proceedings brought by the claimant to set aside a statutory demand. The basis for the application was that the solicitors had previously represented the claimant in matrimonial proceedings and during the early stages of her negotiation with the bank. The solicitors refused to release the files to the claimant's new solicitors as the claimant had failed to pay their legal fees. The judge directed that the files be produced to the court in order to ascertain whether or not they contained confidential information that was germane to the unresolved issues. The judge decided that there was no such material. The claimant objected to the solicitors' files being inspected by the judge without her own solicitors having access to the same files on the basis that it would be procedurally unfair to her and in breach of Article 6. Peter Smith J. accepted that it would have been procedurally unfair for the court to have had regard to documents deployed by one side without the other side having access to them and such would have been an arguable breach of Article 6. However, this was not an absolute rule and in the present case to disclose the files to the claimant's solicitors would have entirely circumvented the solicitors' lien. He found that there was no Article 6 infringement of the claimant's rights as the court had to balance her rights against those of the solicitors. It was relevant that the solicitors did not have any relevant confidential information concerning the issues between the claimant and the bank and there was no risk of disclosure of any confidential information to the bank.

Add new heading (c) and new paragraph **7–035B**:

(c) *Freedom of expression*

7–035B   The conviction of a defence lawyer in criminal proceedings for negligent defamation as a result of a memorandum denouncing the tactics of a public prosecutor as "manipulation and unlawful presentation of evidence" was a violation of Article 10 since it was only in exception cases that restriction of defence counsel's freedom of expression could be "necessary in a democratic society": *Nikula v. Finland* Application No. 31611/96, March 21, 2002.

6. MEDICAL PRACTITIONERS

(b) *Relevant articles in relation to Medical Practitioners*

(i) *Article 2*

7–041   Add to sub-paragraph (a) Abortion: In *R. v. Secretary of State for Health, ex parte John Smeaton (on behalf of the Society for the Protection of Unborn Children)* [2002] 2 F.L.R. 146, Admin. Ct., the legality of the sale and use of the morning after pill was unsuccessfully challenged.

Add to sub-paragraph (b) Euthanasia: Diane Pretty's case and the issue of euthanasia has now been considered by the House of Lords and the European Court: see *Pretty v. Director of Public Prosecutions and Home Secretary* [2001] 3 W.L.R. 1598; [2002] 1 All E.R. 1, HL and *Pretty v. United Kingdom* [2002] 35 E.H.R.R. 1.

The House of Lords held that:

(a) the right to life set out in Article 2 could not be interpreted as conferring a right to die or to enlist the aid of another in bringing about one's death;

(b) the Article 3 right not to be subjected to inhuman or degrading treatment did not bear on an individual's right to live or die; it could not plausibly be suggested that the respondent was inflicting such treatment on Mrs Pretty whose suffering derived from her disease;

(c) the Article 8 right to respect for private life covered protection of personal autonomy in living; it did not extend to the choice to live no longer. Further, even if Article 8 applied, the present legislative regime was justifiable under Article 8(2) and it was notable that the United Kingdom's response to this problem was in accordance with a broad international consensus;

(d) a belief in the virtue of assisted suicide could not found a requirement pursuant to Article 9(1) for Mrs Pretty's husband to be absolved from the consequences of criminal conduct and the same arguments on justification applied in any event;

(e) even if one of the ECHR Articles was engaged and Mrs Pretty could therefore rely in principle on Article 14, section 2 of the Suicide Act 1961 did not discriminate against the disabled whilst allowing the able-bodied to commit suicide; the law conferred no right on anyone to commit suicide.

The European Court largely agreed with the English courts' interpretation of the Convention, holding that:

(a) Article 2 did not impose on States a positive obligation to protect a "right to die";

(b) A State's obligation to prevent ill treatment pursuant to Article 3 could not be considered to include permitting actions designed to cause death. Nor was the State required to provide a means of lawfully committing assisted suicide;

(c) Whilst the right to refuse medical treatment was within Article 8, the interference with Mrs Pretty's ability to end her life was legitimate and "necessary in a democratic society";

(d) Article 9 did not protect all convictions or beliefs: a strongly held belief about assisted suicide did not fall within its meaning;

(e) The State had an objective and reasonable justification for not distinguishing in law between individuals who were and were not capable of committing suicide and therefore there had been no violation of Articles 8 and 14.

In contrast to the *Pretty* case, in *Ms B v. An NHS Hospital Trust* [2002] 2 All E.R. 449 a patient's right to refuse treatment and have the ventilator which kept her alive switched off even if this would result in her death was upheld on the ground that this amounted to refusal of treatment as opposed to active ending of life. Many commentators have called for reform of the law in light of the anomalies which arguably arise as a result of the two cases.

For further analysis of the recent case law in this area see *"Assisted Suicide under the European Convention on Human Rights: a Critique"* [2003] E.H.R.L.R. 65.

Add to sub-paragraph (d) Right to information on life-threatening risks: Contrast *Patricia Howard & another v. Secretary of State for Health* [2002] 3 W.L.R. 738, *The Times*, March 28, 2002, Admin. Ct. in which Mr Justice Scott Baker held that the Secretary of State for Health had been entitled to refuse public access to two inquiries that he had instigated into serious malpractice by doctors, although it was relevant that the Secretary of State had conceded access by interested parties and their representatives throughout the oral hearings and there was no prohibition on witnesses communicating with the media. The judge noted that Article 10(1) did not confer a right on individuals to receive information that others were not willing to impart and the Secretary of State's decision had not interfered with the applicants' ability to impart information by any means available to them. He also held that Article 3 was not engaged because clinical negligence was not a sufficient foundation for such a claim.

Add a new sub-paragraph (e)

(e) *Inquests*: There has been a great deal of case law in this area since the HRA came into force.

In *R. (On the Application of Mohammed Farooq Khan) v. Secretary of State for Health* [2003] EWHC 1414, the claimant applied for judicial review of the investigations carried out into the death of his daughter in an NHS hospital. He contended that the inquiries into his daughter's death did not comply with the State's obligations imposed by Article 2 to properly investigate the same. Silber J. held that following decisions in the Strasbourg court, in cases where a patient died in hospital, the obligation of the State, adjectival to Article 2, was satisfied where the State had an independent system to ascertain the cause of death and had an effective judicial system to establish responsibility and to obtain civil redress. Whilst it was regrettable that the child's family had not been involved in any of the four investigations into the events of her death, it was doubtful that family participation in the investigative process was required to comply with the Article 2 obligation. Further the State was not obliged to fund legal representation at the inquest for the child's family as the inquest would effectively scrutinise the evidence without lawyers for the family as its purpose was inquisitorial and not adversarial.

However, the House of Lords has now overturned this decision and re-emphasised the scope of Article 2 protection in the case of deaths post the Human Rights Act coming into force: see *R. (on the application of Khan) v. Secretary of State for Health* [2003] 4 All E.R. 1239. Their Lordships held that the State's investigatory obligation included a duty to require a public inquiry with the participation of the deceased's family and that the holding of an inquest would not satisfy that obligation as the claimant was in no fit state to take part in it himself unless he had legal representation. It was emphasised that a public investigation had to be held which was both judicial and effective. See also *R. v. Secretary of State for the Home Department, ex p. Amin* [2004] 1 A.C. 653 in which the House of Lords again re-emphasised the importance of proper (namely an independent public) investigation under Article 2 where a death occurs in custody.

It is important to note that this protection will only be applicable in respect of deaths which have occurred after October 2, 2000. In *R. (on the application of Christine Hurst) v. HM Coroner for Northern District London* [2003] A.C.D. 361 L.T.L. 4/7/2003, it had been stated that a coroner owed a duty to consider whether the State's investigative duties under Article 2 had been complied with irrespective of whether or not the Human Rights Act had been in force as at the date of death. However, *in Re McKerr* [2004] 1 W.L.R. 807 the House of Lords overruled this decision and made clear that the duty to investigate an unlawful killing under Article 2 did not arise in domestic law in respect of deaths before October 2, 2000, when the Human Rights Act came into force.

In *R v. Secretary of State for the Home Department, ex p. Amin & Middleton* [2002] 3 W.L.R. 505, CA, the Court of Appeal held that an inquest jury could give a verdict of neglect where necessary so as to comply with Article 2 of the Convention, that is where in the judgment of the coroner it could serve to reduce the risk of repetition of the circumstances that gave rise to the death. However, this decision has was an extremely controversial one and has now been overruled by *R. (on the application of Middleton) v. West Somerset Coroner* [2004] 2 A.C. 182. This decision is now the leading authority on inquests and sets out what detail what compliance with Article 2 requires. Their Lordships have now made clear that where an inquest is the means by which the State discharges its procedural obligation to initiate an effective public investigation into a death involving or possibly involving a breach of the Convention, it has ordinarily to culminate in an expression of the jury's conclusion on the disputed factual issues at the heart of the case in order to be compliant with the Convention which could be achieved by interpreting the word "how" in the Coroners Act 1988, section 11(5)(b)(ii) in a broad sense, meaning "by what means and in what circumstances", rather than simply "by what means" the deceased came by his death. This requires a wider investigation than the narrative verdict approved by the Court of Appeal and the Convention would not be complied with where there was no exploration of the facts surrounding the death or where short verdicts in the traditional form were given. It was for the coroner to decide how best to elicit the jury's conclusion on the central issues and this might be done by inviting an expanded or narrative form of verdict or by inviting the jury's answers to factual questions put by the coroner. On the facts of the case the Convention had not been complied with as the jury's verdict had not expressed their opinion on the crucial matters of whether the deceased ought to have been recognised as a suicide risk and whether appropriate precautions ought to have been taken to prevent him taking his own life. *Middleton* was applied by the House of Lords in a decision made on the same day: see *R. (on the application of Sacker) v. HM Coroner for the County of West Yorkshire* (2004) 1 W.L.R. 796.

Add: In *R. (On the Application of PS) v. (1) Responsible Medical Officer (Dr G) (2) Second Opinion Appointed Doctor (Dr W)* [2003] EWHC 2335 **7–042** forcible administration of anti-psychotic drugs was held to be permissible under the Mental Health Act even where the patient had capacity and had elected not to give consent. The claimant's rights were held not to be engaged under Article 3 because (i) the treatment did not achieve the minimum level of severity to amount to inhuman or degrading treatment, and/or (ii) medical or therapeutic necessity had been convincingly shown to exist. The treatment was also said to be proportionate and justified under Article 8.

(iii) *Article 6*

7–043   Add: In *Hubbard v. Lambeth Southwark & Lewisham Health Authority* [2002] Lloyd's Rep. Med. 8, a decision by the master to order a private pre-trial meeting of both parties' expert witnesses was upheld on the grounds that it would usefully identify and narrow the issues, notwithstanding the genuine sensitivity of the claimants' experts in criticising the professional competence of a distinguished colleague at such a meeting. The Court of Appeal held that the order did not raise any issues under Article 6.

In *William Cassie Powell and Anita Diane Powell) v. Paul Boladz & 6 ors* [2003] EWHC 2160, Article 6 was used to defeat the defendant's application to strike out a libel action on the basis that the interference with the claimant's rights under Article 6 would be more serious if the application was granted than the interference with the defendant's rights under the same Article if the application was refused.

See also *R. (On the Application of Alliss) v. Legal Service Commission* [2002] EWHC 2079 (Admin), in which the claimant succeeded in establishing that the withdrawal of funding by the Legal Services Commission five months before a three-week personal injury and wrongful death claim was in breach of Article 6(1). The Court held that the grant of legal aid might be required pursuant to Article 6 where it was indispensable to ensure effective and fair access to the court which might be by reason of the complexity or type of case. On the facts of that case the claimant was a young man with psychiatric problems and limited education and the trial would be lengthy and complex with the opposing party being represented by leading and junior counsel. In these circumstances having supported the case for five years it had become too late for funding to be withdrawn (although the Court did say that had public funding been discharged at an early stage of the case, that would have been acceptable).

(iv) *Article 8*

7–044   Add: In *Joanna Rose & others v. Secretary of State for Health & others* [2002] 2 F.L.R. 962, EWHC 1593 Admin; L.T.L. 26/7/02, Scott Baker J. held that the desire by a person born as a result of artificial insemination by donor to know details of their origin did engage Article 8 and placed the State under a positive obligation. The information the claimants were trying to obtain was about their biological fathers and was something which went to the heart of their identity and to their make-up as people. Respect for private and family life incorporated the concept of personal identity. However, it should be noted that the issue as to whether Article 8 had in fact been breached was left open.

In *Re R. (A Child) sub nom. Re R. (A Child) (IVF: Paternity of Child)* (2003) 2 All E.R. 131; EWCA Civ 182 it was held that a husband whose sperm had mistakenly not been used in fertility treatment was, as a result of sections 28 and 29 of the Human Fertilisation and Embryology Act 1990, not the legal father of the resultant children. This was held to amount to an interference with his Article 8 rights but it was not necessary to consider the question of incompatibility because within domestic legislation there were remedies which could protect his position in relation to the twins (even if he was not entitled to a declaration of paternity), thereby making any breach of his Article 8 rights proportionate.

In *Natallie Evans v. Amicus Healthcare & Ors* [2004] 2 W.L.R. 713 the Court of Appeal held that the female claimants were not entitled to use frozen embryos created by IVF treatment after the claimants had separated from their male partners who had withdrawn their consent to treatment. Article 2 was said not to be engaged as an embryo was not a human life. However, the wishes of the claimants to continue with the IVF treatment and to have the embryos released from storage and transferred to them was held to engage their right to respect for their private lives under Article 8 which was also engaged by their former partners' opposition to that course of action. The provisions of Schedule 3 to the Human Fertilisation and Embryology Act 1990 which permitted the former partners to refuse to allow the claimants access to the embryos was an interference with their Convention rights but that interference was both necessary for the protection of the rights of all four parties and proportionate.

In *Deep Vein Thrombosis & Air Travel Group Litigation* [2004] Q.B. 234 (2003) TLR 14/7/2003, Nelson J. (whose decision was upheld by the Court of Appeal) held that neither Articles 6 nor 8 of the ECHR gave the claimants a remedy outside of the Warsaw Convention, nor was Article 17 of the latter Convention incompatible with ECHR rights.

In *Collins v. United Kingdom*, App. No. 11909/02, October 15, 2002 a severely disabled claimant had been moved to a purpose built complex within a hospital where she was promised a "home for life". However in 2000 the Health Authority decided to close down that complex and transfer future care to the Social Services Directorate. The claimant unsuccessfully brought judicial review proceedings to challenge that decision. It was held that the decision to move her into alternative care was not disproportionate, gave proper consideration to her interests and was based on relevant and sufficient reasons.

(vi) *Article 12*

Add: Article 12 was unsuccessfully sought to be invoked in *Briody v. St.* **7–046** *Helen's & Knowsley Area Health Authority* [2002] 2 W.L.R. 394, CA in which the Court of Appeal held that damages were not recoverable for surrogacy treatment which, although lawful, had a vanishingly small chance of success (assessed at one per cent). The right to a family founded by marriage set out in Article 12 was held to be quite different from having a right to be supplied with a child.

7. PARTICULAR ISSUES ARISING UNDER THE HRA IN RELATION TO
MEDICAL PRACTITIONERS

(c) *Withdrawal of Treatment*

7–058   Add: In *R. (On the Application of Oliver Leslie Burke) v. General Medical Council & (1) The Disability Rights Commission (Interested Party) and (2) The Official Solicitor to the Supreme Court (Intervener)* [2004] EWHC 1879 it was held that under both the Convention and at common law, if a patient was competent, or although incompetent had made an advance directive which was valid and relevant to the treatment in question, his decision to require the provision of artificial nutrition and hydration during his dying days was determinative of the issue. If neither such circumstances applied, the duty would be to treat the patient in his or her best interests (with there being a strong presumption in favour of preservation of life). It was stated that a failure to provide life-prolonging treatment in circumstances exposing the patient to "inhuman or degrading treatment" would in principle involve a breach of Article 3. Alternatively even if the patient's suffering had not reached the severity required to breach Article 3, a withdrawal of treatment in the same circumstances might still breach Article 8 if there were sufficiently adverse effects on his physical or moral integrity or mental stability. Thus, at the final stage when the patient had lapsed into a coma and lacked awareness of what was happening, there would not be a breach if ANH was withdrawn in circumstances where its continuation was futile and of no benefit to the patient. However, the prior authorisation of the court was required as a matter of law where it was proposed to withdraw or withhold ANH.

(d) *Consent to treatment*

7–059   Add: In *Glass v. United Kingdom* (App. No. 61827/00, March 9, 2004) there was held to be a violation of Article 8 where a hospital imposed treatment on a severely mentally and physically handicapped child contrary to the wishes of his mother. The decision to impose treatment was held to give rise to interference with the right to respect for the child's private life and in particular his right to physical intergrity. It was further stated that, save in emergency situations, the requirement of parental consent required doctors to seek the intervention of the court. Thus the decision to override the mother's objection to the proposed treatment in the absence of authorisation by the court violated Article 8.

(e) *Right of access to confidential information*

7–060   Add: In *MG v. United Kingdom* (App. No. 39393/98, September 24, 2002) the European Court upheld a claim similar to *Gaskin* concluding that there had been a failure to fulfil the State's positive obligation to protect the applicant's rights under Article 8 in respect of his access to his records from April 1995. The applicant had been in local authority voluntary care for five periods during his childhood and he requested access to his social services records relating to his time spent in the local authority care. He specifically requested information on whether he had ever been on the "at risk register", whether his father had been investigated or convicted of crimes against children and about the responsibility of the local authority for abuse he suffered as a child. A year later he was provided with summary information and certain documents from his file. The Court held that this refusal breached his Article 8 rights. However, from March 1, 2000 he could have but had not appealed to an independent authority against the disclosure of certain records on the grounds of a duty of confidentiality to third parties under the Data Protection Act 1998. Therefore the Court held that his rights under Article 8 had been breached between April 1995 and March 1, 2000 only.

In *Rose v. Secretary of State for Health* [2002] EWHC 1593, claimants born as a result of artificial insemination by donor complained that the defendant's refusal to provide them with non-identifying information relating to the donor's medical history, ethnic and cultural identity and with identifying information where possible breached their Article 8 rights. The Court held that the provision of information about the claimants' biological fathers went to the very heart of their identity and to their make-up as people and so the right to respect for private and family life pursuant to Article 8 was engaged.

(f) *Disclosure of confidential information*

Add: See also *H (A Healthcare Worker) v. Associated Newspapers Ltd. and*   **7–061**
H (A Healthcare Worker) v. N (A Health Authority) [2002] Lloyd's Med. Rep. 210, CA in which a health worker with HIV ("H") was held to have a right to confidentiality which could properly be protected by an injunction against the soliciting or publication of information which might lead to deductive disclosure of H's identity. H was also entitled to bring proceedings under a cloak of anonymity because to hold otherwise would have been to frustrate the decision of the court on the issues before it.

In *R. (On the Application of Szuluk) v. HM Prison Sutton* [2004] A.C.D. 45; EWCA 514 (Admin) it was held (on the specific facts of that case) to be a breach of Article 8 to require the content of correspondence between a prisoner with a life-threatening medical condition and his medical advisors outside prison to be examined by a prison medical officer.

(g) *Disclosure of medical records and confidentiality*

Add: Munby J.'s decision has now been considered and upheld by the Court   **7–063**
of Appeal: *A Health Authority v. X & Others* [2002] 1 F.L.R. 1045; [2002] 2 All E.R. 780, CA. The judge was found to have correctly balanced the public interest in effective disciplinary procedures for the investigation and eradication of medical malpractice against the confidentiality of the documents, and to have correctly used his power to attach conditions to disclosure.

The Court of Appeal has also upheld the decision on liability of Morland J. in *Cornelius v. De Taranto* [2002] EMLR 6 (although an appeal against a costs order was allowed). The Court of Appeal reiterated that a client's express consent was required before a medicolegal report was transmitted to a third party.

In *A v. X & B (Non Party)* [2004] EWHC 447 an application was made for disclosure of medical records by a non party. The application arose in circumstances where the main cause of the claimant's injuries in a road traffic accident was a bipolar mood disorder or hypomania. As the disorder could have a genetic origin and C's brother also appeared to suffer from it, the defendant sought disclosure of the brother's medical records in order to seek to prove that the claimant's disorder would have occurred in any event. However, the court refused to make such an order stating that only in a very exceptional factual situation would such disclosure be justified in civil proceedings and this was not such a case. In particular it was noted that there was already clear evidence that the claimant was mentally disturbed whilst at university and disclosure was therefore not necessary for a fair disposal of the claim.

8. Professional Disciplinary Proceedings

7–065   Add: The domestic courts now appear unlikely to find that professional disciplinary proceedings will amount to determination of a "criminal charge" for the purposes of Article 6(1). However, the distinction is of diminished importance because it has been accepted that there is a hierarchy of civil proceedings in relation to the penal element or stigma involved and at the upper end of the hierarchy, due process guarantees similar to those conferred by Articles 6(2) and 6(3) are implied in Article 6(1): *Albert and Le Compte v. Belgium* (1983) 5 E.H.R.R. 533, paras 30, 39; *Official Receiver v. Stern* [2001] 1 W.L.R. 2230, CA at p.2254h and 2257c; *R v. Security & Futures Authority ex p. Fleurose* [2002] I.R.L.R. 297, *The Times*, January 15, 2002, CA, para.14.

Note 46: *Pine v. Law Society* is now reported at (2002) UKHRR 81, CA.

7–066A   In *R. (on the application of Hamilton) v. The United Kingdom Central Council for Nursing, Midwifery and Health Visiting* [2003] EWCA Civ 1600; *The Times*, November 12, 2003, it was argued before the Court of Appeal that registration as a nurse or midwife ranks as a possession protected by Article 1 of Protocol No. 1. The Court did not have to decide the point, and chose not to. It did, however, note that Article 1 of Protocol No. 1 contemplates a range of independent judgment for each state as to how it may deprive citizens of their possessions in the public interest. The court's duty is to gauge whether the state has nevertheless gone beyond what the Article will tolerate. In *Holder v. Law Society* [2003] EWCA Civ 39; [2003] 1 W.L.R. 1059; [2003] 3 All E.R. 62, CA, the Law Society had intervened in the claimant's practice as a solicitor under the provisions of the Solicitors Act 1974 on suspicion of dishonesty. The claimant argued that the society's intervention power infringed his rights under Article 1 of Protocol No. 1. The Court of Appeal accepted that the intervention involved an interference with the claimant's peaceful enjoyment of his possessions, but noted that such interference may be justified, according to Article 1 of Protocol No. 1, if it is in the public interest. While a fair balance must be struck between the demands of the general interest of the community and the requirements of the protection of the individual's fundamental rights, it was said that it is not for the Court to determine what is necessary in the public interest. A discretion must be allowed to the legislature in establishing the statutory regime and to the Law Society as the body entrusted with decisions in individual cases. The Court found that the margin had not been crossed in either case.

Add at end of paragraph:

(a) In *Sadler v. General Medical Council* [2003] UKPC 59; [2004] Lloyd's Rep. Med. 44; (2004) H.R.L.R. 8, the Privy Council stated: "There is no general principle of Convention jurisprudence which prevents professional self-regulation: see *Albert and Le Compte v Belgium* (1983) 5 EHRR 533 especially at pages 541–542, paragraph 29. Whether a tribunal satisfies the requirements of Article 6 depends on all the relevant circumstances, including how the members of the tribunal are appointed, their tenure of office, their protection from outside pressure and their apparent independence (as evidenced by their standing and procedure". In *Aaron v. Law Society* [2003] EWHC 2271 (Admin) the Court stated that, in relation to claims of objective bias the test was whether in the circumstances a fair minded observer would have considered that there had been a real possibility of bias.

(b) In relation to proceedings in a party's absence, see *Das v. General Medical Council* [2003] UKPC 75. The appellant appealed against a determination by the GMC's Committee on Professional Performance. The Committee had made several findings against him in his absence, and had withdrawn his registration for 12 months. The appellant claimed that, by proceeding in his absence, the Committee had breached Article 6(1) of the Convention. Evidence was adduced to show that notice of the hearing was sent to the appellant's address and signed for by him. The Privy Council held that the Committee's determination was a model of its kind and was unassailable. Its findings had been fully particularised, supported by clear evidence that the appellant's performance was seriously defective, and the hearing was eminently fair. The Committee had been entitled to conclude that proper notice of the hearing had been received by the appellant, and its decision to proceed in his absence was a proper exercise of its discretion. On the right to an oral hearing, see *R. (on the application of Thompson) v. Law Society* [2004] EWCA Civ 167; [2004] 2 All E.R. 113; *The Times*, April 1, 2004, CA. In this case, the Office for the Supervision of Solicitors ("OSS") had considered complaints of inadequate professional services against the appellant solicitor. The appellant sought judicial review on the ground that his rights at common law or under Article 6 of the Convention had been infringed by the failure of the OSS to afford him an oral hearing. The Court of Appeal stated that, at common law, the duty of the OSS adjudicator and appellate adjudication panel was to act fairly and what was fair depended on the circumstances of the particular case. Similarly, under Article 6, there might be cases in which an oral hearing was required at first instance and others where it was not. The Court held that no breach of the Convention arose if the tribunal was subject to control by a court which had full jurisdiction and itself complied with the requirements of Article 6. It noted that while some disciplinary proceedings could give rise to disputes over civil rights within Article 6(1) if what was at stake was the right to continue to exercise a profession, a decision to reprimand, as in this case, did not amount to a determination of civil rights.

(f)   In *R. (on the application of Luthra) v. General Dental Council* [2004] EWHC 458 (Admin) the Professional Conduct Committee of the General Dental Council had found the appellant guilty of serious professional misconduct involving dishonesty, and had suspended his registration. The appellant complained that the Committee had erred in law in failing to give any or any sufficient reasons for its finding and had, accordingly, unfairly deprived him of his right to a fair trial under Article 6 of the Convention. The Court accepted that Article 6 was engaged, and required adequate reasons to be given for a decision. However, it expressed the view that, in the instant case, Article 6 added nothing to the common law position. Elias J. held that the basis of the Committee's decision was clear from its conclusions when considered in light of the transcript of evidence and that this was sufficient as giving adequate reasons. He stated there was usually no need for the committee to identify why, in reaching its findings of fact, it accepted some evidence and rejected other evidence.

(h)   The hearing should take place within a reasonable time: *General Medical Council v. Pembrey* [2002] EWHC 1602 Admin, [2002] Lloyd's Rep. Med. 434, L.T.L. August 8, 2002. The GMC was entitled to an extension of an interim conditional registration order against a consultant pending a hearing of complaints by the Professional Conduct Committee where the delay in progressing the matter did not breach Article 6. A stay of proceedings is only necessary if, due to the misconduct of the prosecution, it was unfair for the defendant to be tried or a fair trial was no longer possible: *General Dental Council v. Price* L.T.L. July 19, 2001, DC. See also *Langford v. Law Society* [2002] EWHC 2802 (Admin) where the Divisional Court held that there was a relatively high threshold to be crossed before it could be said in any particular case that a period of delay was unreasonable so as to give grounds for real concern that a Convention right had been violated. In *Aaron v. Law Society* [2003] EWHC 2271 (Admin) the appellant appealed against the Solicitors' Disciplinary Tribunal's finding of "conduct unbecoming a solicitor". The appellant complained, *inter alia*, of unreasonable delay by the Tribunal with reference to Article 6 of the Convention, submitting that the only effective remedy for the delay of up to 14 or 15 years between the first instance of alleged improper conduct and the institution of disciplinary proceedings was to quash the whole of the Tribunal's findings. The Court held that the delays involved in the proceedings did not reach the Article 6(1) threshold, and that none of the delays caused the appellant any prejudice. However, the Court did note that those responsible for regulation of solicitors should now have the "reasonable time" requirement of Article 6 in the forefront of their minds in any disciplinary process.

(i)   Legal aid: Article 6(1) does not necessarily require the provision of legal representation in disciplinary proceedings: *Pine v. Law Society* [2002] 1 W.L.R. 2189; [2002] 2 All E.R. 658; (2002) UKHRR 81, CA.

(j)   Proportionality: The Privy Council held that human rights law did not require a decision of a disciplinary committee to suspend registration to be governed by the principle of proportionality. Accordingly, the General Medical Council's Professional Conduct Committee was entitled to suspend a doctor from sole practice: *Chaudhury v. General Medical Council*, L.T.L. July 16, 2002, PC cf. *Preiss v. General Dental Council* [2001] 1 W.L.R. 1936; [2001] Lloyd's Rep. Med. 434; (2001) H.R.L.R. 56, PC (suspension order excessive and replaced with admonition).

(k) An appeal may cure any unfairness in the disciplinary tribunal procedure: an appeal to the Privy Council was sufficient to cure any alleged unfairness in the composition of the Professional Conduct Committee of the General Medical Council because it was by way of full rehearing: *Ghosh v. General Medical Council* [2001] 1 W.L.R. 1915; [2001] Lloyd's Rep. Med. 443; *The Times*, June 25, 2001, PC. In *R v. Royal Pharmaceutical Society of Great Britain, ex p. Panjawani* [2002] EWHC 1127 Admin; L.T.L., July 10, 2002, the Divisional Court held that an appeal had to be conducted by way of rehearing in order to comply with Article 6 because the statutory procedure for cases before the Statutory Committee of the Royal Pharmaceutical Society allowed for the same body to initiate, prosecute and determine complaints. See also *Preiss v. General Dental Council* [2001] 1 W.L.R. 1926, [2001] Lloyd's Rep. Med. 491, *The Times*, August 14, 2001, PC and *R v. United Kingdom Central Council for Nursing Midwifery & Health Visiting, ex p. Tehrani* [2001] IRLR 208, Ct. Sess. (Scot.). In *Preiss v. General Dental Council* [2001] 1 WLR 1926 the Privy Council said: "Since the coming into operation of the Human Rights Act 1998, with its adjuration in section 3 to read and give effect to legislation, so far as it is possible to do so, in a way compatible with the Convention rights, any tendency to read down rights of appeal in disciplinary cases is to be resisted." Rose L.J. made similar comments in *Langford v. Law Society* [2002] EWHC (Admin) 2802. In *Ghosh v. General Medical Council* [2001] 1 W.L.R. 1915 Lord Millett said: "The Board's jurisdiction is appellate, not supervisory. The appeal is by way of a rehearing in which the Board is fully entitled to substitute its own decision for that of the committee." In *Evans v. General Medical Council* Appeal No 40 of 1984 (unreported) the Board said: ". . . the Board will accord an appropriate measure of respect to the judgment of the committee whether the practitioner's failings amount to serious professional misconduct and on the measures necessary to maintain professional standards and provide adequate protection to the public. But the Board will not defer to the committee's judgment more than is warranted by the circumstances." In cases such as *Chohan v. Law Society* [2004] EWHC 1145 (Admin) and *Hayes v. Law Society* [2004] EWHC 1165 (Admin) the Court has applied this same approach to appeals from solicitors' disciplinary proceedings, treating the case as a rehearing, albeit one within which the decision-making body is accorded appropriate respect. The same approach has been taken to appeals from osteopaths' disciplinary proceedings in *Moody v. General Osteopathic Council* [2004] EWHC 967 (Admin).

NOTE 52: *R v. General Medical Council, ex p. Kyros Nicolaides* is now reported at [2001] Lloyd's Rep. Med. 525. In *R v. United Kingdom Central Council for Nursing, Midwifery and Health Visiting & Nursing and Midwifery Council, ex p. Celia Mary Hamilton* [2002] EWHC 2770 (Admin), a challenge was made to the impartiality of the United Kingdom Central Council ("UKCC") on the grounds that there was insufficient insulation between the prosecutorial and adjudicative functions of the UKCC, the names of professional screeners had not been supplied to the claimant and the requirement that a medical examiner should attend the hearing and could ask questions with the leave of the chairman created an appearance of bias. Crane J. held that the UKCC's procedures did not breach Article 6 because neither the professional screeners nor anyone else had a prosecutorial or even a presentational role in the context of an application for termination of suspension, the screeners' role was limited and the medical examiners were independent experts who acted only as witnesses and advisers. The tenure of the members of the Council did not raise concerns and the committee sat with an independent legal assessor. Although the issue of fitness to practise could involve consideration of the practitioner's ability to comply with professional standards in the context of the code of conduct, this was not sufficient to deprive the committee of independence and impartiality. The case was the subject of an unsuccessful appeal in [2003] EWCA Civ 1600; *The Times*, November 12, 2003, noted at 7–066A above. In *R. (on the application of Mahfouz) v. Professional Conduct Committee of the General Medical Council & The General Medical Council (Third Party)* [2003] EWHC 1695 (Admin), Davis J. held that the Professional Conduct Committee of the GMC did not breach Article 6 in rejecting an application to discharge themselves based on an allegation of unconscious bias following the publication of newspaper articles concerning the claimant during his hearing for professional misconduct. The Court of Appeal (*The Times*, March 19, 2004) allowed the appellant's appeal in part. It stated that knowledge of prejudicial publicity need not be fatal to the fairness of a hearing by the Professional Conduct Committee of the GMC but its effect had to be considered in the context of the proceedings as a whole including the impact of the legal advice available. Where there was a possible breach of the rules of natural justice as well as a potential procedural irregularity, the legal assessor to the committee was under a duty to provide advice, looking at it in the same way as a judge directing a jury. In *Sadler v. General Medical Council* [2003] UKPC 95, *The Times*, September 29, 2003, the Privy Council found that the GMC's Committee on Professional Performance satisfied the requirements of independence, impartiality and fairness under Article 6.

NOTE 61: *Sudesh Madan v. The General Medical Council* is now reported at [2001] Lloyd's Rep. Med. 539, D.C.

Add new heading and new paragraph **7–068**:

Law Society interventions and investigations

7–068   In *Holder v. Law Society* [2002] EWHC 1559; *The Times*, September 9, 2002, Ch.D, Peter Smith J. held that the Law Society's power to intervene in a solicitor's practice is not of itself contrary to the HRA. It is essentially a question of fact and degree in a particular case whether the intervention was in breach of the right to peaceful enjoyment of possessions in Article 1 of Protocol 1. An intervention was not always necessary where a solicitor was suspected of dishonesty and could be a breach of a solicitor's human rights. There were alternative procedures including a short-notice court hearing and reviewing the evidence and considering whether to make an order for intervention or some lesser order such as the appointment of a receiver or manager. However, in *Wright, Goodall, East & Prescott v. Law Society* L.T.L. September 9, 2002, Ch.D, H.H.J. Behrens disagreed with *Holder* finding that the court did not have jurisdiction to adopt the alternative solution to a Law Society intervention proposed by Peter Smith J. where dishonesty was suspected on the part of solicitors. The issue was considered on appeal in *Holder v. Law Society* [2003] 1 W.L.R. 1059; [2003] 3 All E.R. 62, CA. The Court of Appeal held that although intervention by the Law Society in a solicitor's practice involved an interference with the claimant's peaceful enjoyment of his possessions, it was justified in the public interest. The statutory scheme complied with the ECHR. The Court did not rule on whether the alternative procedure suggested by Peter Smith J. was in fact available to the Law Society. It concluded that the judge was wrong to take on himself the task of determining whether the intervention procedure was necessary and therefore proportional. It held that this ignored the all important factor of the "margin of appreciation or discretion" or "area of judgment" allowed to the legislator in establishing the statutory regime of intervention and to the Law Society, as decision-maker, in implementing it. Carnwath L.J. stated that the Law Society's actions must be judged by reference to the procedure laid down by Parliament, not to some hypothetical alternative procedure. The Law Society has a "margin of discretion" and the Court in discharging its separate duty to consider the merits of the case must pay due regard to the views of the Law Society as the relevant professional body. The Court of Appeal held that the Law Society's intervention in the case in question as a matter of the exercise of its discretion was entirely justified. See also *Michael John Harvey v. The Law Society* [2003] EWHC 535 (Ch) in which it was accepted by the claimant that the intervention procedure was in principle compatible with the HRA, both at the stage at which the Law Society comes to decide on intervention and at the stage at which the Court considers whether the intervention should continue.

Add new paragraph **7–069**:

In *R. (on the application of Pamplin) v. Law Society* [2001] EWHC Admin   **7–069** 300, *The Independent*, July 9, 2001, Mr Justice Newman declined to find that the reasonable disclosure of confidential information by the police to the Law Society in connection with an investigation by the Office for the Supervision of Solicitors in the public interest violated Article 8. In *Pal v. General Medical Council* [2004] EWHC 1485, the claimant doctor had brought claims against the GMC and three of its non-medical employees in defamation and under the Data Protection Act 1998 and the HRA. Her claim related to documents and communications outlining the GMC employees' suspicions that she was suffering from an underlying health problem and their investigations into her mental state. The defendants sought summary judgment in respect of parts of the claimant's claims, arguing, inter alia, that their breach of the claimant's right to privacy went only so far as was necessary for the protection of health. The Court held that there were clearly triable issues as to, *inter alia*, whether the defendants' admitted breach of the claimant's human rights was justified within Article 8(2) of the Convention. Such issues were not suitable for summary resolution.

CHAPTER 8

CONSTRUCTION PROFESSIONALS

[55]

1. INTRODUCTION

(a) *The construction professions*

8–006   Add: In *Royal Brompton Hospital NHS Trust v. Hammond* [2002] EWHC
2037 (TCC), (2003) 88 Con.L.R. 1, H.H. Judge Lloyd Q.C. observed that
project management is still an emergent professional discipline, in which professional practices as such have not yet developed or become clearly dis-
cernible. The standard of care required of a project manager is likely to
depend upon his particular terms of engagement and the demands of the
particular project. Nevertheless, it was clear that a central part of the role of
the project manager was to be "co-ordinator and guardian of the client's
interests". Moreover, the terms of engagement of other consultants will be
material in defining the scope of the project manager's duties, since duplica-
tion of function is not expected. Thus, in that case, although the architect was
the contract administrator formally appointed under the building contract,
that function had been transferred *de facto* to the project manager. The judge
also considered the effect of the appointment of a project manager on the
obligations of other professional consultants appointed by the client. The
project manager is the client's primary representative and should be regarded
by other consultants as, in effect, a client (albeit a highly informed client) and
should be kept fully advised by them. The expertise and knowledge of the
project manager will affect only the extent to which such advice needs to be
spelled out; the essential elements of such advice must always be clearly given
even although it may be thought to be pointing out the obvious.

Add to NOTE 17: For further detailed discussion of project managers'
responsibilities, see Leong, C., "The duty of care in project management",
(2001) 17 P.N. 250. For a case where project managers were held liable for

failing to prevent works which created a risk of fire, see *Six Continents Retail Ltd. v. Carford Catering Ltd.* [2003] EWCA Civ 1790.

Add: In *Daejan Investments Ltd. v. The Park West Club Ltd.* [2003] EWHC 2872 (TCC), [2003] B.L.R. 223, it was held that the pre-action protocol applies to Part 20 proceedings. In that case, the Part 20 claimant (which was also the claimant in the main action) was penalised by an adverse costs order for its failure to follow the protocol before issuing Part 20 proceedings.   **8–007**

(b) *Claims against construction professionals*

Add new NOTE 28A: For a review of the effects of implementation of the Civil Procedure Rules upon procedure in the Technology and Construction Court, see Burr, A. and Honey, R., "The Post-Woolf TCC: Any Changes?" (2001) 17 Const.L.J. 378.   **8–008**

2. DUTIES

(a) *Duties to client*

(i) *Contractual duties*

Add: It is common for design and build contractors to take over the appointment of design and other consultants originally engaged by the employer by novation of the consultants' contracts with the employer. In this way, the contractor typically hopes to secure both continuity in the design and other professional services required to complete the project and redress against the relevant consultant if defective services provided to the employer before the novation result in the contractor suffering loss under the building contract. Careful examination of the terms of any novation agreement will be required to determine whether the latter objective is actually achieved. It was not achieved in *Blyth & Blyth Ltd. v. Carillion Construction Ltd.* (2001) 79 Con.L.R. 142, where the Scottish Court of Session held that, on its true construction, a novation agreement made between the employer, the design and build contractor and the consulting engineers originally engaged by the employer only required the engineers to regard the contractor as their client in respect of services provided *after* the date of the novation. Accordingly, the contractor was not entitled to recover damages for loss which it suffered as a result of defective services provided by the engineers to the employer before the novation.   **8–017**

Add: The effect of the Unfair Terms in Consumer Contracts Regulations 1999 upon the terms of the 1999 edition of the RIBA Standard Form of Agreement for the Appointment of an Architect (SFA/99) was considered, *obiter*, by H.H. Judge Toulmin C.M.G., Q.C. in *Picardi v. Cuniberti* [2002] EWHC 2923 (QB), (2002) 94 Con. L.R. 81. The judge regarded the adjudication clause in SFA/99 as deprived of effect by the operation of the Regulations in a case where it had not been individually negotiated. His reasoning suggests that other terms in SFA/99 are also vulnerable to challenge on this basis unless brought specifically to the client's attention and individually negotiated. That decision was distinguished on its facts in *Lovell Projects Ltd.*   **8–022** *v. Legg and Carver* [2003] B.L.R. 452 and in *Westminster Building Company Ltd. v. Beckingham* [2004] EWHC 138 (TCC), [2004] B.L.R. 163. In each of those cases, it was the party who sought to invoke the Regulations which had insisted upon the particular standard form contracts used and had done so in circumstances where it had taken (or had had the opportunity to take) appropriate professional advice.

8-026   Add: In *Consarc Design Ltd. v. Hutch Investments Ltd.* [2002] P.N.L.R. 712, the employer sought to recover damages from its architects for a failure to warn that the completion date agreed in the building contract was unlikely to be achieved. At the relevant time, the architects had not been formally engaged by the employer, although they had provided some preliminary services and were later engaged on the terms of the RIBA Standard Form of Agreement for the Appointment of an Architect, 1992 edition (SFA/92). The employer argued that the terms of SFA/92 had, by implication, retrospective effect so as to govern the parties' prior relationship and import a duty to warn. H.H. Judge Bowsher Q.C. rejected this argument. The judge explained that a contract of engagement may have retrospective effect where the contract so provides either expressly or by necessary implication. An implication of retrospectivity will arise where parties have been conducting themselves as if there is an agreement in place and on the mutual assumption that such agreement will be formalised in due course. But no such implication arises where parties have been proceeding without any certainty as to whether an agreement will ultimately be concluded. Here, although the architects had done some preliminary work for the employer on the project before SFA/92 was executed, there was no such certainty and hence no implication of retrospectivity.

Add to NOTE 81: Even where the circumstances referred to in section 14(1) of the Supply of Goods and Services Act 1982 exist, the facts may render impossible the implication of any meaningful term requiring the performance of services within a reasonable time. For example, in *Munckenbeck & Marshall v. The Kensington Hotel Ltd.* (2001) 78 Con.L.R. 171, it was held that a firm of architects' contract of engagement contained no implied term that they would provide tender drawings within a reasonable time. Since it was not possible to identify the date upon which the architects first came under an obligation to produce such drawings, an implied term that they were to produce them within a reasonable time could not arise.

Add to NOTE 83: For further consideration of the decision in *Chesham Properties Ltd v. Bucknall Austin Project Management Services*, see Leong, C., "The duty of care in project management", (2001) 17 P.N. 250.

8-034   Add to NOTE 1: For further consideration of the decision in *Chesham Properties Ltd. v. Bucknall Austin Project Management Services*, see Leong, C., "The duty of care in project management", (2001) 17 P.N. 250.

8-036   NOTE 8: *Payne v. John Setchell Ltd.* is now reported at [2002] P.N.L.R. 7. Dyson J.'s explanation in *New Islington Health Authority v. Pollard Thomas & Edwards* of the designer's duty to review his design was adopted and applied in *Tesco Stores Ltd. v. Costain Construction Ltd.* [2003] EWHC 1487 (TCC),

[2004] C.I.LL 2062: an architect owed no duty to review his design unless something occurred which would have brought the need to review to the attention of a reasonably competent architect. Accordingly, an architect did not owe a continuing duty to his client to review his design such that a contractual failure to prepare competent designs was a breach that continued until completion of the structure he had designed.

(ii) *Duties independent of contract*

Add: Subsection 1(5) contains an important proviso: if, after completion **8-044** of the dwelling, further work is done to rectify defects in the original work, any cause of action in relation to such further work accrues only when it is finished. Thus in *Alderson v. Beetham Organisation Ltd.* [2003] EWCA Civ 408, [2003] 1 W.L.R. 1686 it was held that the leaseholders of flats acquired a fresh cause of action upon completion of the developer's ineffective works to remedy the originally installed but defective damp proof system in the building. *Payne v. John Setchell Ltd.* is now reported at [2002] P.N.L.R. 7.

Add: *Payne v. John Setchell Ltd.* is now reported at [2002] P.N.L.R. 7. **8-059**

(b) *Duties to third parties*

Add: An issue which commonly arises in connection with a collateral war- **8-062** ranty given by a construction professional to a non-client is whether that warranty has been effectively assigned by the non-client to a third party. Whether a collateral warranty is capable of being assigned will depend upon its terms, and in particular, upon the correct construction of any covenant against assignment which it contains. In *Allied Carpets Group plc v. Macfarlane* [2002] EWHC 1155 (TCC), [2002] P.N.L.R. 812, a collateral warranty was given by a firm of architects and structural engineers which was engaged in the development of a warehouse by its owner to the intended tenant of the warehouse. The tenant assigned its lease to the claimant and purported to assign the collateral warranty. H.H. Judge Bowsher Q.C. held that there had not been any effective assignment of the warranty.

(ii) *Recovery by third parties in respect of personal injury and damage to "other property"*

Add: The decision and reasoning of H.H. Judge Bowsher Q.C. on the issue **8-083** of the architects' duty of care to a subsequent occupier in respect of latent defects in *Baxall Securities Ltd v. Sheard Walshaw Partnership* were upheld by the Court of Appeal: [2002] EWCA Civ 9, [2002] P.N.L.R. 564. A duty of care will exist only in respect of latent defects. A defect is not latent if it is reasonably discoverable by a subsequent occupier with the benefit of such skilled third party advice as he might be expected to obtain before going into occupation. David Steel J. (with whom Brooke and Hale L.JJ. agreed) said, at paragraph 54:

"In my judgment the judge's analysis is correct. Actual knowledge of the defect, or alternatively a reasonable opportunity for inspection that would unearth the defect, will usually negative the duty of care or at least break the chain of causation unless (as is not suggested in the present case) it is reasonable for the claimant not to remove the danger posed by the defect and to run the risk of injury: see *Targett v. Torfaen B.C.* [1992] 3 All E.R. 27 per Sir Donald Nicholls V-C at p. 37.''

8–083A   This decision is the subject of an article by I. N. Duncan Wallace, "Lucky Architects: Snail in an Opaque Bottle?" (2003) 119 L.Q.R. 17. (The architect's appeal on the issue of causation was allowed and that aspect of the case is discussed further at paragraph 8–276, n.32, below).

In *Bellefield Computer Services Ltd. v. E. Turner and Sons Ltd.*, unreported, November 9, 2001, which was decided shortly before the Court of Appeal delivered judgment in *Baxall*, Forbes J. followed the decision of Judge Bowsher Q.C. in holding that architects engaged by a design and build contractor owed a duty of care in tort to a subsequent occupier of the building in respect of latent defects because there had been no reasonable possibility that the claimant would carry out an inspection which was likely to discover those defects before it went into occupation. For the facts, see paragraph 8–124 below. The judge's findings and reasoning were upheld on appeal: [2003] Lloyd's Rep. P.N. 53. Potter L.J. (with whom May L.J. and Sir Anthony Evans agreed) identified the following four principles concerning the existence and scope of an architect's duty to a subsequent owner or occupier:

(1)   An architect may, in appropriate circumstances, owe a duty of care in tort and be liable to a subsequent occupier of the building which the architect has designed and/or the construction of which he has supervised in respect of latent defects in the building of which there is no reasonable possibility of inspection: *cf.* the duty of the negligent builder as expounded by Lord Keith in *Murphy v. Brentwood District Council* [1991] A.C. 398 at 460–465 and as applied to the position of architects by H.H. Judge Bowsher Q.C. in *Baxall Securities Ltd v. Sheard Walshaw Partnership* (2001) TCC 36 at paragraphs 107 and 111.

(2)   The question whether a particular defect in a building comes within the scope of an architect's duty of care to a subsequent occupier will depend upon the original design and/or supervisory obligations of the architect in question. The architect will not owe a duty of care in respect of defects for which he never had any design or supervisory responsibility in the first place: *cf.* the observations of Windeyer J. in the Australian High Court in *Voly v. Inglewood Shire Council* [1963] A.L.R. 657 at 662.

(3)   If a dangerous defect arises as the result of a negligent omission on the part of the architect, he cannot excuse himself from liability on the grounds that he delegated the duty of design of the relevant part of the building works, unless he obtains the permission of his employer to do so: see Keating: Building Contracts (7th ed.) paragraph 13–40 and *Moresk Cleaners Ltd. v. Hicks* [1966] 2 Lloyd's Rep. 338.

(4)   The detailed duties of an architect in relation to his design function depend upon the application of the general principles above stated to the particular facts of the case, including any special terms agreed. The precise ambit of such duties will usually depend upon expert evidence from members of the profession as to what a competent, experienced architect would do in the circumstances.

The question whether a construction professional owed a duty of care to a   **8–083B**
subsequent owner came before the court again in *Sahib Foods Ltd. v. Paskin
Kyriades Sands* [2003] EWHC 142 (TCC), [2003] P.N.L.R. 30. A fire in a food
production factory spread beyond the room in which it ignited because
combustible panels had been used to line that room. The subsequent purchaser of the factory claimed damages from the architects who designed the
refurbishment of the factory. Applying the principles identified in *Baxall* and
Bellefield, H.H. Judge Bowsher Q.C. held that the architects owed a duty of
care to the purchaser in respect of latent defects in the factory of which there
had been no reasonable possibility of an inspection. The purchaser's claim
failed, however, because there was no evidence to suggest that the use of the
combustible panels was a defect which would not have been revealed by a pre-
purchase survey. This point was not taken upon the appeal: [2003] EWCA
Civ 1832, [2003] P.N.L.R. 403.

It should be noted that the loss claimed in *Baxall*, *Bellefield* and *Sahib* was
physical damage to property. In *Bellefield*, May L.J. expressly reserved for
future consideration the question whether or to what extent the scope of an
architect's duty of care to a subsequent owner or occupier extended to loss
associated with physical damage.

(iv) *The English exceptions to the general exclusionary rule*

Add: *Payne v. John Setchell Ltd.* is now reported at [2002] P.N.L.R. 7.   **8–094**

Replace the first four sentences with the following: In *Machin v. Adams*   **8–098**
(1997) 84 B.L.R. 79, an architect was asked by his clients, who were in the
process of selling their house to the plaintiff for use as a care home, to write
a letter setting out the then state of alteration and refurbishment works at the
house together with the amount of time necessary to complete them. The
defendant knew that the letter was to be shown to persons other than his
clients, probably including the purchaser of the house. The Court of Appeal
held that the defendant owed no duty of care to the plaintiff in respect of the
letter. Simon Brown L.J. considered that the defendant would have owed a
duty of care to the plaintiff in respect of the letter but for the fact that he
understood that he would be required to return on completion of the works
in order to certify the same before the completion of the sale. Because of this
understanding, the defendant could not have anticipated that the plaintiff
would take some irrevocable step based upon the letter. Morritt L.J. agreed
with this reasoning but added that no duty of care would have been owed
even had the defendant not intended to return for final certification. There
was no identifiable harm from which the defendant assumed responsibility to
guard the plaintiff in writing the letter: it was not a signal to her to proceed
with the purchase without further enquiry. On this basis, Sir Brian Neill
agreed with Morritt L.J.

Add: *Payne v. John Setchell Ltd.* is now reported at [2002] P.N.L.R. 7.   **8–099**

Add to NOTE 9: An attempt to rely upon *Junior Books Ltd. v. Veitchi Co.*   **8–100**
Ltd. failed in *Architype Projects Ltd. v. Dewhurst Macfarlane & Partners*
[2003] EWHC 3341 (TCC); [2004] P.N.L.R. 38. The claim was brought by a
building owner against an engineer which had been a sub-consultant to the

owner's architect. There had been no contract between the owner and the engineer. H.H. Judge Toulmin C.M.G. Q.C. regarded himself as bound by *Junior Books* only if the facts if the case were identical to the facts in *Junior Books*. They were not (for example, the engineer was not a nominated sub-contractor) and there was no other factor to negative the general rule that, in the context of construction contracts, a sub-contractor owes no duty of care to the building owner.

8–102   Add: The existence of a *Hedley Byrne* duty of care owed by a construction professional to a purchaser from the professional's client was also considered in *Machin v. Adams* (1997) 84 B.L.R. 79 and in *Lidl Properties v. Clarke Bond Partnership* [1998] Env.L.R. 622. Both cases are considered at paragraph 8–098 in the main text and above. No such duty was found to exist in *Howes v. Crombie* [2002] P.N.L.R. 60, Sc. Ct. Sess. The defendant chartered engineer was asked by a house owner to provide a letter confirming the structural integrity of the house. The defendant was not aware that the letter was required by the mortgage lender to a prospective purchaser: he was unaware that the house was for sale. The letter was forwarded to the lender, but not to the purchaser, and the sale proceeded. When structural defects were discovered, the purchaser sued the engineer. Lord Eassie held that the engineer owed no duty of care to the purchaser in providing the letter to the vendor. Important among the reasons for this conclusion were that there was no foreseeable or actual reliance by the purchaser upon the letter and, in any event, reliance by a prospective purchaser without independent enquiry was not foreseeable: any purchaser could be expected to obtain and rely upon his own structural survey.

(v) *The position in Canada*

8–113   NOTE 58: *Ingles v. Tutkaluk Construction Ltd.* is also reported (sub nom *James Ingles v. The Corporation of the City of Toronto*) at (2001) 17 Const.L.J. 540.

(ix) *Problems of scope of duty*

8–124   Add: A recent example of the operation of contract terms agreed between a construction professional and his client to limit the scope of the professional's duty of care to a third party is provided by the decision of the Court of Appeal in *Bellefield Computer Services Ltd. v. E. Turner and Sons Ltd.* [2003] Lloyd's Rep. P.N. 53. The purchaser of a dairy processing plant which was damaged by fire due to defects in the design of its fire-resisting features brought an action against the contractor which had carried out the design and construction of the plant (as to which action, see paragraph 8–081 of the main text). The contractor settled the claim and sought contribution under the Civil Liability (Contribution) Act 1978 from the architects which it had engaged to carry out some of its design duties under the main contract. It was held that the architects were not liable for any contribution because they owed no relevant duty of care to the original claimant (and so were not persons liable in respect of the same damage as the contractor, as required by the Act). The architects owed no relevant duty of care because of the way in which the scope of their design obligations was limited by their contract with the contractor. In particular, they had undertaken no responsibility to provide a detailed design for the critical fire-resisting features and they had not agreed to carry out any supervision or inspection of the works during construction. See further paragraph 8–083A above.

Replace the last sentence of NOTE 5 with the following: The significance of **8–126** this principle in the context of contribution claims was considered by the House of Lords in *Co-operative Retail Services Ltd. v. Taylor Young Partnership* [2002] UKHL 17, [2002] 1 W.L.R. 1419, discussed further at paragraph 8–320A below. In every case where the existence of a policy of insurance in joint names is said to be relevant to liability for breach of contract, it will be important to identify correctly the particular loss(es) covered by the policy. In *Scottish & Newcastle plc v. G.D. Construction (St Albans) Ltd.* (2001) 80 Con.L.R. 75, the claimant engaged the defendant building contractor to refurbish a public house. The defendant's roofing sub-contractor used a blow-torch on the thatched roof of the public house, causing a fire, extensive damage and delay to the opening of the public house for business. The building contract provided that the claimant would take out a policy of insurance in the joint names of the claimant, the defendant and the roofing sub-contractor in respect of loss and damage caused by fire to the existing structure and contents of the public house. H.H. Judge Seymour Q.C. held that this provision was not effective to exclude liability on the part of the defendant to the claimant for damage caused by the fire to the existing structure and contents of the public house, because loss due to negligently caused fire was outside the scope of the policy. Nor was it effective to exclude liability for the claimant's business interruption loss because that was not a type of loss which was covered by the policy. The defendant remained liable to the claimant for the cost of the delay to the opening of the public house for business. On appeal, the judge's decision in relation to damage to the structure of the public house was reversed (there was no appeal against the balance of his decision): [2003] EWCA Civ 16, (2003) 86 Con.L.R. 1.

(d) *The standard of care and skill*

(i) *The ordinary competent and skilled practitioner*

NOTE 32: *Nordic Holdings Ltd. v. Mott MacDonald Ltd.* is now reported at **8–136** (2001) 77 Con.L.R. 88.

(ii) *General practice and knowledge as evidence of the standard*

Add to NOTE 59: See also *Linden Homes South East Ltd. v. LBH Wembley* **8–145** *Ltd.* [2002] EWHC 3115 (TCC), (2003) 87 Con.L.R. 180 (finding of negligence in face of evidence of defendant's expert witness because there was not evidence of two respectable but differing bodies of opinion, merely of differing views as between the two individual experts).

(iii) *Expert Evidence*

Add: For a detailed discussion of the role of expert evidence in claims **8–150** against construction professionals, see paragraphs 16–25 of the judgment of H.H. Judge Lloyd Q.C. in *Royal Brompton Hospital NHS Trust v. Hammond* [2002] EWHC 2037 (TC), (2003) 88 Con.L.R. 1. The judge commented that expert evidence may be needed to assist the court to assess the evidence, for example, by indicating which factors or technical considerations would influence the judgment of a professional person, in cases where the negligence alleged is not a failure to follow an established professional practice. Otherwise, in such cases, expert evidence is not indispensable. The issue of breach of duty may be determined as a matter of common sense. Alternatively, the court may itself possess the necessary expertise to assess the evidence; the Technology and Construction Court has such expertise in disputes arising in the construction industry and in other areas of commerce. Even so, expert evidence may remain desirable in order to satisfy the court that its decision on the required standard of care is in line with the expectations and understanding of the profession. The judge also pointed out that, since the role of the expert witness under the Civil Procedure Rules is to assist the court rather than to make a case for the expert's instructing party, it is not necessary for a party which alleges negligence to adduce supporting expert evidence, provided that in a case where such evidence is necessary or desirable it is available from an expert called by another party.

8–153   Add to NOTE 83: See also *Stephen Donald Architects Ltd. v. Christopher King*, [2003] EWHC 1867 (TCC), (2003) 94 Con.L.R. 1 (evidence of defendant's expert architect unhelpful because he did not address the question whether any reasonably competent architect would have prepared a different design in response to the client's brief).

(iv) *Res ipsa loquitur*

8–154   NOTE 86: For further discussion, see Witting, C., "*Res Ipsa Loquitur*: Some Last Words?" (2001) 117 L.Q.R. 392.

(vi) *Knowledge of the law*

8–161   Add: in *Royal Brompton Hospital NHS Trust v. Hammond* [2002] EWHC 2037 (TCC), (2003) 88 Con.L.R. 1, H.H. Judge Lloyd Q.C. took the view that construction professionals acting as contract administrators or project managers must have both a knowledge of the fundamental principles of construction law and an ability to apply those principles in the administration of building contracts and the management of construction projects. He observed that, in many cases, what is required is not so much knowledge of the general law but rather a good understanding of the operation of the standard forms of building contracts. In that case, both architects and project managers were held to have been in breach of duty to their client in advising on the (incorrect) basis that the building contractor would be entitled to determine its employment under the building contract if it were not given a particular instruction for additional work.

(ix) *Special steps and warranty of reasonable fitness*

8–174   Add: *Payne v. John Setchell Ltd.* is now reported at [2002] P.N.L.R. 7.

(x) *Reliance upon specialists and delegation to them*

8–179   Add to NOTE 60: The judge's finding of breach of duty by the architects was not challenged on the appeal in *Baxall Securities Ltd. v. Sheard Walshaw Partnership* [2002] EWCA Civ 9, [2002] P.N.L.R 564.

3. LIABILITY FOR BREACH OF DUTY

(a) *Examination of site*

Add: in *Linden Homes South East Ltd. v. LBH Wembley Ltd.* [2002] EWHC   **8–186**
3115 (TCC), (2003) 87 Con.L.R. 180, geotechnical and engineering consultants were engaged to carry out an investigation of the site which the claimant
wished to develop, for the purpose of identifying an appropriate foundations
design. Their report negligently failed to disclose that there were reasons why
the design ultimately chosen would not be effective.

(b) *Cost estimates and budgets*

Add: In *Stephen Donald Architects Ltd. v. Christopher King* [2003] EWHC   **8–197**
1867 (TCC), (2003) 94 Con.L.R. 1, H.H. Judge Seymour Q.C. declined to
find that an architect had been in breach of duty in the steps which he took
when he realised that the construction costs of his design would exceed his
client's budget. In those circumstances, any reasonably competent architect
would embark on the process of "value engineering", that is, the consideration with the preferred building contractor and any other members of the
professional team whether there were ways in which the cost of construction
could be reduced to an affordable level. If that failed, the next step was to
inquire of other contractors whether they could build the design within the
client's budget.

(d) *Design and specification*

Add: Similarly, that the defendants' design complied with the Building   **8–203**
Regulations was held to be no defence to the claim that the design was negligently deficient in *Sahib Foods Ltd. v. Paskin Kyriades Sands* [2003] EWHC
142 (TCC), [2003] P.N.L.R. 30. 'This point was not taken upon the appeal:
[2003] EWCA Civ 1832; [2003] P.N.L.R. 403.

Add to NOTE 27: The judge's finding of breach of duty by the architects   **8–207**
was not challenged on the appeal in *Baxall Securities Ltd. v. Sheard Walshaw
Partnership* [2002] EWCA Civ 9, [2002] P.N.L.R 564.

Add to NOTE 33: For further consideration of the decision in *Pride Valley*   **8–209**
Foods Ltd. v. Hall & Partners (Contract Management) Ltd, see Leong, C.,
"The duty of care in project management", (2001) 17 P.N. 250. The use of
combustible panels was also the basis of a successful claim in *Sahib Foods
Ltd. v. Paskin Kyriades Sands* [2003] EWHC 142 (TCC), [2003] P.N.L.R. 30.
It was held that a fire in a food production factory was started as a result of
lack of care by the leasehold owner and occupier, but that its spread beyond
the room where it started was caused by the use of combustible panels to line
that room. The panels had been specified by the defendant architects as part
of their design for the refurbishment of the factory. Although the expert witnesses called by the parties agreed that not all reasonably competent architects would have been aware of the risk of fire spreading as a result of use of
the panels in question, it was found that the defendants were in breach of

duty for specifying the use of such panels because they in fact had knowledge of the risk. The decision is of particular interest because of H.H. Judge Bowsher Q.C.'s analysis of the significance of the client's knowledge of the risk. Holding that the client's knowledge provided the architects with no defence, the judge said (at para.40):

> "A competent architect does not present a design that he knows to be deficient in an important respect and then discuss with the client whether the deficiency should be removed. Still less does he present such a design and say, I did not need to tell the client about the deficiency because the client already knew that such a feature was required. Take a simple example. An architect designs a house as a residence for a client who happens to be a surveyor and forgets to require a damp-proof course under a parapet wall. If after construction the client complains, it is no answer for the architect to say, 'Well you knew about the need for the damp proof course as well as I did'. The architect is employed to use his own skill and judgment. There is no duty on the client who happens to have a particular skill to examine the architect's designs and tell the architect where he has gone wrong. If I, as a lawyer, go to a solicitor for advice and pay him for it, I do not see why I should be criticised if I fail to do that solicitor's work all over again and check whether he has got it right."

The cause of the start of the fire was particularly careless use of equipment by the claimant's employees. The judge found that, in the light of the gravity of the consequences should a fire start in the room in question, the architects had not been entitled to assume that equipment would be correctly used or only slightly misused. This part of the decision upheld on appeal: [2003] EWCA Civ 1832, [2003] P.N.L.R. 403. It seems that if a construction professional charged with design is aware of a serious danger against which his design must guard, he should consider all the ways in which the danger might be brought about, including unusually careless behaviour by the client. In order to avoid liability, he should bring the risks of cost-cutting in design clearly to the attention of the client, making sure that the client (at a suitably senior level) explicitly accepts such risks. For a discussion of this case, see Dugdale, T., "Out of the frying pan, into the fire: how much was the cook to blame?" (2004) P.N. 113.

8–216   Add: In *Royal Brompton Hospital NHS Trust v. Hammond* [2002] EWHC 2037 (TCC), (2003) 88 Con.L.R. 1, project managers were held liable for failing to monitor and co-ordinate the production of drawings by mechanical and engineering services consultants. As a result, they failed to advise the client that it was premature to award the building contract on the basis of the information available and, after award of the contract, they failed to see that the necessary information was provided to the contractor so as to allow it to build to programme.

(h) *Administration of the building contract*

8–232   Add to NOTE 92: The decision in *London Borough of Merton v. Stanley Hugh Leach Ltd.* (1985) 32 B.L.R. 51 was followed in *Sindall Ltd. v. Solland* (2001) 80 Con.L.R. 152: H.H. Judge Lloyd Q.C. held that both as a matter of law and as a matter of established good practice, a contract administrator should always consider whether there are any factors known to him which might justify the grant of an extension of time. This is so even where the contractor has not given written notice of such factors as required by the particular building contract.

Add: The Society for Construction Law has published a Protocol for **8–233** Determining Extensions of Time and Compensation for Delay and Disruption which may be adopted by contracting parties as an aid to interpretation of their building contract and may be used by contract administrators as guidance in dealing with contractors' claims for extensions of time. The Protocol, which was published in final form in October 2002, can be found at *www.eotprotocol.com.* For discussion, see Burr, A. and Lane, N., "The SCL Delay and Disruption Protocol: Hunting Snarks" (2003) 19 Const.L.J. 135.

Add to NOTE 97: For further consideration of the decision in *Pozzolanic* **8–234** *Lytag Ltd. v. Bryan Hobson Associates*, see Leong, C., "The duty of care in project management", (2001) 17 P.N. 250.

(i) *Supervision or inspection of the works*

Add before paragraph 8–236 the following: In *Consarc Design Ltd v. Hutch* **8–236** *Investments Ltd* [2002] P.N.L.R. 712, H.H. Judge Bowsher Q.C. approved and incorporated within his judgment the entirety of paragraphs 8–236 to 8–249 (inclusive) of the main text, including the criticism of his own words in *Corfield v. Grant* (1992) 13 Con.L.R. 58, which appears at paragraph 8–238. In *Consarc Design Ltd. v. Hutch Investments Ltd.*, the judge held that architects engaged to inspect construction works, including the laying of a new floor, were not in breach of duty when they failed to notice defects in the floor. The particular defects were such that a reasonably competent and careful architect could not have been expected to notice them.

Add: Equally, however, a construction professional charged with managing **8–238** construction must take reasonable care to see that the intended result is achieved. In *Six Continents Retail Ltd. v. Carford Catering Ltd.* [2003] EWCA Civ 1790, the defendant project manager was retained for the design and installation of kitchen equipment in a restaurant, which was later damaged by fire arising from the fixing of a rotisserie to a combustible wall. It had warned the owner that the installation might create a fire risk but the owner had taken no steps in response. The Court of Appeal held that the project manager had not discharged its duty to the owner by giving the warning. Its duty was to take care to bring about a safe installation.

(j) *Certification*

Add to NOTE 77: For commentary on the decision in *London Borough of* **8–253** *Barking & Dagenham v. Terrapin Construction Ltd* [2002] B.L.R. 479, see I.N.D. Wallace Q.C., "RIBA/JCT Final Certificates Again (*London Borough of Barking and Dagenham v. Terrapin Construction Limited*)" (2002) 18 Const.L.J. 4.

4. DAMAGES

(a) *The scope of the duty*

8–265   Add: In *HOK Sport Ltd. v. Aintree Racecourse Co Ltd.* [2002] EWHC 3094 (TCC), (2003) 86 Con.L.R. 165, H.H. Judge Thornton Q.C. held that the *BBL* principle applied generally to claims against construction professionals and would be particularly important where (i) a professional is engaged to provide information for a specific project, (ii) the client is to decide whether to proceed with the project, (iii) the information to be provided by the professional is to be relied on by the client as part of its decision-making process and (iv) the decision is neither participated in by nor dependent upon the advice of that professional. In that case, in breach of their appointment, the claimant architect failed to warn the client racecourse owner that various design changes during the development of a new stand would mean that fewer standing places would be available than had been expected. As a result, the racecourse owner was deprived of the opportunity to postpone development of the new stand and redesign the project so as to remedy the loss of places. The arbitrator awarded the racecourse owner damages based on the financial loss which it suffered as a result of the lack of those places. The judge held that, in the light of *BBL*, this was the wrong approach. The architect's duty was to provide information as to the number of places which its design would provide. It was not to advise the racecourse owner on whether it should postpone the project to allow a redesign. The loss which fell within the scope of the architect's duty was limited to the loss attributable to the racecourse owner's decision to proceed with the project on the incorrect assumption that a larger number of places would be provided. The case was remitted to the arbitrator for assessment of this loss.

(b) *Remoteness*

(i) *Causation*

8–267   Add: Unusually, the concept of remoteness operated to increase the claimant's recovery in *Earl Terrace Properties Ltd. v. Nilsson Design Ltd.* [2004] EWHC 136 (TCC); [2004] B.L.R. 273, an architect's negligence case. It was alleged that breach of duty by the architect had caused a delay in completion of a development and that, as a result, the claimant developer had suffered losses. The consequence of the delay in completion of the development was a delay in sale of the developed properties. The architect argued that the developer was obliged to give credit against its recoverable losses for the profit it would make upon the eventual sales of the developed properties, the property market having moved upwards during the period of delay. The judge held that market movements were outside the scope of the architect's duty and too remote. Accordingly, since the developer could not have recovered additional loss if the market had moved downwards during the delay, neither could the architect enjoy the benefit of a rising market.

8–269   Add to NOTE 13: *Nordic Holdings Ltd. v. Mott MacDonald Ltd.* is now reported at (2001) 77 Con.L.R. 88.

Add: Where other specialists are retained by the client, the relative roles of   **8–276**
the construction professional and such specialists will require careful consideration in order to decide whose conduct was the effective cause of the client's
loss. It may be open to the construction professional to argue that the conduct of another specialist was sufficient to break the chain of causation
between his own breach of duty and the client's loss. Such an argument
failed, however, in *Linden Homes South East Ltd. v. LBH Wembley Ltd.*
[2002] EWHC 3115 (TCC), (2003) 87 Con.L.R. 180. Geotechnical and engineering consultants were engaged to carry out an investigation of the site
which the claimant wished to develop, for the purpose of identifying an
appropriate foundations design. When the chosen design was found to be
unsuitable after work had begun, the consultants argued that although they
had recommended that design, the final say on foundations design lay with
the specialist contractor engaged by the client and it was that contractor's
choice of design which was the effective cause of the loss. The argument
failed because the specialist contractor had relied and had been entitled to
rely upon the consultants' site investigation report in choosing the
foundations design. The report had negligently failed to disclose that there
were reasons why the design ultimately chosen would not be effective.

Add to Note 32: But compare *Baxall Securities Ltd. v. Sheard Walshaw
Partnership* [2002] EWCA Civ 9, [2002] P.N.L.R. 564, the facts of which
appear at paragraph 8–082 in the main text. The Court of Appeal decided
that the sole effective cause of both floods was the lack of adequate overflows
in the roof drainage system. That was a patent defect which ought to have
been detected by the surveyors instructed to report to the claimant prior to
the claimant's purchase of the property. Had the architects owed a duty of
care to the claimant in respect of the lack of overflows, the architects would
have been in breach of such duty but the surveyors' failure to detect the lack
of overflows would have broken the chain of causation between the architects' breach and the claimant's loss. However, since the Court of Appeal had
confirmed that the prospect that the claimant would commission a pre-
purchase survey which ought reasonably to have discovered the lack of overflows prevented the architects owing any relevant duty of care, the court's
remarks on the issue of causation were *obiter*.

The Court of Appeal considered what was required before a client could   **8–277**
be said to have broken the chain of causation between its own loss and the
breach of contract or negligence of a construction professional in *Six Continents Retail Ltd. v. Carford Catering Ltd.* [2003] EWCA Civ 1790. The defendant project manager was retained for the design and installation of kitchen
equipment in a restaurant, which was later damaged by fire arising from the
fixing of a rotisserie to a combustible wall. It had warned the owner that the
installation might create a fire risk but the owner had taken no steps in
response. The Court of Appeal held that the project manager had not discharged its duty to the owner by giving the warning. Its duty was to take care
to bring about a safe installation. Further, the owner's failure to heed the
warning had not broken the chain of causation between the project manager's breach of duty and the owner's loss, since the risk of such a fire was
within the range of outcomes which the project manager's contractual
obligations were designed to avoid. Laws L.J. said, at paragraph [22],

". . .it was a warning of an outcome which the respondents themselves should have prevented from happening. I find it very difficult to see how the giving of such a warning ought to transpose the burden of avoiding that very outcome from the respondents, who owed a duty in effect to prevent it, to the appellants who were the beneficiaries of that duty."

(ii) *Foreseeability*

8–282   Note 52: *Alcoa Minerals of Jamaica Inc. v. Herbert Broderick* is now reported at [2002] 1 A.C. 371.

(d) *Heads of damage*

(i) *Costs of rectification*

8–288   Add: An unusual claim for damages representing the costs of rectification was made in *Consarc Design Ltd. v. Hutch Investments Ltd.* [2002] P.N.L.R. 712. The employer discovered that a newly laid floor was defective during the defects liability period provided for by the building contract. Under the contract, the employer was entitled to require the building contractor to rectify the defects before issuing the final certificate or, alternatively, to instruct another contractor to carry out the repair works and deduct the cost from the payment due to the original contractor. The employer took neither course. Instead, it paid the original contractor in full and then put the floor repair works out to tender. The original contractor submitted the lowest tender and was awarded the contract to repair its own defective floor. The employer sought to recover the cost of the repair works as damages from its architects on the grounds that they had failed to prevent the floor being completed with defects during the original construction period. H.H. Judge Bowsher Q.C. dismissed the claim on the basis that the architects were not in breach of their duty to inspect, but he remarked *obiter* that, in effect, the employer had made a voluntary payment of the repair cost to the original contractor by failing to invoke its rights under the original building contract. It could not be right, the judge commented, that there should be a recovery from one wrongdoer of a voluntary payment made to another wrongdoer.

8–290   Add to Note 77: See, for an unsuccessful attempt to apply *Ruxley* so as to reduce a claimant's damages, *McLaren Murdoch & Hamilton Ltd. v. The Abercromby Motor Group Ltd.* [2003] C.I.L.L. 1964, Sc. Ct. Sess. (O.H.): replacement of the underfloor heating system in four car dealership showrooms was not an unreasonable and disproportionate response to the results of the architects' negligent failure properly to design the original system.

8–291   Add: *Nordic Holdings Ltd. v. Mott MacDonald Ltd.* is now reported at (2001) 77 Con.L.R. 88.

8–293   Note 86: *Alcoa Minerals of Jamaica Inc. v. Herbert Broderick* is now reported at [2002] 1 A.C. 371.

(vi) *Consequential losses*

8–303   Add: The recoverability of "holding costs" was addressed in *Earl Terrace Properties Ltd. v. Nilsson Design Ltd.* [2004] EWHC 136 (TCC); [2004]

B.L.R. 273, an architect's negligence case. It was alleged that breach of duty by the architect had caused a delay in completion of a development and that, as a result, the claimant developer had suffered losses. The consequence of the delay in completion of the development was a delay in sale of the developed properties, and that meant that the development capital was "locked into" the development for longer than it otherwise would have been. H.H. Judge Thornton Q.C. held that if a developer can show that it has lost the opportunity to use funds invested for a commercial purpose, it can recover damages (in the form of a reasonable rate of return) for the loss of its opportunity to use those funds elsewhere. It may do so even if it cannot reasonably or readily identify the nature or extent of its loss. Further, the developer was entitled to recover damages for loss of use of funds locked into the development even although its complex funding arrangements meant that some of the holding costs were incurred not by it but by its ultimate parent company. The judge held that since the architect knew that this was a speculative commercial development by a special purpose vehicle company, losses suffered by the parent company were within the scope of the architect's duty and recoverable by the claimant.

Add: A more restrictive approach to the award of damages for the cost **8–304** of managerial time was taken by H.H. Judge Toulmin C.M.G., Q.C. in *Phee Farrar Jones Ltd. v. Connaught Mason Ltd.* [2003] C.I.L.L. 2005. The claimant failed to recover damages for the cost of managerial time spent organising a relocation of its business following a flood caused by the defendant's breach of contract because it could not show that it had incurred a discrete expense, such as overtime, or any specific loss of revenue which it would have enjoyed had its manager not been occupied with the relocation.

(vii) *Liability to third parties*

Replace the last sentence of NOTE 22 with the following: *Royal Brompton* **8–305** *Hospital N.H.S. Trust v. Hammond (No.3)* [2002] UKHL 14, [2002] 1 W.L.R. 1397, is an example of a case where a client sued its professional advisers for impairing its prospects of achieving a favourable settlement with the building contractor: the case is discussed further at paragraphs 8–318 to 8–318B below.

(e) *Mitigation of loss*

NOTE 44: *Alcoa Minerals of Jamaica Inc. v. Herbert Broderick* is now **8–313** reported at [2002] 1 A.C. 371.

5. SHARED RESPONSIBILITY

(a) *Apportionment of liability*

Replace the last sentence of the paragraph with the following: The mean- **8–316** ing of this phrase has been the subject of recent decisions at appellate level: see paragraphs 8–318 and 8–318B below.

same as the building contractor's claim against the insurance broker. H.H. Judge Gilliland Q.C. held that the parties were not liable to the building contractor in respect of the same damage. The damage caused by the sub-contractor was the need for remedial works. The damage caused by the insurance brokers was the financial loss caused by the absence of insurance cover. The Court of Appeal allowed the insurance brokers' appeal, holding that the parties were liable in respect of the same damage, but the House of Lords in *Royal Brompton (No.3)* held that the Court of Appeal had erred. H.H. Judge Gilliland Q.C.'s distinction between the different types of damage was correct and the parties were not liable in respect of the same damage. Similarly, the House of Lords preferred the decision of David Steel J. in *Bovis Construction v. Commercial Union* [2001] 1 Lloyd's Rep. 416, to that of H.H. Judge Thornton Q.C. in the related case of *Bovis Lend Lease Ltd. v. Saillard Fuller & Partners* (2001) 77 Con.L.R. 134. In those cases also, the House of Lords held, damage comprising pure financial loss could not be equated to damage representing the cost of repairing defective construction works, so that the parties were not liable in respect of the same damage.

Add new paragraph **8–318B**:

8–318B   The House of Lords in *Royal Brompton (No.3)* took the opportunity to comment on the proper role of the "mutual discharge" test in determining whether parties are liable in respect of the same damage. This test was first formulated by Sir Richard Scott V.C. in *Howkins & Harrison v. Tyler* [2001] P.N.L.R. 27, as a threshold test. In order to decide whether the Civil Liability (Contribution) Act 1978 applied at all to a contribution claim made by A against B in respect of damage suffered by C, it was said, it was necessary to answer both of the following questions in the affirmative:

(1)   If A pays C a sum of money in satisfaction, or on account of A's liability to C, will that sum operate to reduce or extinguish B's liability to C?

(2)   If B pays C a sum of money in satisfaction, or on account of B's liability to C, will that sum operate to reduce or extinguish A's liability to C?

Thus, unless a payment made by one party to a contribution claim to the party who suffered the damage operated *pro tanto* to reduce the liability to the victim of the other party to the contribution claim, there could be no liability to make contribution under the Act. In *Royal Brompton (No.3)*, the House of Lords confirmed the proper role of the mutual discharge test. It is not a threshold test which determines whether the Act applies. Rather, as Lord Steyn put it at paragraph 28:

"It is best regarded as a practical test to be used in considering the very statutory question whether two claims under consideration are for 'the same damage'. Its usefulness, however, may vary depending on the circumstances of individual cases. Ultimately, the safest course is to apply the statutory test."

It is very difficult, however, to imagine circumstances in which the mutual discharge test will not be met but in which the parties will be liable in respect of the same damage, or *vice versa*. For example, on the facts in *Royal Brompton (No.3)*, the Hospital's claim against the Architects would be reduced *pro tanto* by any recovery which the Hospital made against the Contractor, but the converse would not be true.

Add new paragraph **8–320A**:

The House of Lords also dismissed the professionals' appeal in *Co-operative Retail Services Ltd. v. Taylor Young Partnership* [2002] UKHL 17, [2002] 1 W.L.R. 1419. The professionals sought in two ways to avoid the difficulty created by the fact that the claimant (CRS), Wimpey and Hall were joint insured in respect of the fire damage. First, they argued that the main building contract did not exclude the liability of Wimpey or Hall for loss caused by the fire if the fire was caused by their breach of duty to CRS. Rather, Wimpey remained liable to pay compensation to CRS for the loss caused by the fire save to the extent that such loss was recoverable from insurers under the joint names policy. This was important because the policy did not entirely cover CRS's losses: it excluded consequential loss and it was also subject to an excess. Secondly, the professionals argued that the question whether persons are liable in respect of the same damage for the purposes of the 1978 Act is to be determined at the date when the damage occurs. At the date of the fire, no claim had yet been made under the insurance policy, so that CRS could then have recovered damages from Wimpey and Hall. Accordingly, they were persons liable to CRS in respect of loss caused by the fire. **8–320A**

Both arguments failed. The first argument provided the main issue in the House of Lords. Their Lordships subjected to close analysis the manner in which the main building contract (JCT 80) allocated loss in the event of fire damage to the contract works. They held that, on the true construction of the main contract, neither CRS nor Wimpey were entitled to sue each other for loss caused by fire damage to the contract works. Such liability was wholly excluded; it was not merely the case (as the professionals had argued) that Wimpey's liability was reduced by the amount of any insurance payment. In other words, the main contract provided a complete scheme for dealing with loss caused by fire damage which could not co-exist with a right in either party to the contract to recover damages for such loss from the other. If Wimpey could not be held liable under the contract for CRS's fire-related loss, it followed that Wimpey was not a person who could be held liable to CRS in respect of the same damage as the professionals and their claim for contribution failed. Since the sub-contract between Wimpey and Hall incorporated the provisions of the main contract, the claim against Hall failed in the same way.

Although not necessary for their decision, the House of Lords also considered, and rejected, the professionals' second argument. As had the Court of Appeal, they held that the relevant time for deciding whether persons are liable in respect of the same damage is the time when contribution is sought and *not* the time when the damage is suffered. However, the court did not distinguish between the date when contribution proceedings are brought and the date when judgment is given on the claim for contribution: that question remains for decision.

Add new NOTE 60A: The analysis deployed by the House of Lords in this case (*viz.*, examination of the main contract to see whether there is an implied exclusion of liability between the joint insureds) is obviously sensitive to the particular terms of the main contract. Different contract terms can be expected to produce different results. Thus no exclusion of liability was found so that a contribution claim could proceed in *Surrey Heath Borough Council v. Lovell Construction Ltd.* (1990) 48 B.L.R. 108 (where the contract was the JCT Standard Form of Building Contract With Contractor's Design: JCT WCD 81) and in *Bovis Lend Lease Ltd. v. Saillard Fuller & Partners* (2001) 77 Con.L.R. 134 (where the contract was a tailor-made construction management contract).

Add new paragraph **8–325A**:

8–325A   **Costs as damage.** The settlement of a claim will typically involve the payment of some sum (which may or may not be separately identified) on account of the claimant's legal costs. The question whether the paying party may recover contribution from a third party under the Civil Liability (Contribution) Act 1978 to sums paid on account of costs has been considered in two recent cases concerning construction professionals. The facts in *J. Sainsbury plc v. Broadway Malyan* (1998) 61 Con.L.R. 31, are summarised at paragraph 8–324 of the main text. In that case, H.H. Judge Lloyd Q.C. dismissed a claim brought by architects against engineers for a contribution to the sum which the architects had paid to settle the building owner's claim for negligent design, on the grounds that the engineers had committed no relevant breach of duty. The judge went on to consider whether, if the claim for contribution had been a good one, the architects would have been entitled to a contribution to the sums paid on account of the building owner's legal costs. He thought not, for two main reasons. First, costs were not properly characterised as "damage" and the right to recover costs was not the right to recover "compensation in respect of ... damage", within the meaning of section 1 of the Act. Secondly, the fact and amount of the owner's legal costs arose from the architects' decision to contest liability for the owner's loss, and not from the negligence upon which the owner's claim was based. These remarks were, of course, *obiter*.

In *Parkman Consulting Engineers v. Cumbrian Industrials Ltd.* (2001) 79 Con.L.R. 112, the Court of Appeal took a different view. In that case, BICC plc engaged both Parkman (engineers) and Cumbrian (a building contractor) to decontaminate and develop some land, which involved making the sub-soil layers watertight. The scheme which was designed by Parkman and built by Cumbrian for this purpose failed. Parkman settled BICC plc's claim for £1.95 million including unspecified sums for statutory interest and BICC plc's costs, and then claimed contribution under the 1978 Act from Cumbrian. Cumbrian argued that £1.95 million should not be the starting point for the claim against it because that sum included an element on account of BICC plc's legal costs which should first be deducted. H.H. Judge Thornton Q.C. rejected this argument and the Court of Appeal upheld his decision. It held that the judge had been entitled to regard the whole of the settlement sum, which was admitted to be a reasonable settlement, as the basis and starting point for the claim for contribution. It was a global settlement and, accordingly, the entire sum paid should be regarded as paid in settlement of Parkman's liability to BICC plc. (The remarks of Judge Lloyd Q.C. in *J. Sainsbury plc v. Broadway Malyan* were distinguished: in that case the settlement had been held to be an unreasonable one). The Court also suggested a way to recover a contribution to costs without invoking the 1978 Act: it held that the power of the court under section 51(3) of the Supreme Court Act 1981 to order the payment of costs was wide enough to allow an order that the defendant in contribution proceedings make a payment in respect of the original claimant's costs. It was irrelevant that the original claimant (BICC plc, in this case) was not a party to the proceedings in which the court would make such an order.

(b) *Contributory Negligence*

Add new paragraph **8–329A**:

The analysis provided by Sedley L.J. in *Pride Valley Foods Ltd. v. Hall &*   **8–329A**
Partners (Contract Management) Ltd. (see paragraph 8–329 of the main work) was applied in *Sahib Foods Ltd. v. Paskin Kyriades Sands* [2003] EWHC 142 (TCC), [2003] P.N.L.R. 30. A fire in a food production factory started because of negligence on the part of the claimant leaseholder's employees. It spread beyond the room in which it started because combustible panels had been used to line that room. The use of those panels was the result of negligent design by the defendant architects. H.H. Judge Bowsher Q.C. held that there was no contributory negligence by the leaseholder so far as its loss attributable to spread of the fire beyond the combustible panels was concerned, since the risk that fire would not be contained by the panels was the very risk against which the architects had a duty to guard in formulating their design. The correct analysis, the judge held, was that the parties were respectively responsible for two distinct elements of the claimants' loss: the leaseholder for loss caused by the fire inside the panels and the architects for loss caused by spread of the fire beyond the panels. The leaseholder's damages would be assessed as its entire loss as a result of the fire less the loss which it would have suffered had the fire been contained in the room in which it started (as would have been the case but for the architects' negligent choice of combustible panels). This part of the decision was reversed on appeal: [2003] EWCA Civ 1832; [2003] P.N.L.R. 403. It was held that the leaseholder was partly responsible for spread of the fire beyond the room where it started, because it had misinformed the architects as to the use to which the room would be put and that misinformation had contributed to the architects' decision to use combustible panels. Further, it was held that the judge ought to have adopted the conventional approach to contributory negligence and made a percentage deduction from the leaseholder's entire loss to reflect its contributory negligence in relation to both start and spread of the fire. Considering the analysis offered by Sedley L.J. in *Pride Valley Foods Ltd. v. Hall & Partners (Contract Management) Ltd.* (see paragraph 8–329 of the main work), the Court of Appeal commented that a claimant may be guilty of contributory negligence even if the defendant in breach of duty has failed to protect the claimant against the very damage which it was employed to guard against. Only in a case where the whole of the responsibility for the damage was the defendant's failure to protect the claimant against his own negligence would it be appropriate not to hold the claimant guilty of contributory negligence. It is a matter of fact in each case: it may or may not be reasonable of the claimant to rely entirely upon the defendant

rather than in part upon his own efforts to protect his person or property. For a discussion of this case, see Dudgale, T., "Out of the frying pan, into the fire: how much was the cook to blame?" (2004) P.N. 113.

6. Adjudication

8–332   Add: A professional engagement to administer a building contract was held to be a construction contract in *Gillies Ramsay Diamond v. PJW Enterprises Ltd.* [2003] B.L.R. 58 (Sc. Ct. Sess. O.H.). Lady Paton rejected the argument that issues of professional negligence were not within the scope of adjudication under the Act but recognised that:

> ". . . it may on one view seem startling that a professional person acting as an Adjudicator should be invited to rule within 28 days on the important and often difficult and delicate question as to whether a fellow-professional has failed in his or her duty to such an extent that there has been professional negligence . . . .".

A reclaiming motion was refused by the Inner House: [2004] B.L.R. 131.

Add to Note 87: Where novation of a contract takes place after May 1, 1998, the novation agreement may itself be a construction contract within the meaning of s.104. If the novated contract was made before May 1, 1998, the curious result will be that the parties have a right to refer to adjudication disputes which arose before the Act came into effect. In *Yarm Road Ltd. v. Costain Ltd.*, unreported, July 30, 2001, Judge Havery Q.C. recognised that this construction of the Act created anomalies but regarded it as inescapable.

Add to Note 88: In *R.J.T. Consulting Engineers Ltd. v. D.M. Engineering Ltd.* [2002] B.L.R. 217, the Court of Appeal considered the question of precisely what must be evidenced in writing for a construction contract to exist under s.107(2)(c). The majority held that the whole agreement had to be evidenced in writing. Written evidence of the existence (as opposed to the terms) of the agreement would not suffice. Nor would written evidence of only some of the terms, even if those terms (*e.g.*, as to the identity of the parties, the scope of the works or the price) formed the substance of the agreement. This decision can be expected to exclude a wide range of contracts from the operation of the Act. It was followed in *Carillion Construction Ltd. v. Devonport Royal Dockyard* [2003] B.L.R. 79, where an oral agreement to vary the payment terms of a written contract was held not to be a construction contract. Section 107(3) brings within the definition of a construction contract an oral agreement which refers to a written document: in *Total M and E. Services Ltd. v. ABB Building Technologies Ltd* [2002] EWHC 248 (TCC), (2003) 87 Con.L.R. 154, it was held that orally agreed variations to the scope of works under a building contract referred to the written terms of the building contract for this purpose. Section 107(4) provides that an agreement is evidenced in writing if it is recorded by one of the parties, or by a third party, with the authority of the parties to the agreement. In *Connex South Eastern Ltd. v. M J Building Services Group plc* [2004] EWHC 1518 (TCC), a contractor's tender was accepted by an oral instruction to proceed with the works which was given at a meeting. That instruction was recorded in the minutes of the meeting, which were written with the parties' authority. It was held that this was sufficient to evidence the contract in writing within the meaning of section 107.

Add: A further important exception is made by section 106 of the Act, **8–333** which excludes from the scope of the statutory adjudication scheme a construction contract with a residential occupier which principally relates to operations on a private dwelling-house or flat.

Add to NOTE 90: For examples, see the cases cited at para.8–338, NOTE 4, below.

Add to NOTE 91: In *Connex South Eastern Ltd. v. M J Building Services* **8–334** *Group plc* [2004] EWHC 1518 (TCC), it was held that an adjudication provision survived even the discharge of a contract by acceptance of a repudiatory breach.

Add to NOTE 92: In an article, "Adjudicators' Time Defaults" (2001) 17 Const.L.J. 371, David Blunt Q.C. notes that neither the Act nor the Scheme for Construction Contracts provides for the consequences in law when an adjudicator fails either to reach or to deliver his decision within the statutory time limits and considers what those consequences might be. See also paragraph 8–338 below.

Add to NOTE 93: The juridical basis for the enforcement of adjudicators' **8–335** decisions was considered further in *David McLean Housing Contractors Ltd. v. Swansea Housing Association Ltd.* [2002] B.L.R. 125, where H.H. Judge Lloyd Q.C. preferred to say that the cause of action enforced is not a debt created by the parties' agreement in their construction contract to be bound by the adjudicator's decision but, rather, the cause of action which underlay the dispute decided by the adjudicator. This remains the minority view at first instance, however. The more common view is that there is an express contractual agreement to be bound by the adjudicator's decision: see *VHE Construction plc v. RBSTB Trust Ltd* [2000] B.L.R. 187 (H.H. Judge Hicks Q.C.), *Bovis Lend Lease Ltd. v. Triangle Development Ltd.* [2002] EWHC 3123 (TCC), [2003] B.L.R. 31 (H.H. Judge Thornton Q.C.) and, in Scotland, *Construction Group Centre Ltd. v. The Highland Council* [2002] B.L.R. 476 (Lord MacFadyen).

Add: The principles set out by H.H. Judge Thornton Q.C. in *Sherwood and* **8–336** *Casson Ltd. v. Mackenzie* and listed in the main work were approved by the Court of Appeal in *C.& B. Scene Concept Design Ltd. v. Isobars Ltd.* [2002] B.L.R. 93. The adjudicator decided in favour of the claimant's claims to interim payments on the grounds that, under the contract, the defendant's failure to give notice of non-payment meant that it had no defence to the claims. The defendant sought to resist enforcement of this decision on the basis that the adjudicator had failed to appreciate that the Act operated to replace the relevant contract terms with the terms of the Scheme for Construction Contracts. It followed, argued the defendant, that the adjudicator had addressed himself to the wrong question and so exceeded his jurisdiction. The challenge succeeded at first instance but failed on appeal. It was held that the adjudicator had indeed mistaken the effect of the Act, but that this was an error of law which did not go to his jurisdiction. The Court of Appeal emphasised that an error of law, unless it be as to the scope of the dispute referred, does not take the adjudicator outside his jurisdiction. Stuart-Smith L.J., with whom Rix and Potter L.JJ. agreed, said at paragraph 30:

"It is important that the enforcement of an adjudicator's decision by summary judgment should not be prevented by arguments that the adjudicator has made errors of law in reaching his decision, unless the adjudicator has purported to decide matters that are not referred to him. He must decide as a matter of construction of the referral, and therefore as a matter of law, what the dispute is that he has to decide. If he erroneously decides that the dispute referred to him is wider than it is, then, in so far as he has exceeded his jurisdiction, his decision cannot be enforced. But in the present case there was entire agreement as to the scope of the dispute, and the Adjudicator's decision, albeit he may have made errors of law as to the relevant contractual provisions, is still binding and enforceable until the matter is corrected in the final determination."

Thus in *Gillies Ramsay Diamond v. PJW Enterprises Ltd.* [2003] B.L.R. 48 (Sc. Ct. Sess. O.H.), Lady Paton held that an adjudicator's decision awarding damages for professional negligence by a contract administrator was not justified on the material before him, but that his errors were within his jurisdiction and so his decision was enforceable. A reclaiming motion was refused by the Inner House: [2004] B.L.R. 131. In *Joinery Plus Ltd. (in Administration) v. Laing Ltd.* [2003] EWHC 213 (TCC), (2003) 87 Con.L.R., H.H. Judge Thornton Q.C. distinguished the decision in *C. & B. Scene Concept Design Ltd. v. Isobars Ltd.* (above) to find that an adjudicator who decided the dispute by reference to the wrong contract terms (as opposed to the wrong construction of the right terms) lacked jurisdiction. Similarly, in *Galliford Try Construction Ltd. v. Michael Heal Associates Ltd.* [2003] EWHC 2886 (TCC), an adjudicator's decision which was based on an erroneous conclusion that there was a contract between the parties was not enforced. Since the statutory regime of adjudication does not apply unless there is a (written) contract between the parties, the adjudicator had lacked jurisdiction. For the same reasons, an adjudicator's erroneous decision that there was a written contract between the parties led to a refusal to enforce his decision in *Thomas-Fredric's (Construction) Ltd. v. Keith Wilson* [2003] EWCA Civ 1494, [2003] B.L.R. 23.

Add to NOTE 97: For a further case where the court granted only partial enforcement of an adjudicator's decision, see *Griffin v. Midas Homes Ltd.* (2000) 78 Con.L.R. 152 (some of the disputes decided by the adjudicator were not properly identified in the notice of adjudication and others had not arisen at the date of his decision). However, partial enforcement will be possible only where it is possible to distinguish between several disputes decided by the same adjudicator. It is not open to a party to accept only part of an adjudicator's decision on a *single dispute*: see *K.N.S. Industrial Services (Birmingham) Ltd. v. Sindall Ltd.* (2000) 75 Con.L.R. 71 and *Shimizu Europe Ltd. v. Automajor Ltd.* [2002] EWHC 103 (TCC), [2002] B.L.R. 113. The particular terms of the construction contract may allow the unsuccessful party in the adjudication to set off against the sum due from him under the adjudicator's decision some other claim which was not determined by the adjudicator: see, for example, the Court of Appeal's decision in *Parsons Plastics (Research and Development) Ltd. v. Purac Ltd.* [2002] B.L.R. 334. But where such other claim is regulated by the payment provisions of the Act and the defendant has failed to comply with those provisions, set off will not be permitted: see, for example, *Solland International Ltd. v. Daraydan Holdings Ltd.* [2002] EWHC 220 (TCC), (2003) Con.L.R. 109, cf. *Shimizu Europe Ltd. v. L.B.J. Fabrications Ltd.* [2003] EWHC 1229 (TCC), [2003] B.L.R. 381 and *Conor Engineering Ltd. v. Les Constructions Industrielles de la Mediterranee* [2004] B.L.R. 212. In *Ferson Contractors Ltd. v. Levolux A. T. Ltd.* [2003] EWCA Civ 11, [2003] B.L.R. 118, the Court of Appeal held that the particular terms of the contract did not permit an unsuccessful party in an adjudication to set off other contractual claims against the adjudicator's award and said, further, that where contractual provisions cannot be construed so as to give effect to the adjudication scheme required by the Act, such provisions will be struck out of the contract. In *Pegram Shopfitters Ltd. v. Tally Wiejl (UK) Ltd.* [2003] EWCA Civ 1750, [2004] 1 All E.R. 818, another one of the relatively few adjudication cases to have reached appellate level, May L.J.'s judgment contains a reminder that the Court's approach will normally be to enforce adjudicators' decisions in recognition of the policy of the legislation, although there will be cases "when legal principle has to prevail over broad brush policy" [9].

Add to NOTE 98: The parties may confer jurisdiction upon an adjudicator   **8–337** in various ways. At the time when they make their construction contract, they may adopt procedural rules for adjudication which expressly confer upon the adjudicator the power to decide his own jurisdiction: see, for example, *Farebrother Building Services Ltd. v. Frogmore Investments Ltd.* [2001] C.I.L.L. 1762. Alternatively, at the time of the adjudication they may reach an express or implied *ad hoc* agreement that the adjudicator shall have such power: see, for example, *Nordot Engineering Services Ltd. v. Siemens plc* [2001] C.I.L.L. 1778. An estoppel by convention may arise to prevent one or other party from denying that the adjudicator had jurisdiction: see *Oakley v. Airclear Environmental Ltd.* [2002] C.I.L.L. 1824 (where, however, no estoppel was found on the facts). A party which participates in an adjudication without expressing its objection to the jurisdiction of the adjudicator is likely to be held to have submitted to that jurisdiction: see, for example, *Cowlin Construction Ltd. v. CFW Architects* [2003] B.L.R. 241. In *Thomas-Fredric's (Construction) Ltd. v. Keith Wilson* [2003] EWCA Civ 1494, [2003] B.L.R. 23, the Court of Appeal enunciated the following principles: (1) if the defendant has submitted to the adjudicator's jurisdiction in the full sense of having agreed not only that the adjudicator should rule on the issue of his own jurisdiction but also that he would then be bound by that ruling, then he is liable to enforcement even if the adjudicator's decision on jurisdiction is plainly wrong, (2) even if the defendant has not submitted to the adjudicator's jurisdiction in that sense, he still liable to enforcement if the adjudicator's decision on jurisdiction was plainly right. On appeal in *Pegram Shopfitters Ltd. v. Tally Wiejl (UK) Ltd.* [2003] EWCA Civ 1750, [2004] 1 All E.R. 818, it was held that the defendant had advanced its argument that the adjudicator lacked jurisdiction in the adjudication and so was not estopped from taking the same point in subsequent enforcement proceedings. By contrast, in *Shimizu Europe Ltd. v. Automajor Ltd.* [2002] EWHC 103 (TCC), [2002]

B.L.R. 113, H.H. Judge Seymour Q.C. remarked *obiter* that by paying part of the sum which the adjudicator had decided was due from it to the claimant and by asking the adjudicator to make a correction to his decision under the slip rule, the defendant had elected to treat the entire decision as made within the adjudicator's jurisdiction. Remarks to similar effect had been made by H.H. Judge Lloyd Q.C. in *K.N.S. Industrial Services (Birmingham) Ltd. v. Sindall Ltd.* (2000) 75 Con.L.R. 71 and by H.H. Judge Gilliland Q.C. in *Farebrother Building Services Ltd. v. Frogmore Investments Ltd.* (above). No such election occurred in *Joinery Plus Ltd. (In Administration) v. Laing Ltd.* [2003] EWHC 213 (TCC), (2003) 87 Con.L.R. 87, where a party which was partly successful in an adjudication was not estopped from challenging the adjudicator's jurisdiction as to the balance of the decision by its conduct in banking a cheque sent in compliance with the decision: it made clear before doing so that the adjudicator's jurisdiction was disputed. Moreover, as H.H. Judge Seymour Q.C. emphasised in *R. Durtnell & Sons Ltd. v. Kaduna Ltd.* [2003] B.L.R. 225, a party will not be held to have submitted to the adjudicator's jurisdiction unless he knew of the matters which meant that the adjudicator lacked jurisdiction.

8–338   Add: An adjudicator who fails to decide the dispute referred to him commits an error of jurisdiction and any award which he makes will be a nullity: see, for examples, *Ballast plc v. The Burrell Company (Construction Management) Ltd* [2001] B.L.R. 529, Sc. Ct. Sess., *Dean & Dyball Construction Ltd. v. Kenneth Grubb Associates Ltd* [2003] EWHC 2465 (TCC), [2003] C.I.L.L. 2045 and *McAlpine PPS Pipeline Systems Ltd. v. Transco plc* [2004] EWHC 2030 (QB), (H.H. Judge Toulmin C.M.G. Q.C., May 5, 2004, unreported). It seems that there must be a failure to decide the entire dispute; the mere failure to consider a submission made by one or other party will not normally amount to an error of jurisdiction (although a serious failure of this sort may amount to a breach of the rules of natural justice so as to take the adjudicator outside his jurisdiction: see Paragraph 8–339 below). In *SL Timber Systems Ltd. v. Carillion Construction Ltd.* [2001] B.L.R. 516, the adjudicator awarded payments to the pursuer purely on the grounds that the defender had failed, contrary to section 110 of the Act, to serve withholding notices in respect of those payments. The adjudicator decided that this was sufficient to entitle the pursuer to payment and that it did not have to establish any entitlement under the contract. The Court of Session accepted the defender's argument that the adjudicator's approach was wrong in law, but rejected its contention that this error had led the adjudicator to exceed his jurisdiction by declining to decide a dispute which was properly before him. It was simply an error of law as to the terms of the contract. In accordance with the decision of the Court of Appeal in *Bouygues UK Ltd. v. Dahl-Jensen UK Ltd.* (for which, see paragraph 8–336 in the main work), it was an error within his jurisdiction. (For further discussion of *SL Timber Systems Ltd. v. Carillion Construction Ltd.*, see the article by I.N.D. Wallace Q.C., "The HGCRA: A Critical Lacuna?" (2002) 18 Const.L.J. 117). Similarly, an adjudicator's error as to whether the Act operated to imply an entitlement to stage payments into a construction contract was merely an error of law as to the terms of the contract and did not go to the adjudicator's jurisdiction: see *C.& B. Scene Concept Design Ltd. v. Isobars Ltd.* [2002] B.L.R. 93 (discussed at paragraph 8–336 above) and *Tim Butler Contractors Ltd. v. Merewood Homes Ltd.*

(2002) 18 Const.L.J. 74, *cf. Barr Ltd. v. Law Mining Ltd.* (2001) 80 Con.L.R. 134, Sc. Ct. Sess. Errors of law by the adjudicator did not prevent the enforcement of his decisions in *William Verry Ltd. v. North West London Communal Mikvah* [2004] EWHC 1300 (TCC), (2004) 26 E.G. 192 (CS) and in *London & Amsterdam Properties Ltd. v. Waterman Partnership Ltd.* (2003) EWHC 3059 (TCC), [2004] B.L.R. 179. The latter was a dispute arising out of allegations of professional negligence against structural engineers. H.H. Judge Wilcox held that it was strongly arguable that the adjudicator had failed properly to address the issue of professional negligence, appearing to regard an error as necessarily negligent, but that this was an error of law which was within his jurisdiction. The judge commented at [190],

> "The resolution of questions of professional negligence within the limited timescale by an adjudicator is not best suited to deciding such matters, particularly when the adjudicator's professional qualifications are not of the same or a similar discipline as that of the professional he seeks to judge. Neither is the impugning of a professional's standards something to be desired. However, that clearly is a matter ultimately for Parliament."

Finally, the failure by an adjudicator or by a party to the adjudication to comply with the procedural rules governing the adjudication process may deprive the adjudicator of jurisdiction so that his decision will not be enforced: see, for example, *IDE Contracting Ltd. v. R.G. Carter Cambridge Ltd.* [2004] B.L.R .172. In two cases, however, it has been held that an adjudicator's failure to issue his decision within the time period stipulated by the statutory scheme did not render his decision unenforceable: see *Barnes & Elliott Ltd. v. Taylor Woodrow Holdings Ltd.* [2004] B.L.R. 111 and *Simons Construction Ltd. v. Aardvark Developments Ltd.* [2003] EWHC 2474 (TCC); [2004] B.L.R. 117.

Add to NOTE 2: The question whether and when a dispute can be said to exist for the purposes of adjudication has been considered in several recent cases. In *Sindall Ltd v. Solland* (2001) 80 Con.L.R. 152, H.H. Judge Lloyd Q.C. said that for a dispute to exist, it must be clear that a point has emerged in the process of discussion or negotiation between the parties which needs to be decided. In *Watkin Jones & Son Ltd v. Lidl UK GmbH* [2002] C.I.L.L. 1834, H.H. Judge Moseley Q.C. regarded himself as bound by the decision of the Court of Appeal in *Halki Shipping Corporation v. Sopex Oils Ltd.* [1998] 1 W.L.R. 726, a decision on when a dispute can be said to exist for the purposes of arbitration, to hold that a dispute may arise in the absence of a positive rejection of the claim or a refusal to meet it. A passive failure to admit a claim will suffice in certain circumstances. Forbes J. took the same approach in *Beck Peppiatt Ltd. v. Norwest Holst Construction Ltd.* [2003] EWHC 822 (TCC), [2003] B.L.R. 316, as did H.H. Judge Bowsher Q.C. in *Carillion Construction Ltd. v. Devonport Royal Dockyard* [2003] B.L.R. 79 and H.H. Judge Kirkham in *Cowlin Construction Ltd. v. CFW Architects* [2003] B.L.R. 241 and in *Orange EBS Ltd. v. ABB Ltd.* [2003] B.L.R. 326. The grounds for the claim must be adequately communicated to the defendant before a dispute can be said to have arisen, however, and any fundamental alteration to those grounds may result in a finding that the dispute ultimately decided by the adjudicator did not exist at the time of the referral to adjudication: *Edmund Nuttall Ltd. v. R.G. Carter Ltd.* [2002] B.L.R. 312. In that case, H.H.

Judge Seymour Q.C. refused to enforce the adjudicator's decision on the grounds that the claimant, after starting the adjudication, had abandoned wholesale the facts and arguments upon which it had previously relied in support of its claim to an extension of time and submitted new facts and arguments to the adjudicator, albeit in support of a claim to the same extension of time. The result was that the adjudicator decided a dispute which was different to that which existed at the time of the referral and which, therefore, he had no jurisdiction to decide. If correct, this decision means that a party wishing to refer a claim to adjudication must first make sure that the other party has been given full information and an adequate opportunity to answer the claim. As such, it should reduce the ability of a claiming party to use adjudication to "ambush" the other party to the contract. On the other hand, the decision significantly widens the scope for jurisdictional challenge to adjudicators' decisions. In many cases, the difference between (a) the refinement of a party's arguments and the abandonment by it of unmeritorious points after the referral to adjudication (both processes which are to be encouraged) and (b) the abandonment of facts and arguments originally relied upon to such a degree that the nature of the dispute is altered, may not be at all obvious. No dispute capable of reference to adjudication will exist, of course, if the same claim has been determined in a previous adjudication: *Watkin Jones & Son Ltd. v. Lidl UK GmbH (No.2)* [2002] EWHC 183 (TCC), (2003) Con.L.R. 155.

Add to NOTE 4: *Gibson Lea Retail Interiors Ltd. v. Makro Self Service Wholesalers Ltd.* is now reported at [2001] B.L.R. 407. For further examples of contracts held not to be for "construction operations", see *Mitsui Babcock Energy Services Ltd. v. Foster Wheeler Energia O. Y.* [2001] S.L.T. 1158 (installation of boilers held to be an activity concerned with a site occupied primarily with oil and chemicals processing, exempted by s.105(2)(c)(ii) of the Act) and *Fence Gate Ltd. v. James R. Knowles Ltd.* [2001] C.I.L.L. 1757 (a dispute over fees for litigation support services provided by architects and surveyors was not a dispute "in relation to construction operations", even although the litigation in question concerned such a dispute).

NOTE 5: *Atlas Ceiling and Partition Co. Ltd. v. Crowngate Estates (Cheltenham) Ltd.* is now reported at (2002) 18 Const.L.J. 49.

Add to NOTE 6: For further cases where decisions were not enforced because they were made outside the scope of the dispute referred to the adjudicator, see *Dean & Dyball Construction Ltd. v. Kenneth Grubb Associates Ltd.* [2003] EWHC 2465 (TCC), [2003] C.I.L.L. 2045 and *McAlpine PPS Pipeline Systems Ltd. v. Transco plc* [2004] EWHC 2030 (QB), H.H. Judge Toulmin C.M.G. Q.C., May 5, 2004, unreported).

8–339   Add: The court also refused to enforce an adjudicator's decision on the grounds of an appearance of bias in *Balfour Beatty Construction Ltd v. Borough of Lambeth* [2002] B.L.R. 288. In deciding that the claimant building contractor was entitled to a substantial extension of time and therefore to repayment of liquidated damages and payment for loss and expense caused by delay, the adjudicator relied upon his own analysis of the causes and nature of the relevant delay. The claimant had supplied no sufficient delay analysis of its own, so that the adjudicator was effectively making good a major deficiency in the claimant's case. Furthermore, he had given neither party an opportunity to comment upon the approach which he adopted. The failure of the adjudicator to allow the parties a fair hearing within the necessary constraints of the adjudication procedure also led to refusals to enforce decisions in *Shimizu Europe Ltd. v. L.B.J. Fabrications Ltd.* [2003] EWHC 1229 (TCC), [2003] B.L.R. 381, *RSL (South West) Ltd. v. Stansell Ltd.* [2003] EWHC 1390 (TCC), [2003] C.I.L.L. 2012, *Buxton Building Contractors Ltd. v. The Governors of Durand Primary School* [2004] EWHC 7233 (TCC), [2004] C.I.L.L. 2117, *AWG Construction Ltd. v. Rockingham Motor Speedway Ltd.* [2004] EWHC 888 (TCC) and *McAlpine PPS Pipeline Systems Ltd. v. Transco plc* [2004] EWHC 2030 (QB), (H.H. Judge Toulmin C.M.G. Q.C., May 5, 2004, unreported). However, a similar challenge failed in the Scottish case of *Karl Construction (Scotland) Ltd. v. Sweeney Civil Engineering (Scotland) Ltd.* (2003) 85 Con.L.R. 59. In that case, the adjudicator decided a sub-contractor's claim for payment on the basis that the sub-contract did not contain an adequate mechanism for deciding when payment was due, contrary to the requirements of the Act, so that the Scheme for Construction Contracts was implied into the contract and governed the claim. This approach had not been ventilated in submissions but the Court of Session held that the adjudicator's adoption of it was not a matter which vitiated her jurisdiction. *Balfour Beatty v. Lambeth* was also distinguished on the facts in *Try Construction Ltd. v. Eton Town House Group Ltd.* [2003] EWHC 60 (TCC), (2003) 87 Con.L.R. 71. A challenge to an adjudicator's appointment on the grounds that he had been appointed in an earlier adjudication between the same parties and so could not be relied upon to be impartial was rejected in *R.G. Carter Ltd. v. Edmund Nuttall Ltd.* [2002] B.L.R. 359 (see references to previous decisions between the same parties at paragraph 8–330 Note 85 and 8–338 Note 2, *supra*). H.H. Judge Bowsher Q.C. held that the court had no power to revoke the appointment of an adjudicator and, in any event, there was no appearance of bias. The adjudicator was a surveyor. The judge observed that professionals such as surveyors and architects commonly act as certifiers under construction contracts and so are used to making decisions which they may later revise in the light of different evidence. *AMEC Capital Projects Ltd. v. Whitefriars City Estates Ltd.* [2004] EWHC 393 (TCC) was a case in which a challenge on grounds that there was a real possibility of bias on the part of the adjudicator succeeded.

Add: Following Dyson J.'s indications at an earlier stage of this case, as set   **8–341**
out in the main text, the defendant in *Herschel Engineering Ltd. v. Breen Property Limited (No.2)*, unreported, July 28, 2000, applied to H.H. Judge Lloyd Q.C. for a stay of execution on the basis of evidence which it claimed showed that the claimant was or might be unable to repay the adjudicator's award if that award was reversed in subsequent arbitration or litigation. The application failed, in part because the claimant's financial position was the same as it had been, to the knowledge of the defendant, when the defendant contracted with it. The defendant had thus accepted the risks which attached to contracting with a party in that financial position. A stay of execution was also refused in *Total M. and E. Services Ltd. v. ABB Building Technologies Ltd.* [2002] EWHC 248 (TCC), (2003) Con.L.R. 154, in that case because of the lack of compelling and uncontradicted evidence that the successful party

in the adjudication would be unable to repay the award in the event that the adjudicator's decision was reversed in subsequent arbitration or litigation. By contrast, the Court of Appeal granted a stay of execution in *Bouygues UK Ltd. v. Dahl-Jensen UK Ltd.* [2000] B.L.R. 522. The defendant in that case was already in liquidation by the time of the claimant's application to enforce the adjudicator's award. That was a special circumstance which justified a stay pending the outcome of arbitration or litigation to achieve a final determination of the parties' dispute. In *Baldwins Industrial Services plc v. Barr Ltd.* [2003] B.L.R. 176, where the claimant was in administrative receivership, a stay on enforcement of an award was granted on terms that the defendant paid the sum at stake into court and issued legal proceedings on the dispute within one month. For further discussion of the issues created in the context of the enforcement of adjudication decisions by a party's insolvency, see *Construction Act Review* (2002) 18 Const. L.J. 39.

Note 19: *Rainford House Ltd. (In Administrative Receivership) v. Cadogan Ltd.* is also reported at [2001] B.L.R. 416.

CHAPTER 9

SURVEYORS

1. GENERAL

(a) *Bases of liability*

9–014 Add: The decision in *Merrett v. Babb* was distinguished by McKinnon J. in *Bradford & Bingley Plc v. Hayes*, unreported July 25, 2001. A lender relied on a mortgage report signed by an individual valuer employed by a limited company. The instructions had been addressed by the limited company. The judge found no basis to impose a duty of care on the individual valuer. He pointed out that *Merrett* had been based on the decision of the House of Lords in *Smith v. Bush* and that both cases had been concerned with individuals relying on mortgage reports in order to consider the purchase of domestic property. It therefore appears likely that the decision in *Merrett* will be confined to situations where the claimant is an individual contemplating the purchase of modest domestic property.

(b) *Duties to client*

(i) *Contractual duties*

9–023 An example of a failure to follow the provisions of the Red Book is provided by the facts of *Montlake v. Lambert Smith Hampton* [2004] EWHC 938. The claimants were the owners of the Wasps rugby ground and wished to raise money for expansion. They decided to form a company and float on the AIM market. The defendant valuers were asked to prepare a valuation. Given the length of time which the club had occupied the ground, there was concern as to possible Capital Gains Tax liability on a sale and the defendant valuers sought to maintain that establishing whether such liability existed was the only purpose of the valuation. The judge held however, that the defendants appreciated that they were being asked to confirm the current value of the ground for fund raising purposes. The defendants had previously provided a valuation some two years previously for "accounting purposes" on a depreciated replacement cost basis. The new valuation was provided on the same basis and ignored the possibility of gaining planning consent. It was accepted at trial, that, even had the valuation only been for the purposes of calculating any Capital Gains Tax liability it should have been on an Open Market basis.

(c) *Duties to third parties*

(i) *General principles*

Add new paragraph **9–038A**:

9–038A One important consideration in deciding whether or not a duty of care should be imposed in a particular factual situation is whether or not a claimant has alternative remedies available. In *Raja v. Austin Gray* [2003] Lloyd's Rep. P.N. 126, the claimant was the administrator of the owner of a property portfolio. Sixteen of the properties had been charged to a property development company which had itself borrowed money from a bank secured by a debenture. The bank appointed administrative receivers who, in turn, appointed the defendant valuers to carry out valuations and to act and advise and assist in relation to the sale of the properties. The question as to whether the defendants owed a duty of care to the deceased was tried as a preliminary issue. It was accepted for the purposes of the issue that the defendants knew that the deceased owned the properties and that the price obtained on sale would directly affect his equity in the properties. At first instance, Buckley J. held that a duty of care was owed. In doing so he relied on the facts: a) that the interests of the receiver and the deceased were essentially co-terminous in that they both wished to obtain the best price; b) that the deceased had no valuable remedies against anyone else as the receivers would be entitled to maintain that they had acted on the expert advice of the defendants; and c) that there was no substance in drawing a distinction between the property company's rights and those of the deceased. The judge did, however, consider that the valuers were bound to put their duty to the bank above any tortious duty to the deceased. It followed that the defendants could not be in breach of duty in the event of any conflict between the interests of the bank and those of the deceased.

The Court of Appeal reversed the decision and followed the earlier decision of H.H. Judge Jack Q.C. in *Huish v Ellis* [1995] BCC 462. It found that the claimant was within the group of persons to whom the receiver owed a duty in equity when exercising a power of sale. The Court considered the question as to whether the receiver was entitled to rely on the advice of apparently competent valuers in effecting the sale and found, notwithstanding the absence of binding authority, that the answer was "no". It followed that the claimant was not without a remedy. Clarke L.J. stated:

> "Given that [the claimant] has an adequate remedy against [the receivers] and (on my view of the case) the receivers, I can see no reason why he should also have a remedy against the appellant valuers. I do not subscribe to the principle: 'the more the merrier'. Valuers in their position perform their services under a contract with the receivers which may contain limitations and restrictions of different kinds which may not be at all easy to fit into the concept of a duty of care in tort. I recognise Mr Douthwaite's point that the scope of any duty owed by the valuers would be limited by the scope of their instructions from their principals, the receivers, and that it would be likely to be a defence to valuers that they acted in accordance with the scope of their instructions. For that reason, I would not, for my part, regard problems of conflict as a conclusive consideration; but they do seem to me to be relevant factors."

Given the limitation on the duties sought to be imposed, it highly arguable that the Court was wrong, as a matter of principle, to regard the existence of an alternative remedy as being decisive. The practical effect of the Court's decision may well be to impose the risk of insolvency of the receiver (who may be an individual) on the claimant. In many cases it may well be that the primary responsibility for selling at an undervalue will lie with the advisers to the receiver. Nevertheless both the question as to whether the receiver is liable even if he has taken apparently competent advice and whether the valuer owes a direct duty of care must be regarded as settled in England below the House of Lords. (The valuers sought and were refused leave to appeal by the House.)

(ii) *Knowledge of reliance*

9–041   Add to NOTE 68: In *Cohen v. TSB Bank plc* [2002] BCLC 32, the claimant was the guarantor of certain secured borrowings. Upon default, two partners in a surveying firm were appointed receivers and a separate firm of valuers appointed as selling agents. The claimant sued both the receivers and the agents for failing to obtain a proper price. The receivers accepted that they owed a duty of care subject to an exclusion clause. The agents denied the existence of any duty to the claimant. Having rejected the claim on its facts, the judge left open the questions as to whether any duties were, in fact, owed.

(iii) *Duty of mortgagee's valuer to purchaser*

9–049   Add: In normal circumstances, a claim by a mortgagor against a lender's valuer will arise from the terms of the written report provided by the valuer. It is, of course, possible for the scope of the duty to be widened as a result of direct contact between the valuer and the mortgagor. Thus in *Frost v. James Finlay Bank* [2001] Lloyd's L.R.P.N. 629, it was alleged that a valuer had provided express assurance to the mortgagor following an inspection at the property. Hart J. rejected the claim on its facts.

(d) *The standard of care and skill*

(iii) *Not every error is negligence*

9–058   Add to NOTE 55: In *Frost v. James Finlay Bank* [2001] Lloyd's L.R.P.N. 629, Hart J. rejected a claim brought by a mortgagee against a valuer who had noticed and reported on cracking but considered it to be insignificant. He found that there was no basis upon which it could be shown that the valuer's conclusion was one to which no reasonably competent valuer could have come.

(iv) *The relevance of "the bracket"*

9–059   Add: In *David Goldstein v. Levy Gee* [2003] EWHC 1574, which was a case concerning the valuation of shares by an accountant, Lewison J. considered the rival strands of authority at some length and stated that he found them difficult to reconcile. He found that he was bound by the decision in *Merivale Moore* so that the valuation had to be outside an acceptable bracket before it was found to be negligent. In this respect he followed the earlier decision of Mr Harvey Q.C. in *Currys Group v. Martin* [1999] 3 E.G.L.R. 165. It now appears unlikely that the observations in *Lion Nathan* and *Arab Bank v. John D. Wood* will be followed by first instance judges. However it also appears that the matter is open to review although probably only in the House of Lords unless the Court of Appeal can be persuaded to distinguish *Merivale Moore* on appropriate facts.

9–060   Add to NOTE 60: This case was followed by H.H. Judge Richard Seymour Q.C. in *Lloyds TSB Bank v. Edwards Symmons* [2003] EWHC 346 where it was alleged that the defendant valuers had negligently undervalued a shopping centre for a bank with the result that it was sold by the bank at too low a price. The judge considered a large number of alleged errors in methodology by the valuers but found that, as the result of the valuation was within the appropriate bracket, no case had been made out. He did not consider whether the terms of the valuers' retainer were such that they were required to do more than simply produce an end figure.

Add new NOTE 61A after "characteristics": The above passage was cited   **9–061**
with approval by H.H. Judge Heppel Q.C. in *John D Wood & Co. v. Knatchbull* [2003] P.N.LR. 351, in the context of advice by an estate agent to a vendor as to the appropriate asking price for a house. The agent had advised an asking price of £1.5 million. The judge concluded that the true value of the property was £1.7 million at the material time. He nonetheless held that the initial advice was not negligent both because of the limited information available to the agent and because the agent was entitled to a margin of error. He went on to hold that the agent was in breach of duty in that he should have informed the vendor when he became aware that a nearby similar property was on the market at £1.95 million. See further paragraphs 9–078 and 9–176 below.

(e) *Limitation of liability*

Add to NOTE 13: A similar conclusion was reached by Lord Eassie in *Bank*   **9–071**
of Scotland v. Fuller Peiser [2002] P.N.LR. 289. It appears that although the relevant English authorities were cited to him, he was not informed of the decision in *Commercial Funding Services v. McBeth*. A borrower had commissioned a valuation of a hotel which she sent to her bank who were considering making a loan in connection with the purchase. The valuation contained an exclusion clause. Lord Eassie held that the effect of the exclusion clause was to prevent any duty of care from arising. He distinguished the decision in *Smith v. Bush* on the grounds that was a case concerned with domestic conveyancing where different considerations applied.

He pointed out that this case was set in a commercial context (albeit of modest value). Amongst the factors pointing to the reasonableness of the disclaimer were: the size of the claimant; its ability to obtain legal advice; the fact that the claimant could easily have obtained its own report (or paid a fee to the defendant to enable it to rely on his report); the lack of any time constraint upon obtaining alternative advice and the fact that the bank was of at least equal bargaining power with the defendant.

2. LIABILITY FOR BREACH OF DUTY

(a) *Failing to carry out instructions*

Add: The decision of the House of Lords in *Farley v. Skinner* permitting   **9–077**
the recovery of general damages is now reported at [2001] UKHL 49.

Add: Where estate agents are employed for the sale of properties, they will   **9–078**
be subject to the usual obligations of such agents. Thus in *John D Wood &*
Co. v. Knatchbull, [2003] P.N.LR. 351, agents had given an initial valuation of

a property at £1.5 million which the judge found to have been competent. The property was then marketed. During the course of the marketing campaign the agents became aware that a nearby similar property was on the market at £1.95 million. H.H. Judge Heppel Q.C. found that the agents were in breach of duty in not bringing this knowledge to the attention of their principal. He stated:

> ". . . the agent has a duty to exercise reasonable care when marketing a property for sale and if in the course of so doing he becomes aware of a significant event in the market which might influence his principal's instructions to inform the principal thereof and to advise him accordingly".

See further paragraphs 9–061 above and 9–176 below.

(c) *Failing to inspect properly*

(iii) *Failing to observe*

9–096   Note 15: *Hoadley v. Edwards* is now reported at [2001] P.N.L.R. 965.

(d) *Failing to make sufficient inquiries*

9–100   Add: A further recent example of the negligent failure to make proper enquiries is provided by the facts of *Montlake v. Lambert Smith Hampton*, [2004] EWHC 938 (see further paragraph 9–023) above, where the defendant surveyors did not make proper enquires of the local planning authority before updating a valuation made two years previously. In the course of the two years, the local authority had changed the designation of a rugby ground from "Public and Private Open Space/Playing fields" to undesignated land. The consequence was that no allowance was made for the possibility of profitable residential development.

9–101   Note 38: The decision of the House of Lords in *Farley v. Skinner* is now at [2001] UKHL 49.

3. Damages

(c) *Remoteness*

(i) *Causation*

9–121   Add: In *Speshal Investments Ltd. v. CorbyKane Howard Partnership*, [2003] EWHC 390, Hart J. considered whether reliance on a valuation had to be reasonable in order for liability to be found (see further paragraph 9–172 below). Having found that it was necessary for a claimant to establish that he believed a valuation before reliance could be found, the judge summarised the relationship between duty, reliance and contributory negligence as follows:

> "So far as concerns the proposition that, even if the claimant did rely on the valu- ations believing them to be reliable, they were unreasonable in doing so, there is in

my judgment some danger of confusion. The claim is based on the premise that the defendants owed the claimant a duty of care in tort . . . If the defendants did owe the claimants a duty of care in providing the valuations, and the claimant in fact relied on those valuations believing them to be reliable, the question whether it was "reasonable" for the claimant to have relied appears to me to arise only in the context of considering whether it was contributorily negligent. If the proposition is that the caveats in the valuation report . . . had the effect of negativing the existence of a duty of care, or of excepting the defendants from liability for a breach of it, then the issues relate to the nature of the relationship said to give rise to the duty of care and the true construction of the provision alleged to exempt from liability. The question of the reasonableness of the reliance which was in fact placed on the valuations does not, it seems to me, arise at this stage. As I understand it, the defendants conceded the existence of a duty of care, and did not seek to argue that liability had effectively been excluded by the terms of the caveats. My approach is therefore to consider, first, whether there was actual reliance in the relevant sense and secondly to consider whether a case of contributory negligence has been made out."

9–122   Add: The Courts have also consistently refused to require a lender to give credit for a mortgage indemnity guarantee on the basis that it represents a policy of insurance for which the law does not require the claimant to give credit—see *Arab Bank v. John D Wood* [1999] Lloyd's Rep. P.N. 173. Similarly a claimant does not have to give credit for its own building insurance policy or NHBC guarantee—see *Hanley Smith v. Darlington* [2001] E.G. 160.

(d) *Measure of damages*

(i) *Negligent survey or valuation for a purchaser who completes a purchase*

9–131   Add: In *Smith v. Peter North* [2001] P.N.L.R. 274, the Court of Appeal again rejected an attempt to distinguish previous authorities so as to claim the costs of repair. The claimants, who ran an equestrian business, instructed the defendants to advise as to the costs of repairing a property to bring it up to their required standard as well as on its value. The defendant surveyor advised that the property was in substantially good repair whereupon the claimants purchased it for £330,000. They then claimed that £130,000 was required to bring the property up to the required standard although the Court appointed valuer stated that the property was worth £340,000 (*i.e.* £10,000 more than the claimants paid for it) at the time of purchase. The judge struck out the claim for the cost of repairs although allowed to remain a claim for the costs of seeking alternative accommodation together with the costs of moving and storing furniture during the repair works. The Court of Appeal upheld the judge's conclusion. Jonathan Parker L.J. considered the case to be straightforward and emphasised (at paragraph 50) that the effect of permitting the cost of repairs to be claimed would be to place them in a better position than had the valuer given a competent report.

9–131   In *McKinnon v. E Surv Ltd.* [2003] P.N.L.R. 174, the Court was asked to consider the interesting question as to the appropriate damages where a surveyor negligently failed to report on the true extent of structural movement and recommend monitoring but where it was possible to show that the movement had, in fact, finished. The question arose as to whether the property should be valued as at the date of purchase, in which event, there would necessarily be uncertainty as to the position with a consequential effect on value or in the knowledge of the true facts, namely that movement had stopped. Mr Jonathan Gaunt Q.C. held, it is submitted correctly, that in order to give effect to the overall compensatory rule in the assessment of damage, it was necessary to take account of information available at trial.

NOTE 71: *Hoadley v. Edwards* is now reported at [2001] P.N.L.R. 965.

9–139   Add: The Courts have also had to consider the nature of a claim for damages against a negligent valuer in the context of limitation. In *Hamlin v. Evans* [1996] 2 E.G.L.R. 106 , the defendant valuers settled a claim based upon the presence of dry rot and were then presented with a claim based upon a fracture in one of the walls. The Court of Appeal considered that the only relevant damage was the diminution in value caused by purchasing the property in reliance on the negligent report. It followed that the second claim was statute barred. Waite L.J. distinguished cases brought against building contractors out of separate defects. *Hamlin* was followed by the Northern Irish Court of Appeal in *McKillen v. Russell*, [2002] P.N.L.R. 29, where a claimant first discovered that a garage had been built without Building Regulations approval and made a claim against his surveyor which was settled. He later discovered that there had also been extensive works done to the house without the relevant approval. Kerr J. held that the claim was statute barred as the claimant knew of the relevant damage when he first discovered that he had purchased the house at an over-value as a result of his surveyor's negligence.

9–140   Add: The position may, of course, be different in a situation where a survey is carried out after exchange or where special contractual provisions apply. Thus in *Hanley Smith v. Darlington* [2001] E.G. 160, a purchaser was entitled to have defects remedied by the vendor under a contract of sale. The survey was instituted after exchange and the measure of damages was held to be the costs of repair on the basis that but for the surveyor's negligence the claimant would have been entitled to have the defects remedied free of charge.

9–141   NOTE 33: *Hoadley v. Edwards* is now reported at [2001] P.N.L.R. 965.

9–148   Add to NOTE 56: Similarly a claimant does not have to give credit for an NHBC guarantee—see *Hanley Smith v. Darlington* [2001] E.G. 160.

(iii) *Negligent survey or valuation for lender*

9–172   **(d) Contributory negligence by lender**. In *Speshal Investments Ltd. v. CorbyKane Howard Partnership* [2003] EWHC 390, the defendant valuers made grossly negligent valuations which, as the lender knew although the valuer did not, exceeded the amount of the purchase price of the properties concerned and were also called into question by other valuations (of which both the valuer and the lender were aware). Hart J. found that the lenders should have either withdrawn from the transaction or made further inquiries. He assessed the appropriate reduction for contributory negligence as 20 per cent stating:

"A higher reduction would in my view be unjust. A valuer who gives negligent valuations as egregiously wrong as these cannot lightly be excused any part of his prima facie liability to pay for the full consequences of his negligence. A lesser reduction would risk appearing to be a recognition of an almost token nature only of some minor carelessness on the claimant's part."

(v) *Undervaluation for vendor*

There have been two recent cases concerning damages awarded to a vendor **9–176** who has received inadequate advice on sale. In *John D Wood & Co. v. Knatchbull* [2003] P.N.LR. 351 (for facts see paragraphs 9–061 and 9–078 above), H.H. Judge Heppel Q.C. awarded damages to a vendor based upon the lost chance of a sale at a higher price. The property had been marketed and sold, in accordance with advice from estate agents, at a price of £1.5 million. Although this advice was competent, the judge found that the agents were in breach of duty in failing to inform the vendor, prior to exchange of contracts, that they had learned that a nearby property was on the market at £1.95 million. The judge further found that had this knowledge been imparted, the property would not have been sold for £1.5 million but that there was a 66 per cent chance that it would have sold at £1.7 million and awarded damages accordingly.

In *Montlake v. Lambert Smith Hampton* [2004] EWHC 938, (for facts see paragraphs 9–023 and 9–100 above), the judge concluded that, if properly advised, Wasps Rugby Club would have received the difference between the value placed upon its ground and that which should have been put given a competent valuation. Much of the difference in value was explained by the fact that the negligent valuation did not take into account the possibility (although not the certainty) of obtaining planning permission but the judge regarded the "chance" of obtaining planning permission as being only a check on his assessment of quantum. The judge also rejected, on the facts, suggestions that the claimants had been contributorily negligent in failing to minimise the loss that they had suffered. He emphasised that the club had been entitled to proceed on the basis that they had a proper valuation.

(vii) *Inconvenience and discomfort*

Note 84: The decision of the House of Lords in *Farley v. Skinner* is **9–181** reported at [2001] UKHL 49.

Add: In *Holder v. Countrywide Surveyors* [2003] P.N.L.R. 29, an award of **9–189** £2,000 was made to a claimant against a negligent surveyor where the claimant had to move out of accommodation and clean dirty man-hole covers.

Note 31: *Hoadley v. Edwards* is now reported at [2001] P.N.L.R. 965.

(viii) *Incidental expenses*

Add to Note 34: In *Holder v. Countrywide Surveyors* [2003] P.N.L.R. 29, **9–190** the judge stated that although the logic of the statement by H.H. Judge Hicks in *Bigg v. Howard Son and Gooch* [1990] 1 E.G.L.R. 173 was unassailable, nevertheless the courts had awarded damages for the costs of accommodation during repair and proceeded to make an award under this head.

CHAPTER 10

SOLICITORS

1. GENERAL

10–003　　Add to NOTE 13: The Law Society has powers to intervene in a solicitor's practice, which the Court of Appeal in *Holder v. Law Society* [2003] 3 All E.R. 62 held raised no issue under the Human Rights Act 1998.

NOTE 18, replace with the following: The updated *Guide* can be found on the Law Society website.

(a) *Duties to client*

(i) *Contractual duties*

10–008　　Add to NOTE 39: *Pilbrow* was applied by the Court of Appeal in *Adrian Alan Ltd. v. Fuglers* [2003] P.N.L.R. 14, where a former solicitor had fraudulently deceived the client into believing that he was qualified.

10–010　　Add to NOTE 48: Also followed by the Hong Kong High Court in *National Commercial Bank Ltd v. Albert Hwang, David Chung & Co.* [2002] 2 H.K.L.R.D. 409.

10–011　　Add: A retainer may determine because it is impossible for the solicitors to carry out their retainer, see *Morfoot v. W F Smith & Co.* [2001] Lloyd's Rep. P.N. 658, Ch.D. See paragraph 10–75, n. 95 on whether the retainer to a company continues although it may be impossible to obtain instructions from it.

Add to NOTE 52: In *Perotti v. Collyer-Bristow* [2003] W.T.L.R. 1473, Lindsay J. doubted whether a retainer to conduct litigation was an entire contract, and concluded that old authority established that there was no such entire retainer in a complicated matter such as the administration of an estate. In any event, the defendant solicitors had reason in that case to determine their retainer because there was a conflict of interest and serious breakdown in confidence between client and solicitor, and a natural break had been reached.

Add to NOTE 56: There was no continuing duty in *Morfoot v. W F Smith &* **10–012**
Co. [2001] Lloyd's Rep. P.N. 658, Ch.D., where it was held that the duty to
obtain a deed of release was broken as soon as it was possible to obtain such
a deed.

NOTE 57, replace reference to *Hines v. Willans* with the following: [2002]
W.T.L.R. 299.

(ii) *Tortious duties*

Add to NOTE 75: The New Zealand Court of Appeal emphasised in *Frost* **10–015**
& Sutcliffe v. Tuiara [2004] 1 N.Z.L.R. 782 that the duties in contract and tort
would usually be concurrent and coextensive.

(iii) *Fiduciary duties*

General. Add to NOTE 78: Fiduciary duties may be owed by a solicitor to **10–016**
his partner or employer, which he must be careful not to breach when leaving
a firm to set up business elsewhere, see for example *Kao Lee & Yip v. Koo Hoi*
Yan [2003] W.T.L.R. 1283, Hong Kong High Court.

(2) Personal dealings with clients. Add: In *Johnson v. EBS Pensioner* **10–018**
Trustees Ltd. [2002] Lloyd's Rep. P.N. 309, a solicitor acting for undisclosed
lenders arranged a loan to his clients, but did not disclose that his firm would
benefit from a 1.5 per cent service charge paid by the lenders. The Court of
Appeal held: (i) that the law of personal dealings with the client, described as
the doctrine of abuse of confidence, applied in cases where property did not
pass; by a majority that (ii) the solicitor had failed to prove the transaction
was a fair one as a result of the non-disclosure of the service charge; but that
(iii) the remedy was an account of the service charge and rescission of the
transaction was disproportionate. In *Longstaff v. Birtles* [2002] 1 W.L.R. 470,
the Court of Appeal held that a solicitor seeking to buy or sell property from
a present or former client must insist that the client obtains independent legal
advice. However, in that case the judge had found that the clients had not
been given full information about the transaction.

Add to NOTE 98: See also *Peterco Holdings v. Calverton Holdings* (2003) 11
B.C.L.R. (4th) 280, British Columbia C.A., where it was held that, on the
facts, the other partners trusted and relied on the solicitor as a partner but
not as a solicitor, and there was no relationship sufficient to establish a
fiduciary duty.

(6) Accepting inconsistent engagements. NOTE 14, replace reference to
Hines v. Willans with the following: [2002] W.T.L.R. 299.

Add to NOTE 17: In *R v. Neil* (2003) 218 D.L.R. (4th) 671 the Supreme **10–023**
Court of Canada made it clear that the duty of loyalty went beyond the issue
of confidentiality, and included a duty to avoid conflicting interests, a duty of
commitment to the client's cause, and a duty of candour. There may be a
breach of fiduciary duty even if the two retainers are unrelated if one client's
interests are directly adverse to the immediate interests of another client.

10–024   Add to NOTE 17: The rule applies not only to acting for clients with conflicts in the same transaction, but where the conflict arises from different transactions, providing that there is a reasonable relationship between them. As a result, in *Marks & Spencer plc v. Freshfields Bruckhaus Deringer* [2004] 1 W.L.R. 2331 Lawrence Collins J. injuncted the defendants from acting for a third party.

Add to NOTE 18: In *Leeds & Holbeck Building Society v. Arthur & Cole (a Firm)* [2002] P.N.L.R. 23, the claimant building society failed to prove that the solicitor had known that he ought to disclose the lack of any deposit passing through his hands and that his failure had been intentional and conscious. Morland J., having heard the solicitor's evidence, found him to be frank, fair and honest.

10–026   **(7) Confidence.** Add to NOTE 36: Similar duties will be owed to a solicitors' partners, which may be breached by misusing confidential information to their own benefit, see *Deacons v. White & Case Ltd. LLP* [2003] HJKLRD 670, Hong Kong High Court. In *Marsh v. Sofaer* [2004] P.N.L.R. 24 the Vice-Chancellor held that the duty to keep communications confidential extend to the conclusions a solicitor draws from the material communicated, and thus a solicitor cannot communicate his conclusion that the client did or might lack capacity even to another solicitor acting for the client in a different matter, and lack of capacity did not provide implied consent for such disclosure.

Add to NOTE 37: Thus there would be no duty to disclose to a subsequent client relevant information revealed in a prior retainer by another client, as the duty to disclose matters did not cover matters which solicitors were obliged to treat as confidential, see *Hilton v. Parker Booth & Eastwood (a Firm)* [2003] P.N.L.R. 32, C.A., and see para. 10–217 below.

Add to NOTE 39: In exceptional circumstances a lawyer may be restrained from acting even where there is no confidential information, see *Geveran Trading Co. Ltd. v. Skjevesland* [2003] 1 W.L.R. 912 (C.A., noted at Chap. 11 paragraph 11–005 n. 20), and *Re Recover Ltd. (in liquidation)* [2003] 2 BCLC 186, Pumfrey J.

10–027   Add to NOTE 42: See also Stafford, Andrew: "Chinese walls and confidential information." (2003) 19 P.N. 306.

10–028   Add to NOTE 43: For another illustration see *Ball v. Druces & Attlee (a Firm)* [2002] P.N.L.R. 23. The defendant solicitors acted for the Eden Trust in litigation brought by the claimant. He alleged that the solicitors had acted for him in setting up the Eden project, and that there was a risk that they would give their clients confidential information to his prejudice. Burton J. held that there was an arguable case that the claimant's retainer of the solicitors had existed and that confidential information imparted to the solicitors might remain in their hands. He therefore granted an injunction, as he was not satisfied that there was no risk of disclosure. The injunction was interlocutory as the question of whether there had been a breach of confidence would be finally determined in the trial of the action the claimant had brought against the solicitors. It was granted on the basis of a cross-undertaking and guarantee in relation to the solicitors' potential lost profits and the Eden Trust's potential expense of instructing new solicitors. *Cf. Re Recover Ltd (in liquidation)* [2003] 2 BCLC 186, where Pumfrey J. required the alleged confidential information to be properly particularised, which it was not, and thus no injunction was granted.

Add to NOTE 46: For a contrasting case, see *Koch Shipping Inc. v. Richards Butler (a Firm)* [2003] P.N.L.R. 11, where the partner handling the applicant's shipping arbitration left her firm and joined Richards Butler, who acted for the opposing party. There were detailed undertakings from all the solicitors involved, and the Court of Appeal held that this made the risk of inadvertent disclosure of confidential information fanciful, and discharged the injunction which had been granted at first instance. *Cf Marks & Spencer plc v. Freshfields Bruckhaus Deringer* [2004] 1 W.L.R. 2331, where Lawrence Collins J. held that no effective barriers could be put in place because of the very large numbers of people concerned. **10–030**

Add: In *Carter Holt Harvey Forests Ltd. v. Sunnex Logging Ltd.* [2001] 3 N.Z.L.R. 343, the solicitors acted for Sunnex in proceedings against Carter Holt. An injunction was granted by the New Zealand Court of Appeal against the solicitors, as they had acted in a very similar claim by Rua against Carter Holt. While the injunction was not sought by a former client, the earlier litigation had ended in a mediation in which the lawyers had participated, and where they had signed a comprehensive confidentiality agreement on which Carter Holt were entitled to rely. **10–031**

Add to NOTE 48: *Bank of Montreal v. Dresler* (2003) 224 D.L.R. (4th) 337, New Brunswick C.A.

Add to NOTE 49: However, in *Spincode Pty Ltd. v. Look Software Pty Ltd.* (2001) 4 V.R. 501, the Victoria Court of Appeal rejected the English law that an injunction could only be granted where there was a risk of disclosure of confidential information, and considered that an order could be made on the basis of a duty of loyalty or a solicitor's conduct being offensive to fairness and justice.

Add: See also the guidance of the House of Lords in *Porter v. Magill* [2002] 2 A.C. 357. **10–033**

(iv) *Trust duties*

Add: In *Twinsectra v. Francis John Yardley* [2002] 2 A.C. 164, the House of Lords held that when solicitors receive monies from a lender on an undertaking that they will be retained until they are applied in the acquisition of property on behalf of the client, and will only be used for that purpose, a trust was created. The power to apply the money "in the acquisition of property" was sufficiently certain to create a trust, and the fact that the lender had not intended to create a trust was irrelevant. **10–035**

Replace the last four sentences with the following: In *Twinsectra v. Francis John Yardley* [2002] 2 A.C. 164, the House of Lords applied *Royal Brunei Airlines v. Tan* in a case against a solicitor. Monies were paid by the claimant lender to a Mr Sims under an express purpose trust to be applied in the acquisition of **10–038** property, most of which monies were paid to the defendant solicitor without the imposition of any restriction, although the solicitor knew of the restriction. The solicitor acquiesced in a short term advance of £34,000 for another venture, and used other parts of the money for the payment of his fees and other uses which were not the anticipated acquisition of property. A majority of the House of Lords (Lord Millett dissenting) held that the test for dishonesty was a combined one: the defendant's conduct must be dishonest by the ordinary standards of reasonable and honest people; and he must in fact have realised that by those standards his conduct was dishonest. The trial judge had applied that test and had held that the solicitor was mistaken rather than dishonest, as he believed that the undertaking was not his concern. The House of Lords held that in the light of the judge's findings, the Court of Appeal should not have substituted its own findings of dishonesty. For a helpful commentary on the case see T.M. and Tjio H.: "Knowing what is dishonesty" (2002) 118 L.Q.R. 502.

10–039   Add: All the cases in this paragraph must now be read subject to the House of Lords decision in *Twinsectra v. Francis John Yardley* [2002] 2 A.C. 164, discussed in the previous paragraph (10–038).

Add to NOTE 83: In *Mortgage Express Ltd. v. S Newman & Co. (a Firm)* [2001] Lloyd's Rep. P.N. 605, Etherton J. found, on the retrial, that the solicitor was not dishonest.

(b) *Duties to third parties*

(i) *General*

10–041   Add to NOTE 99: A similar suggestion was made in *Yazhou Travel Investment Co. Ltd.* [2004] 1 HKLRD 969, purporting to apply the English cases cited in the next note.

10–042   Add to NOTE 2: See also *Wakim v. HIH Casualty & General Insurance Ltd.* [2001] 182 ALR 353, discussed at Ch.11, para.11–006, where a duty of care was owed by a solicitor to the principal creditor of his client, the trustee in bankruptcy; the issue of reliance was not discussed.

10–044   NOTE 11, replace the second sentence with the following: In *Harris v. Nantes & Wilde* [1997] N.P.C. 7, the defendant solicitors acted for stepmother and stepson in the acquisition of property. She later instructed the firm to convey the estate into her sole name, which they did without informing him. In fact she was involved in a fraudulent enterprise and forged his signature. The Court of Appeal declined to strike out an action by the stepson against the stepmother's solicitors in part because it was arguable that they owed him a duty of care, it being arguable that the instructions from the stepmother purported to be joint instructions from both of them.

Add to NOTE 13: In *Esser v. Brown* (2003) 223 D.L.R. (4th) 560, the British Columbia Supreme Court came to the same result on very similar facts in an action brought against a notary public.

(ii) *Liability to beneficiaries without reliance*

Add to NOTE 43: While the Court of Appeal did not have to determine **10–048** whether any duty was owed to the beneficiary or the personal representative of the deceased, they decided in *Daniels v. Thompson* [2004] P.N.L.R. 33 that, where the solicitor's negligence caused the payment of inheritance tax, the testator could not suffer loss.

Add to text: There is no requirement to prove that the testamentary intention **10–049** continued until death, see *Humblestone v. Martin Tolhurst Partnership (A Firm)* [2004] P.N.L.R. 26, Mann J.

Add to NOTE 54: For an argument that the disappointed beneficiary has an **10–052** action in restitution against the unintended recipient, see O'Dell, Eoin: "Restitution, Rectification, and Mitigation: Negligent Solicitors and Wills, Again" (2002) 65 M.L.R. 360.

Add: *Chappell v. Somers & Blake (a firm)* [2004] Ch 19 shows an interest- **10–053** ing and ingenious application of *White v. Jones*. An executrix instructed the defendant solicitor to act in the administration of the estate. She alleged that they did nothing for five years, and thus the beneficiaries lost the opportunity to obtain the properties five years earlier. The solicitor's application to strike out the claim on the grounds that the loss had been suffered by the benefici- aries was refused by Neuberger J. Relying on Lord Goff's speech in *White v. Jones,* the beneficiaries might have no claim, but it would be wrong for there to be a black hole with the duty owed to the executrix and the loss suffered by the beneficiaries. The judge therefore considered that the executrix could be treated as representing the interests of the owners of the property and thus would be entitled to recover damages. The beneficiaries were willing to be joined to the action, so there was no risk of double recovery. For a commen- tary see O'Sullivan, Janet: "Solicitors, executors and beneficiaries,: Who can sue and who can be sued?" (2003) 19 P.N. 507.

Add to NOTE 62: For further consideration of whether duties are owed to ben- eficiaries in relation to inter vivos transaction see the accountant's negligence case of *Richards (T/A Colin Richards & Co.) v. Hughes* [2004] P.N.L.R. 35, C.A.

Add after the first sentence the following: *White v. Jones* was followed in **10–054** the Scottish case of *Davidson v. The Bank of Scotland* [2002] P.N.L.R. 740, Outer House.

NOTE 73: *Earl v. Wilhelm* is also reported at [2001] W.T.L.R. 1275.

(iii) *Duty of care to the other side*

Add to NOTE 88: While none of the cases referred to in this and the pre- **10–059** ceding paragraphs were cited to the Court, the result in *347671 B.C. Ltd. v. Heenan Blaikie* (2002) 10 C.C.L.T. (3d) 306; British Columbia CA, is consis- tent with them. There, the lawyers acting for the borrower made specific representations to the lender in a telephone conversation.

10–061   Add to NOTE 97: *Patriquin v. Laurentian Trust of Canada Inc.* (2002) 96 B.C.L.R. (3d) 318, British Columbia CA.: broker's solicitor owed no duty to investor where he told investor that he did not represent his interests and the investor had own lawyer. *Gerling Global General Insurance Co. v. Siskind, Cromarty, Ivey & Dowler* (2002) 59 O.R. (3d) 555, Ontario Superior Ct.: solicitor assisting client in filling out proof of loss for insurance claim which was then sworn in front of him did not represent that the document was true. He only represented as true the identity of the deponent, the place and time of swearing, and that the deponent had sworn that the contents were true.

10–062   Add to NOTE 1: A similar result was reached by the Ontario Superior Court in *Baypark Investments Inc. v. Royal Bank of Canada* (2002) 57 O.R. (3d) 528.

(iv) *Solicitors' liability on undertakings*

10–068   NOTE 45, replace the last two sentences with the following: An undertaking to apply the monies received in a particular way is likely to create a trust, see *Twinsectra v. Francis John Yardley* [2002] 2 A.C. 164 and para.10–035 above.

10–072   Add: In *Hole and Pugsley (a Firm) v. Sumption* [2002] P.N.L.R. 502, Hart J. made it clear that disclosure of a material change in circumstance would not relieve solicitors from liability in every case. In that case, the undertaking was to send proceeds of sale to the respondents or their bank. Disclosure of the change in circumstance, which was that the solicitors' client's bank now required the full net proceeds of sale to be paid to it, did not relieve the solicitors of their obligation.

(v) *Other liabilities*

10–075   Add to NOTE 95: Such a claim failed in *Donsland Ltd. v. Van Hoogstraten* [2002] P.N.L.R. 26, where it was alleged that proceedings were continued in breach of warranty of authority after the sole director of the claimant company had died. The Court of Appeal held that the retainer continued, as the company continued in existence, although there was no one to give instructions. The solicitors had authority to take all necessary steps to preserve the claim. The case was applied by Cooke J. in *Euroafrica Shipping Lines Co. Ltd. v. Zeguila Polska SA* [2004] 2 BCLC 97, where there were difficulties in obtaining instructions as there was a dispute about the constitution of the client company.

10–076   Add to NOTE 98: In *Folland v. Ontario* (2003) 225 D.L.R. (4th) 50, the Ontario Court of Appeal declined to strike out an action for malicious prosecution brought by a victim of a miscarriage of justice against a crown prosecutor.

10–076A   Lawyers have some limited duties to report matters to the authorities. In particular, under the Proceeds of Crime Act 2002 Parts 7 and 8, lawyers may commit a criminal offence if they are concerned in an arrangement which facilitates the use or control of criminal property by another person. There is protection if disclosure is made to the National Criminal Intelligence Service. There is also an offence of "tipping off" the other person about a potential investigation by the NCIS. These provisions are potentially wide-ranging and go beyond what may ordinarily be considered to be money laundering. They are of particular concern in ancillary relief applications arising from divorce although they can arise in other circumstances. In *P. v. P. (Ancillary Relief: Proceeds of Crime)* [2004] Fam 1 the wife's lawyers were concerned that the husband's assets were derived from untaxed income, the provisions of the Act therefore applied to the settlement of the ancillary relief proceedings, and they sought the guidance of the Court. The President gave helpful guidance as to the statutory regime. Negotiating an ancillary relief settlement would amount to being concerned in a prohibited arrangement which facilitated the use or control of criminal property, which required reporting to the NCIS. The relevant provisions apply even to small amounts of money which have been illegally obtained. However, lawyers who have reported a matter to the NCIS, and then make disclosure to the client or other side after seven days (or a further 31 if the NCIS does not consent) will generally not commit an offence of "tipping off", unless done for an improper purpose. See also the Law Society's Money Laundering Warning Card, which can be found on the Law Society's website.

(c) *The standard of skill and care*

(ii) *General practice as evidence of reasonable skill and care*

Replace the last two sentences with the following: In *Patel v. Daybells (a Firm)* [2002] P.N.L.R. 6, solicitors completed a sale on the basis of undertakings given by the vendor's solicitors. The Court of Appeal held that this practice was not negligent, and distinguished *Wong* on the basis that the undertaking in *Wong* was wider, there was no official indemnity scheme in place, and the Law Society of Hong Kong had already warned its members of the risk. They held that the principle in *Wong* was correct, which was that if a practice exposes clients to a foreseeable and avoidable risk, it may not be capable of being defended on rational grounds, and in those circumstances the fact that the practice is commonly or universally followed will not exclude liability. The principle in *Wong* was applied in *National Commercial Bank Ltd. v. Albert Hwang, David Chung & Co.* [2002] 2 H.K.L.R.D. 409. The lender's solicitor released monies without verifying the authority of the person who purported to sign the agreement for the sale of property on behalf of the vendor company. This exposed the lender to a foreseeable risk that the mortgage would not be effective, which could have been avoided by making inquiries about the signer. The Hong Kong High Court held that the solicitors had been negligent. **10–088**

(iii) *The specialist solicitor and the inexperienced solicitor*

NOTE 59, replace the final reference with the following: [2002] Lloyd's Rep. P.N. 23. **10–094**

(iv) *Mitigating factors*

Add to NOTE 68: On appeal, the finding of negligence was upheld, but the Court of Appeal held that the negligence caused no loss, see [2001] 2 H.K.L.R.D. 342. In *Carew Counsel Pty Ltd. v. French* (2002) 190 A.L.R. 690, the Victoria Court of Appeal took account of the fact that the solicitors had **10–097** only two days in which to decide how to protect their client in relation to complex bankruptcy provisions, and the solicitors were held not to be negligent.

(v) *Aggravating factors*

10–100   Add to NOTE 81: The Hong Kong Court of Appeal condemned this practice in *Yau Chin Kwan v. Tin Shui Wai Development Ltd.* [2003] 2 H.K.L.R.D. 1.

Add to NOTE 82: A solicitor was held to be liable where he did not mention to his clients that there was a possible conflict of interest in *Lizotte v. Lizotte* (2002) 249 N.B.R. (2d) 70, New Brunswick C.A.

10–102   Add to NOTE 95: Applied by the New Zealand Court of Appeal in *Niak v. Macdonald* [2001] 3 N.Z.L.R. 334.

(d) *Specific defences to a claim for breach of duty*

Add new paragraph **10–105A**:

10–105A   **Illegality**. It is no defence to a claim in negligence that the solicitor and client were both engaged on a fraud, if the action could be pleaded and proved without reliance on the alleged fraud—see *Sweetman v. Nathan* [2004] P.N.L.R. 7, C.A.

(i) *Immunity*

10–107   NOTE 19, replace the reference with the following: [2002] 1 A.C. 615.

(ii) *Abuse of process*

10–108   NOTE 21, replace the reference with the following: [2002] 1 A.C. 615.

10–109   Replace NOTE 32 with the following: [2002] 1 A.C. 615 at 703G.

Replace NOTE 33 with the following: *ibid.* 706E.

10–110   NOTE 39, replace the reference with the following: [2002] 1 A.C. 615.

10–113   Add to Note 41. *Hunter* was relied on by the Saskatchewan Court of Appeal in *Fischer v. Halyk* (2003) 239 D.L.R. (4th) 67. The plaintiff was convicted of theft and her appeal failed. Her action against her defence lawyer was an improper collateral attack on a criminal conviction, and was struck out as an abuse of process.

NOTE 42, replace the reference with the following: [2002] 1 A.C. 615, 685B *per* Lord Browne-Wilkinson; 702G *per* Lord Hoffman.

Replace NOTE 43 with the following: *ibid.* 679G.

Replace NOTE 44 with the following: *ibid.* 685C.

Replace NOTE 45 with the following: *ibid.* 727B–C.

Replace NOTE 46 with the following: *ibid.* 706E.

Replace NOTE 47 with the following: *ibid.* 722G–H.

Replace NOTE 48 with the following: *ibid.* 753A.

Replace NOTE 49 with the following: *ibid.* 751C–D.

NOTE 50, replace the second reference with the following: [2002] 1 A.C. 615 at 706E.

Replace NOTE 51 with the following: *ibid.* 679H.

Replace NOTE 52 with the following: *ibid.* 685D.

Replace NOTE 53 with the following: *ibid.* 753A.

Replace NOTE 55 with the following: *ibid.* 703H.

NOTE 56, replace the reference with the following: 722H.

Replace NOTE 57 with the following: *ibid.* 680A–B.

Replace NOTE 58 with the following: *ibid.* 680B.

Replace NOTE 59 with the following: *ibid.* 706G–H.

Replace NOTE 60 with the following: *ibid.* 701A–G.

Replace NOTE 61 with the following: *ibid.* 706H–707B.

Add: In *Gribbon v. Lutton* [2002] P.N.L.R. 19, solicitors acted as stake- **10–115** holder in relation to a deposit paid to their clients on the proposed sale of land. No contract was entered into, and a dispute arose between vendor and purchaser. The solicitors issued interpleader proceedings, in which it was held that the deposit was non-refundable. When later sued by the clients, the solicitors sought to argue that the deposit was refundable. The Court of Appeal held that this was an abuse of process. While the solicitors could not plead or argue a case in the interpleader proceedings, by taking out such proceedings they sought a binding ruling and the benefits which flowed to them from such a ruling, and they were parties to such proceedings.

NOTE 65, replace the first reference with the following: [2002] 2 A.C. 1.

(iii) *Acting on counsel's advice*

Add new NOTE 65A: at the start of the paragraph: For a helpful explana- **10–116** tion of the law see Bartle, Philip: "The defence of reasonable reliance on counsel" (2002) 18 P.N. 111.

10–118   NOTE 70, replace the first reference with the following: [2002] Lloyd's Rep. P.N. 23 at 29.

10–119   NOTE 74, replace the last reference with the following: [2002] Lloyd's Rep. P.N. 23.

Add to NOTE 75: In *Darvall McCutcheon v. H.K. Frost Holdings Pty Ltd.* (2002) 4 V.R. 570, the underlying litigation concerned a breach of contract claim, considered by the judge, and a breach of confidence claim, which was not. The Victoria Court of Appeal held that the solicitors on the appeal were negligent in failing to take steps to have the breach of confidence claim remitted to the judge. The defence of reliance on counsel failed because counsel was not in fact asked to advise about the breach of confidence claim, but in any event the solicitors should have turned their mind to any advice which was given and examine it to ensure that it was sound, and should have sought and considered the reasons for such advice.

10–120   Add to NOTE 76: See also *Firstcity Insurance Group Ltd. v. Orchard* [2003] P.N.L.R. 9, summarised at Ch.11 paragraph 11–050A where neither counsel nor solicitors were held to be negligent in making an error of judgment. The solicitors additionally succeeded on the basis that they were entitled to rely on counsel, applying the law as set out in paragraph 10–118 above. In *Afzal v. Chubb Guarding Services Ltd. (Wasted Costs Order)* [2003] P.N.L.R. 33 H.H. Judge Bowsher Q.C. held that solicitors were entitled to rely on counsel's opinion on whether the client was likely to establish that he was suffering genuine psychiatric injuries rather than making his symptoms up. While the case involved personal injury, it was very difficult, and the solicitors were entitled to rely heavily on specialised counsel. In *Sherman v. Perkins* [2003] P.N.L.R. 39 the solicitors issued proceedings on behalf of the executrix as to what the defendant was entitled to in the testator's estate. The Court of Appeal held that they were not negligent and no wasted costs order was made against them as there was no easy solution to their client's dilemma to be found in the textbooks, and the solicitors relied on specialist Counsel.

10–121   NOTE 80, replace the last reference with the following: [2002] Lloyd's Rep. P.N. 23.

(iv) *Acting on client's instructions*

10–123   Add to NOTE 84: See also *Fraser v. Gaskell* [2004] P.N.L.R. 32, H.H. Judge Rich Q.C.

Add to NOTE 87: Thus in *Sutton v. Mishcon de Reya* (2004) 1 FLR 837, the claimant and another man agreed that they would enter a master-slave relationship, with the slave handing over his property and money to the claimant master. The claimant instructed the first defendant solicitors to draw up a deed to put into effect the agreement. They correctly advised that the agreement might not be enforceable. Hart J. struck out a claim (*inter alia*) that the deed should have been sanitised by not incorporating references to a "statement of trust." The instructions were to incorporate that reference, and as the "statement of trust" was part of the matrix of the cohabitation deed, it would have made no difference to the enforceability of the agreement to exclude reference to it.

(e) *Solicitor's liability for costs*

NOTE 96, replace the reference to *Harley v. McDonald* with the following: **10–126**
[2001] 2 A.C. 678.

Add to NOTE 5: As to attempts to limit the scope of the jurisdiction, see **10–127**
Ch.11, paragraph 11–027A. As to the last clause of subs. 51(7), this may be
relevant, for instance, where costs were reasonably incurred on behalf of a litigant but the action was later struck out as a result of the litigant's solicitors'
defaults—see *Snowden v. Ministry of Defence* [2002] Costs L.R. 249, CA.

Add: For the potential difficulties of contribution proceedings in relation **10–128**
to wasted costs between solicitors and barristers, see the *obiter* remarks of
the Court of Appeal in *Fletamentos Maritimos SA v. Effjohn International
SA* [2003] Lloyd's Rep. P.N. 26, and H. Evans *Lawyers' Liabilities* (2nd ed.,
2002), paragraph 7–06. If only some of the potentially defaulting lawyers
are respondents to a wasted costs application, the fact that others may be
to blame does not prevent the Court from making the respondents liable
for all the wasted costs—see *Gandesh v. Nandra* [2002] Lloyd's Rep. P.N.
558, Jacob J.

Add to NOTE 6: The same applies to any costs incurred by the solicitors in
successfully resisting a wasted costs application.

Add to NOTE 12: *Ridehalgh* was endorsed by the House of Lords *Medcalf* **10–129**
v. Mardell [2003] 1 A.C. 120, subject to *Hall v. Simons* [2002] 1 A.C. 615, and
subject to further amplification in relation to privilege, discussed at Ch.11,
paragraph 11–028A.

Add new paragraph **10–130A**

The limits of the jurisdiction. In *Byrne v. Sefton Health Authority* [2002] 1 **10–130A**
W.L.R. 775, it was alleged that solicitors had negligently failed to issue proceedings within the limitation period, where subsequent solicitors had done so,
and the action was then dismissed on limitation grounds. The Court of Appeal
held that there was no jurisdiction to make a wasted costs order under section
51(6) as the solicitors had not conducted litigation. A similar result was
reached on similar facts but slightly different grounds in *Radford & Co. v.
Charles* [2004] P.N.L.R. 25. The solicitors negligently failed to issue an appeal
against the local authority decision on the claimant's housing needs within
the permitted time. Neuberger J. held that the solicitors were not in breach of
a duty owed to the court, but only to their client, so no wasted costs order
could be made, and further the case was indistinguishable from *Byrne*.

Add to NOTE 16: However, it may be possible to infer that lawyers acting **10–131**
for legally aided claimants advised that there was a reasonable prospect of
success or were in breach of their duties to the Legal Aid Board or Legal Services Commission—see *e.g. B v. B (Wasted costs: abuse of process)* [2001] 1
F.L.R. 843, Wall J., and *Gandesha v. Nandra* [2002] Lloyd's Rep PN 558,
Jacob J. But see *Persaud v. Persaud* [2003] P.N.L.R. 26, noted at Chap. 11,
paragraph 11–029A.

Add to NOTE 17: The protection of the lawyer who is unable to give his full account due to privilege has been developed further in *Medcalf v. Mardell* [2003] 1 A.C. 120, discussed at Ch.11 paragraph 11–028A. In *Dempsey v. Johnstone (Wasted Costs Order)* [2004] P.N.L.R 25 the Court of Appeal were unwilling to infer from the fact that legal aid had been extended to trial that the lawyers were asserting that there were good prospects of success.

10–132   NOTE 21, replace the reference to *Re G (Minors) (Care Proceedings: Wasted Costs)* with the following: [2000] Fam 104.

NOTE 22, replace the reference to *Harley v. McDonald* with the following: [2001] 2 A.C. 678. Add before the last sentence: Turner J. refused to allow a wasted costs application to proceed even to the first stage in *B v. Pendelbury* [2003] P.N.L.R. 1, because there was substantial dispute on the facts, and the allegations which were based on impropriety and fraud were unsuitable to be determined in a summary jurisdiction. However, the fact that complex issues might arise in the wasted costs application did not preclude use of the procedure; account had to be taken of the prospects of success and how far time could be saved by appropriate case management—see *Wagstaff v. Colls (Wasted Costs Order)* [2003] P.N.L.R. 29, CA.

10–133   Add to NOTE 25: Subsection 51(6) of the Supreme Court Act states that wasted costs applications can be made "in the proceedings", but this is a reference to the Court of Appeal Civil Division, High Court and County Court, and does not mean an application has to be made during the currency of the proceedings, see *Wagstaff v. Colls (Wasted Costs Order)* [2003] P.N.L.R. 29, CA. In that case in any event proceedings were extant as they had merely been stayed, and the Court would have lifted the stay if necessary, which it was not.

Add to NOTE 29: These cautionary warnings were repeated by the Court of Appeal in *Persaud v. Persaud* [2003] P.N.L.R. 26.

10–134   Add: The court must ask whether the costs in question would have been incurred on the balance of probabilities but for the lawyers' conduct, not whether there was a substantial possibility that they would not have been incurred, see *Brown v. Bennett (No.2)* [2002] 1 W.L.R. 713, Neuberger J.

Add to NOTE 34: An example of a wasted costs application failing on causation is *Afzal v. Chubb Guarding Services Ltd. (Wasted Costs Order)* [2003] P.N.L.R. 33. It was alleged that solicitors failed to put contrary views contained in other experts' reports to the key psychiatric expert in good time. However, when they were put to the expert, she did not waiver in her views, and causation was not established. In assessing the quantum of wasted costs it is necessary to consider whether the costs claimed were reasonable, and in *R. (on the application of DPP) v. Cheshire Justices* [2002] P.N.L.R. 36, the Administrative Court reduced the wasted costs order made in relation to an adjournment of a speeding offence from £2,084.45 to £400.

10–135   Add to NOTE 37. As to the relationship between acting negligently or unreasonably in bringing a hopeless case and the question of abuse of process, see further *Dempsey v. Johnstone (Wasted Costs Order)* [2004] P.N.L.R 25 and Chap. 11. paragraph 11–029A.

Add to NOTE 38: In *Isaacs Partnership (a firm) v. Umm Al-Jawaby Oil Service Co. Ltd. (Wasted Costs)* [2004] P.N.L.R. 9 a wasted costs order was upheld by Gross J. against solicitors who had pursued hopeless litigation against the wrong defendant for breach of an employment contract, when they had both documentary evidence and a letter from the defendants pointing out that the claimant had been employed by another company. Wasted cost orders were made by Henrique J. in *Secretary of State for the Home Department v. Zinovjev & Ors (Wasted Costs Order)* [2004] P.N.L.R. 4 in four immigration appeals, all abandoned on the day of the appeal, where the appeal was made out of time without any explanation and on formulaic and unfocussed grounds.

Add to NOTE 42: In *Gandesh v. Nandra* [2002] Lloyd's Rep. P.N. 558, Jacob **10–136** J. held that it may not be unreasonable to bring proceedings on behalf of a legally aided claimant who was later found to be a liar, in a case which depended on her credibility; for a similar factual case where the same conclusion was drawn, see *Persaud v. Persaud* [2003] P.N.L.R. 26, C.A. In *Terence Daly v. Martin Bernard Hubner* [2002] Lloyd's Law Rep. P.N. 461, some of the allegations made by the successful defendant against the claimant's legal advisers were that the pleaded claim was manifestly unsustainable in law. Etherton J. held that if this were so the defendant could have applied to have the action struck out. Other allegations were dismissed for other reasons, and in refusing to permit the wasted application to continue to the second stage the judge also relied on the fact that the costs spent so far on the application were larger than the alleged wasted costs.

Add to NOTE 45: See also *Fletamentos Maritimos SA v. Effjohn International SA* [2003] Lloyd's Rep. P.N. 26 (a case decided in 1997). The Court of **10–137** Appeal made a wasted costs order against a solicitor for making a misconceived appeal against an arbitrator's decision refusing disclosure, which made allegations of actual or a risk of bias by the arbitrator, as it was an abuse of process.

Add to NOTE 52: *cf. Wasted Costs Order (No.5 of 1997), The Times,* **10–139** September 7, 1999, discussed at Ch.11, paragraph 11–031.

Add to NOTE 53. In *Sherman v. Perkins* [2003] P.N.L.R. 39 the solicitors issued proceedings on behalf of the executrix as to what the defendant was entitled to in the testator's estate. This was not the correct procedure, but it was caused by the defendant unreasonably threatening proceedings but not commencing them, there was no easy solution found in the textbooks, and the solicitors relied on Counsel. While the solicitors did not pass on the Master's views about the procedural difficulties, this was not improper, unreasonable or negligent within the meaning of section 51(7) of the Supreme Court Act 1981. The Court of Appeal held that no wasted costs order should be made.

(g) *Practice and Procedure*

(i) *Expert evidence*

Add to NOTE 72: Subsequently, at trial, the expert's evidence was ruled **10–142** inadmissible because of the close relationship between him and the defendant, see *Liverpool Roman Catholic Archdiocese Trustees Incorporated v. Goldberg (No.3)* [2001] Lloyd's Rep. P.N. 823, Evans Lombe J.

2. LIABILITY FOR BREACH OF DUTY

(a) *General*

10–146   Add to NOTE 87: the relevant principles of vicarious liability are now to be found in *Lister v. Hesley Hall Limited* [2001] 2 W.L.R. 1311; for an application to solicitors see *Balfron Trustees Limited v. Karsten Peterson* [2002] Lloyd's Rep. P.N. 1, Laddie J. See generally Evans, H.: "Attribution and professional negligence" (2003) 19 P.N. 470.

10–147   Replace third and fourth sentences with the following: That case has been overruled by the recent decision of the House of Lords in *Dubai Aluminium Co. Ltd. v Salaam* [2002] 2 A.C. 366, and all subsequent cases must be reconsidered in the light of this case. Their lordships held that "wrongful acts" in section 10 included equitable wrongs such as dishonest assistance in a breach of trust, as well as tortious liability. They also held that such acts would be done in the ordinary course of the business of the firm if it could fairly and properly be so regarded, which was a question of law. Thus the drafting of an agreement by a partner to assist in a fraudulent scheme was so closely connected with acts which he was authorised to do that he could be regarded as having acted in the ordinary course of the firm's business, and his innocent partners were liable for his assumed dishonest assistance. The case was applied by the Court of Appeal in *J.J. Coughlan Ltd. v. Ruparella* [2004] P.N.L.R. 4. where it was held that the motive or purpose of the solicitor was irrelevant, but one should not shut one's eyes to the true nature of the solicitor's acts when determining whether they fell within the ordinary business of a solicitor. It was necessary to look at the substance and detail of the transaction. In that case, the rogue solicitor attended meetings and acted as stakeholder, but the transactions promised absurd rates of return, and it was not part of a solicitor's business to be involved in such a scheme.

Add to NOTE 94: There would have to be special circumstances to find that liabilities of the old firm were novated to the new firm, see *Re Burton Marsden Douglas (a firm)* [2004] 3 All E.R. 222, Lloyd J.

10–148   Add to NOTE 97: *Quaere* how this case should be reconciled with principles of agency and *Gregory v. Shepherds* [2000] P.N.L.R. 769, CA.; see further Evans, H.: "Attribution and professional negligence" (2003) 19 P.N. 470 at 471–477.

(c) *Failing to give advice*

10–156   Add to NOTE 26. For another example see *Campbell v. Imray* [2004] P.N.L.R. 1, where the solicitors correctly advised the client that her action for damages for personal injury was statute-barred, but negligently failed to point out that there was a possibility of an application under the equivalent of section 33 of the Limitation Act 1980.

Add to NOTE 47: In *Pickersgill v. Riley* [2004] P.N.L.R. 31 the Privy Coun- **10–160** cil held that this sentence correctly states the position. In that case, the defendant solicitors owed no duty to an experienced businessman who was entering a personal guarantee. They advised him in general terms about the risk of taking a guarantee from a limited company, but owed no duty to advise on the financial prudence of the project.

Add to NOTE 49. The Privy Council's decision was applied by Harrison J. in *Bindon v. Bishop* [2003] N.Z.L.R. 136. The defendant solicitor's retainer in that case was to provide advice on the legal risks and liabilities of the proposed guarantor, and he had no obligation to proffer advice on the legal wisdom of the transaction.

Add to NOTE 58. In *John Mowlem Construction plc v. Neil F. Jones & Co.* **10–162** *(A Firm), The Times,* August 27, 2004, the Court of Appeal similarly found that the defendants had no duty to inquire into and advise the clients about insurance issues, but the Court emphasised that the professional obligations in this regard were fact specific.

Add: In *Ezekiel v. Lehrer* [2002] Lloyd's Rep. P.N. 260 the Court of Appeal **10–164** suggested that there was a duty upon a solicitor to advice his client that he had been negligent or ought to seek alternative advice to establish whether he had been negligent, but only where the solicitor knew or ought to have known that he was guilty of an earlier breach of duty.

Add: In *Queen Elizabeth's Grammar School Blackburn Ltd. v. Banks Wilson* **10–165** *(a Firm)* [2002] P.N.L.R. 14, a solicitor advised a school that the meaning of a restrictive covenant, which limited the construction of any building to no greater in height than the buildings already existing on the property, should be construed as including the chimney pots and not just the roofline. The solicitor knew that a dispute was potentially to emerge with a neighbour about the effect of the clause. The Court of Appeal held that he was negligent in failing to advise that there was a risk about what was the true construction of the clause, as the arguments against his construction were of sufficient significance. For a criticism of the decision, see Gee, Steven: "The Solicitor's duty to warn that a court might take a different view" (2003) 19 P.N. 363.

Add to NOTE 68: In *Credit Lyonnais SA v. Russell Jones & Walker (A Firm)* [2003] P.N.L.R. 2, Laddie J. relied on this dictum, and held that it was not in conflict with the principle set out in *Clarke Boyce v. Mouat* (see paragraph 10–160 above) or the dictum of Bingham M.R. in *Mortgage Express Ltd v. Bowerman & Partners* (see paragraph 10–208 below). In any event, the terms of the particular solicitor's retainer when instructed in relation to the exercise of a break option in the lease included reading the break clause, and he should have advised that the payment required under it was a condition precedent. The dictum was also applied in *Keith v. Davidson Chalmers* [2003] P.N.L.R. 10 (Outer House of the Court of Sessions), where a solicitor acting for the pursuer, who was setting up a property venture, failed to warn him that he may be in breach of his duties as director of an established property company.

Add to NOTE 69. For another example, see *Yazhou Travel Investment Co. Ltd.* [2004] 1 HKLRD 969, where the solicitors realised that the right to name a building would not run with the land, and devised a scheme to make the right enforceable, without advising that the validity of the scheme was open to question.

Add to NOTE 76: In *May v. Mijatovic* (2002) 26 WAR 95, Hasluck J. held that a solicitor who was instructed to apply for an injunction at short notice with insufficient time to read the documents presented to him should have warned the plaintiff of the risks associated with the application and the signing of an undertaking as to damages, and should have reviewed the documents in the time available and given a view as to the merits.

10–167 Add to NOTE 82. However, there are obviously limits as to how far an explanation should go. In *Masons (a firm) v. W D King Ltd.* (2004) 92 Con.L.R. 144 the claimant solicitors adapted a clause in a standard building project to provide further mechanisms to enable the project manager to ensure that the contractor constructed the building in time, as it was vitally important that there was no significant delay in completion. They explained how the new clause worked in some detail, but did not say whether breach of the clause would give rise to unliquidated damages, or only the agreed liquidated damages. H.H. Judge Humphrey Lloyd Q.C. held that they had no such duty, particularly as the extent of the actual losses were only known after the condition had been drafted, and it was quite unclear what the answer would be.

10–168 Add to NOTE 89: for another illustration see *Atkins v. Dunn & Baker (a firm)* [2004] W.T.L.R. 477, where the Court of Appeal held that a solicitor who had sent a draft will to the testator had no duty to chase the client up, although there may be such a duty in some circumstances.

10–174 Add to NOTE 12: Although there are many circumstances in which it is desirable to give advice in writing, it is not necessary to do so as a matter of law—see *Harwood v. Taylor Vinters (a Firm)*, *The Times*, April 1, 2003, Ch.D.

Add new paragraph **10–174A**:

10–174A **Funding of litigation**. The Client Care Code 1999, reproduced in chapter 13 of the *Guide,* suggests at paragraph 4(j) that the solicitor should discuss with the client how and when costs are to be met, and consider whether the client may be eligible for legal aid, covered by insurance, should take out after the event insurance ("ATE"), or whether the costs may be paid by another person such as an employer. In the context of a claim by a passenger injured in a vehicle driven by someone in the same household, the Court of Appeal gave guidance as to what should be done in *Sarwar v. Alam* [2002] 1 W.L.R. 125, relying on paragraph 4(j). A solicitor should normally advise the client to bring to the first interview any relevant motor insurance policy, household insurance policy, or before the event ("BTE") policy belonging to him or any partner living in the same household. It is desirable for solicitors to send a standard form letter requesting sight of such documents. In most cases worth less than £5,000, the solicitor should refer the client to any BTE insurer, rather than seek ATE insurance. The solicitor should enquire whether a third person such as an employer might pay the costs, and should generally ask a passenger to obtain a copy of the driver's insurance if reasonably practicable. The solicitor's enquiries should be proportionate to the amount at stake.

(d) *Misconduct of litigation*

Add to the end of the paragraph: In *Jemma Trust Co. Ltd. v. Kippax* **10–176** *Beaumont Lewis* [2004] W.T.L.R. 533, the solicitors acted for the executors of the husband. His landed estate was left to his nephew upon trust for the wife, who suffered from severe senile dementia, for life, and then his nephew. On the solicitors' advice, the executors decided to mitigate liability to inheritance tax on the wife's death by advancing a sum to her on her releasing her life interest, and an application was made to the Court of Protection to enable this, which was opposed. That application was improper, as the executors and solicitors owed fiduciary duties to all those beneficially interested in the landed estate, and the application made it impossible to satisfy those duties to the wife and the nephew. As a result, the solicitors were negligent.

Add to NOTE 26: Similarly, Gray J. held in *Brinn v. Russell Jones & Walker* [2003] P.N.L.R. 16 that the defendant solicitors were not negligent in failing to join the editor and journalist as defendants in libel proceedings, as there was nothing to put them on notice that the publisher may be in financial difficulties and the claim was not a large one.

Add: In *Beswarick v. Ripman* [2001] Lloyd's Rep. P.N. 698, the defendant **10–178** solicitors acted for the claimant in divorce proceedings against her husband, which settled. H.H. Judge Griffith Williams Q.C., sitting as a High Court judge, found the defendants negligent in two major respects. First, they had erred in concluding that her half interest in a boat should be taken into account in calculating her assets for the purposes of eligibility for legal aid. However, if legally aided she would have had to repay the cost of her legal aid at some time, and no loss flowed. Secondly, they were aware of the prospects of the claimant's children returning to live with her, and should have advised her to obtain a nominal periodical payment to ensure that she could apply to vary the order if this happened. Damages were awarded of £30,000 under this head. The defendant solicitors were not negligent with regard to an application for interim maintenance, which was not a sustainable claim, nor for settling the lump sum provision for £35,000 when an appropriate sum may have been as much as £40,000.

Add to NOTE 37: In *Noble v. Lourensse* (2003) 253 N.B.R. (2d) 293, the New **10–180** Brunswick Court of Appeal upheld a decision that solicitors were not negligent in failing to obtain expensive evidence to contest one part of a relatively small claim. Contrast *Henderson v. Hagblom* [2003] 7 W.W.R. 590, where the Saskachewan Court of Appeal held a lawyer negligent for failing to obtain expert evidence which was needed to prove that a fire was caused by the negligent construction of a chimney.

10–183   Add: For an example where a solicitor acted as advocate at a criminal trial, and various allegations of negligence before and at trial were examined and dismissed, see *Paquet v. Getty* (2002) 253 N.B.R. (2d) 256, New Brunswick CA.

10–184   Add to NOTE 58: For another illustration see *Darvall McCutcheon v. H.K. Frost Holdings Pty Ltd.* (2002) 4 V.R. 570, summarised at paragraph 10–119 above.

10–190   Add to NOTE 85: See also *Phippen v. Palmers* [2002] 2 F.L.R. 415, Fam. Div., where solicitors were negligent in recommending acceptance of the husband's offer in ancillary relief proceedings. They should not have advised a clean break settlement which left the wife, who had no earning capacity, with inadequate income.

(e) *Misconduct of non-contentious business*

(i) *Conveyancing*

10–193   Add to NOTE 1: In *Feerni Development Ltd. v. Daniel Wong & Partners* [2001] 2 H.K.L.R.D. 13, Hong Kong High Court, the solicitors who acted for the purchaser failed to inspect an earlier assignment of the property; if they had done so they should have noticed that the person who signed as the vendor-administrator and the purchaser was the same, and thus that the transaction was avoidable under a Hong Kong ordinance.

10–198   Add: In *Rickards v. Jones (No. 2)* [2003] P.N.L.R. 13, the defendant solicitors acted for the purchaser in the conveyance of a newly built house. The National House Building Council has a guarantee scheme for such properties. The defendants sent off the paperwork to the NHBC after completion, but they replied that the builder had ceased to be a member of the scheme. The house was defective and worthless. The Court of Appeal held that the defendants were negligent in failing to consider the NHBC paperwork properly. They should have confirmed with the NHBC that the builder was a member of the NHBC scheme and that cover would be granted once the paperwork was completed, and indeed as the house was already completed they should have obtained an NHBC certificate before completion of the purchase.

10–199   Add to NOTE 19: In *Boateng v. Hughmans (A Firm)* [2002] P.N.L.R. 40, the claimant entered a property transaction where he sold a house to builders who were to convert it into flats, eventually conveying one of the flats back to the claimant. The builders required a mortgage to carry out the work. The Court of Appeal held that the claimant's solicitors were negligent in failing to explain to him that he was exposed to the inherent risk of being left without any interest in the property or remedy if the builders became insolvent, as happened.

10–200   Add before the last sentence: However, in *Patel v. Daybells (a Firm)* [2002] P.N.L.R. 6, the Court of Appeal distinguished *Wong*, and held that it was not negligent to complete a sale on the basis of undertakings given by the vendor's solicitors, see further paragraph 10–088 above.

NOTE 28: Delete second sentence which refers to *Patel*.

Add: In *Gribbon v. Lutton* [2002] P.N.L.R. 19, solicitors acting for a   **10–201**
prospective vendor received a deposit as stakeholder. No contract was
entered, and the purchaser successfully argued that the deposit was not
refundable. The Court of Appeal held that the solicitors were negligent in
failing to secure an enforceable agreement under which the deposit was for-
feit if the vendor failed to purchase. The agreement actually obtained in
relation to the deposit was unenforceable as there was no consideration.

Add to NOTE 40: In *Finley v. Connell Associates (a Firm)* [2002] Lloyd's   **10–203**
Rep. P.N. 62, the claimant acquired a building licence from the local council
to build a hotel in 18 months. When he was running out of time and money,
the council demanded a large premium for a change to a residential development. Ousley J. held that the defendant solicitor negligently failed to advise
that on its true construction the building licence permitted such change, not
to be unreasonably withheld, with recourse to arbitration in the event of a
dispute.

Replace NOTE 51 with the following: [2001] 3 W.L.R. 1021.   **10–205**

Add to NOTE 53: Lord Scott concluded that in general the nature and effect
of the documents had to be explained, although the facts of a particular case
may add to or reduce the duty. Following this, it was held in *Colton v.
Graysons* [2003] Lloyd's Rep. P.N. 80, Ch.D., that there was nothing reckless
or obviously imprudent in the transaction in question which required the
solicitor to urge the clients to think hard against entering the transaction and
to hunt around for alternatives.

(ii) *The investment of money and claims by lenders*

Add to NOTE 11: A solicitor should verify the authority of the person who   **10–215**
signed a sale agreement on behalf of a vendor company—see *National
Commercial Bank Ltd. v. Albert Hwang, David Chung & Co.* [2002] 2 H.K.L.R.D.
409, Hong Kong High Court.

Add: In a slightly different context, in *Hilton v. Parker Booth & Eastwood*   **10–217**
(a Firm) [2003] P.N.L.R. 32, the solicitors acted for vendor and purchaser in
a contract to purchase flats. The Court of Appeal held that there was no duty
to disclose to a client confidential information about the criminal proceedings
and conviction of the purchaser, as the duty to disclose to the vendor did not
cover matters which they were obliged to treat as confidential.

(iii) *Wills*

NOTE 27: *Earl v. Wilhelm* is also reported at [2001] W.T.L.R. 1275.   **10–218**

Add to NOTE 30: *cf. Re Praught Estate* (2002) 208 Nfld. & P.E.I.R. 64,   **10–219**
where the Prince Edward Island Supreme Court held that a solicitor had to
satisfy himself as to the testator's capacity, knowledge and approval, particularly if elderly or apparently suffering from delusions or lack of capacity. In
Hall v. Estate of Bruce Bennett [2003] W.T.L.R. 827, the Ontario Court of

Appeal held that a solicitor has a duty to inquire into the client's testamentary capacity and be satisfied that it exists, particular care being required in suspicious circumstances such as the client being ill and elderly. The relevant question on liability in that case was not whether the client had capacity, but whether a reasonable and prudent solicitor could have concluded that he did not. Similarly, the Manitoba Court of Appeal held in *Slobodianik v. Podlasiewicz* (2003) 173 Man.R.(2d) 287 that if there were suspicious circumstances as to testamentary capacity, the solicitor had to satisfy himself that capacity did exist, and if there were any possible doubt a note of the observations and conclusions should be made.

10–221   Note 39: *Earl v. Wilhelm* is also reported at [2001] W.T.L.R. 1275.

10–222   Add to Note 47: In *Humblestone v. Martin Tolhurst Partnership (A Firm)* [2004] P.N.L.R. 26, Mann J. also held that there was a duty to check the attestation of a will where the solicitor did not supervise the execution.

10–223   Add to text: In *Atkins v. Dunn & Baker (a firm)* [2004] WTLR 477 the Court of Appeal held that a solicitor who had sent a draft will to the testator had no duty to chase that client for a response, although there may be such a duty in some circumstances.

Replace Note 51 with the following: [2002] Lloyd's Rep. P.N. 18; Pumfrey J.

3. Damages

(a) *Breach of fiduciary duty and breach of trust*

10–229   Add to Note 67: For a helpful discussion on whether remoteness criteria are required in equity, see Elliott, S. B. "Remoteness Criteria in Equity" (2002) 65 M.L.R. 588.

10–230   Add before last sentence: In *Youygang Pty Ltd. v. Minter Ellison Morris Fletcher* [2003] W.T.L.R. 751, the High Court of Australia reached the same conclusion. In that case solicitors had instructions to release $500,000 to a third party to purchase a bearer deposit certificate. They released the monies in breach of trust in a number of respects, and as a result the monies were lost. Causation needed to be proved, but it was proved. If a trustee wished to assert that there was no loss because the beneficiary would have authorised the breach, there was an evidentiary onus on the trustee to prove that.

(b) *Remoteness*

(i) *Causation*

10–234   Add to Note 83: In *Boateng v. Hughmans (A Firm)* [2002] P.N.L.R. 40, the Court of Appeal emphasised that in all cases where failure to advise was alleged against a solicitor, the claimant had to plead and prove what he would have done if he had been properly advised. The claimant in that case failed to prove that he would have acted differently.

Add to NOTE 84: For another case where the claimant failed to prove causation, see *Westbury v. Sampson* [2002] 1 F.L.R. 166. The defendant solicitors acted for the claimant husband in ancillary relief proceedings, and failed to inform him that any lump sum settlement could be later varied by the court pursuant to section 31 of the Matrimonial Causes Act 1973, as in fact happened. The Court of Appeal held that the claimant could not establish causation as there was no way to protect him from the effect of section 31.

Replace NOTE 99 with the following: [1994] 1 W.L.R. 1360, C.A., on which **10–236** see Ch.15, paragraph 15–123, and see *Bernasconi v. Nicholas Bennett* [2000] Lloyd's Rep. P.N. 285, discussed in Ch.11, paragraph 11–053. See also *MacMahon v. James Doran & Co.* [2002] P.N.L.R. 33 where the Northern Ireland Court of Appeal, relying on *Galoo,* held that the defendant solicitors were not liable for the plaintiff running up a sizeable overdraft, as the incurring of a capital obligation to repay was not a loss as it was balanced by the receipt of the sum advanced.

Add new paragraph **10–239A**

Intervening act of the defendant. As a matter of public policy, defendant **10–239A** solicitors cannot rely on their own intervening negligence to break the chain of causation, as the Court of Appeal held in *Normans Bay Ltd. v. Coudert Brothers (a Firm) The Times*, March 24, 2004. The point will seldom arise as the claimant would normally amend to plead the alleged negligence. In that case, the claimant lost its investment in a Russian firm when a Russian court declared invalid its tender offering a five year investment period, as the government had decreed a three year maximum. The defendants could not rely on the allegation that no loss had been caused because they had failed to seek anti-monopoly permission.

(ii) *Foreseeability*

Add: In *McLoughlin v. Jones* [2002] Q.B. 1231, the Court of Appeal held **10–240** that the question of the foreseeability of psychiatric injury, caused by the defendant solicitors' allegedly negligent handling of his criminal trial which resulted in his imprisonment, should be determined with the assistance of expert medical evidence.

Add to NOTE 9: In *Cadoks Pty Ltd. v. Wallace Westley & Vigar Pty Ltd.* (2000) 2 V.R. 569, Victoria Sup. Ct., the loss was foreseeable in tort, but not contract. The defendant solicitors negligently failed to ensure their clients had finance in place for the purchase of a farm, causing a delay in purchase of 15 months. The solicitors knew that the plaintiff intended to resell, but the loss of the opportunity to sell at a favourable time was too remote in contract although not in tort.

(iii) *The scope of the duty*

Add: *Cf. Michael Gerson Investments Ltd v. Haines Watts (a Firm)* [2002] **10–245** P.N.L.R. 34, where Rimer J. did not strike out an action where it was alleged that the defendant solicitors, by releasing documents in a tax saving scheme, impliedly advised that good title was available to the containers which underlay the scheme. The solicitors gave no tax advice but were only concerned with the question of good title. It was arguable that they gave advice rather than information, and were responsible for the wasted expenditure of the scheme which failed.

10–248   Add: In *Petersen v. Personal Representatives of Rivlin* [2002] Lloyd's Rep. P.N. 386, the claimant purchased property which was subject to litigation with a neighbour, and in respect of which he gave an indemnity for 90 per cent of any liability and of the costs of the proceedings from the date of the contract. The defendant solicitor negligently failed to explain the indemnity provision properly, and the claimant would have withdrawn from the transaction if it had been explained. The failure to advise was a failure to provide information, and the claimant's claim for legal fees in the proceedings with the neighbour were not within the scope of the duty, as he did understand and accept that the indemnity applied to costs liabilities incurred by the vendors after the exchange of contracts. In *McLoughlin v. Jones* [2002] Q.B. 1312, the claimant alleged that as a result of the defendant solicitors' negligent handling of his criminal trial he was imprisoned, which caused his psychiatric illness. The Court of Appeal held that it was arguable that the purpose of the defendants' engagement was to minimise the risks of wrongful conviction and of suffering psychiatric illness. They applied the tests of the scope of duty or purpose, and also the assumption of responsibility and the tripartite test of foreseeability, proximity and justice and reasonableness.

Replace NOTE 32 with the following: [2000] P.N.L.R. 110.

(c) Measure of damages

10–249   Add to NOTE 34: In *Welburn v. Dibb Lupton Broomhead (A Firm)* [2003] P.N.L.R. 28, the claimant alleged that his solicitors had lost him the fruits of an arbitration by delay. The Court of Appeal held that he could claim no damages where the beneficial interest of the claim had been vested in the claimant's supervisor under an individual voluntary arrangement, although he retained the legal interest.

(i) Date of assessment

10–250   Add: In *Aylwen v. Taylor Joynson Garrett* [2002] P.N.L.R. 1, the claimant purchased a property subject to a £1m mortgage from her estranged husband for £1.8m. She alleged that the defendant solicitors had negligently failed to complete the purchase or inform her of possession proceedings by the mortgagee, which sold the property for £1.2m in June 1993. The Court of Appeal held that damages should be assessed at the date of breach, and thus the action was struck out as there was no evidence that the mortgagee sold the property at an undervalue. The claimant was not entitled to claim for the loss of an opportunity to redevelop or enfranchise the property, which would entail valuing the case at a date of her choosing, and there was nothing to suggest that this property could not be replaced. *Cf. Cadoks Pty Ltd. v. Wallace Westley & Vigar Pty Ltd.* (2000) 2 V.R. 569, summarised at paragraph 10–240, NOTE 9.

Add to Note 43: See also *Griffiths v. Last Cawthra Feather (a Firm)* [2002] P.N.L.R. 27, TCC, following *Wapshot*.

Add to Note 44: For a case similar to *McElroy* where damages were **10–251** assessed at the date of an aborted sale in 1996 after a purchase by the plaintiff in 1994, see *Feerni Development Ltd. v. Daniel Wong & Partners* [2001] 2 H.K.L.R.D. 13, Hong Kong High Court.

(iii) *Evaluation of a chance*

Add to Note 57: Reid, Graham: "The hypothetical outcome in profes- **10–256** sional negligence claims: Part II" (2001) 17 P.N. 262, and Stapleton, Jane: "Cause-in-fact and the scope of liability for consequences" (2003) 119 L.Q.R. 388 at 402–411.

Add: In *Channon v. Lindley Johnstone* [2002] P.N.L.R. 41, the claimant **10–259** alleged that the defendant solicitors had failed to prepare and present his case in an application for ancillary relief. The Court of Appeal held that it should consider the best order that the claimant was reasonably likely to have obtained if his case was properly presented. The Court held that on the basis of the revised figures which should have been presented to the District Judge, which showed that the claimant had a smaller income than had appeared originally, the split with the claimant's wife would have been 50:50, and not 60:40 in her favour as had actually been ordered. Damages were reduced by 20 per cent to reflect the fact that the claimant was a bad witness who would not have inspired sympathy in the court, and that the court might have continued to award a split of 60:40.

Add to Note 63: *Finley v. Connell Associates (a Firm)* [2002] Lloyd's Rep. P.N. 62 (if properly advised, development 60 per cent likely to commence by May 1990, profits reduced by £30,000 if development started later, damages reduced by £12,000).

Add to Note 69: In *Prosser v. Castle Sanderson Solicitors (A Firm)* [2003] Lloyd's Rep. P.N. 584, the defendant solicitors negligently failed to advise the claimant, during a hostile creditors' meeting in relation to his proposed indi- vidual voluntary arrangement, that he could seek and obtain an adjournment of the meeting. However, the Court of Appeal upheld the judge's conclusion that no loss was suffered, as there was no realistic chance of the decision of the creditors' meeting being any different if adjourned.

Add to Note 71: In *Brown v. Bennett (No.2)* [2002] 1 W.L.R. 713, **10–260** Neuberger J. held that the applicant had to prove that the lawyers' conduct had caused the waste of costs on the balance of probabilities.

(d) *Heads of damage*

(i) *Loss of opportunity to acquire or renew an interest in property*

Add to Note 88: A similar approach was adopted in *Aran Caterers Ltd. v.* **10–265** *Stephen Lake Gilbert & Paling* [2002] 1 E.G.L.R. 697, Judge Howarth sitting as a High Court Judge. The defendant solicitors negligently failed to make an application for a grant of a new tenancy under Part II of the Landlord and Tenant Act 1954. The judge determined that if an application had been made, a four-year term would have been granted as the landlord intended to redevelop the building. Damages were calculated on the basis of the likely profits from the business, adjusted to £95,000, with a year's purchase multiplier of 2.75, and with a deduction of £30,000 for the lease that the claimant had been forced to take from the landlord. Loss of disturbance compensation under the Act was added, discounted for accelerated receipt, and a total of £315,000 was awarded. Uncertainty of tenure forced the claimant to acquire a lease of alternative property, but no costs of relocation were awarded, in part because they would have been incurred in due course anyway.

(ii) *Difference in value of property*

10–275   **(5) Radical change in circumstances**. Add to Note 25: This was not considered by the Court of Appeal, which overturned the finding of liability—see *Patel v. Daybells (a Firm)* [2002] P.N.L.R. 6.

(iii) *Loss of opportunity to bring proceedings*

10–277   Add to NOTE 30. Lost opportunity claims encompass more than cases which are wholly lost as a result of proceedings not being issued in time or being struck out. This is illustrated by three recent cases. In *Moffat v. Burges Salmon (A Firm)* [2004] P.N.L.R. 13 the claimants did recover damages in the original action in relation to the operation of an unlawful milk quota scheme, but only for the six years before proceedings were commenced. They sued their solicitors for failing to issue proceedings earlier. The Court of Appeal held that they were entitled to rely on the findings of the original judge, including his determination that the losses which were more than six years old had been statute-barred, unless there was evidence that the judge had been capricious or irrational, because the issue was simply whether, if the claimants had brought proceedings earlier, they would in fact have recovered more. In *Somatra Ltd. v. Sinclair Roche & Temperley* [2003] 2 Lloyd's Rep. 855 (C.A.) the claimants lost confidence in their lawyers shortly before trial as a result of numerous breaches by them, and settled the claim for 66 per cent of its full worth. The claimants succeeded in proving that, but for the negligence, the case would have been settled for 75 per cent of its full worth, and they obtained damages accordingly. In *Browning v. Brachers (A Firm)* [2004] P.N.L.R. 28 the claimants were unable to rely on evidence in the original action which had been served out of time because of the negligence of the defendants solicitors. The claim was compromised for £5,000, but the claim valued by the judge at over £46,000.

10–278   Add to text: That case and others establish that the essence of the jurisprudence is not to fight out a trial within a trial; thus where an essential part of the original litigation was what the claimant would have done, he or she will not have to establish that fact in the actual trial on the balance of probabilities, see *Dixon v. Clement Jones Solicitors (a Firm), The Times,* August 2, 2004, C.A.

Add to NOTE 39: Applied in *Stealth Enterprises Ltd. v. Hoffman Dorchik* (2003) 11 Alta.L.R. (4th) 201, Alberta CA. However, in *Henderson v. Hagblom* [2003] 7 W.W.R. 590, the Saskachewan Court of Appeal rejected that approach in favour of the English one.

Add to NOTE 52: In *Hatswell v. Goldbergs* [2002] Lloyd's Rep. P.N. 359, the **10–282** Court of Appeal distinguished cases where there was a loss of a right of value, and those which were bound to fail. In that case, the claimant and his witnesses had no possibility of establishing the correctness of their recollection that he was suffering night sweats which were reported to his doctor at the material time, giving rise to a claim for clinical negligence, given the doctor's notes which had no such record. Sir Murray Stuart-Smith suggested that the court should consider a two-stage process: the court should be satisfied that the claimant had lost something of value; and if that was satisfied, the court should evaluate the lost claim in percentages.

Add to NOTE 58: A similar discount of 10 per cent for the small prospect **10–283** of the original defendant establishing contributory negligence in the claimant's personal injury action was made by Garland J. in *Hunter v. Earnshaw* [2001] P.N.L.R. 42.

Add to text: It is often the case that the claimant faces a potential liability **10–285** to pay the costs of the other party against whom the original action failed. In such cases, it is common for the courts to award an indemnity to the claimant, sometimes subject to a percentage deduction where appropriate, as in *Browning v. Brachers (A Firm)* [2004] P.N.L.R. 28, Jack J.

Add to NOTE 13: See also *Parry v. Edwards Geldard (a Firm)* [2001] P.N.L.R. 44, where Jacob J. held that it was not foreseeable that, as a result of losing a right of pre-emption to purchase adjacent land, the claimant farmer would lose a milk quota which he would not have to pay for, as an earlier error by the valuer in failing to take account of the quota attached to the land was not foreseeable.

This approach was largely followed by Gray J. in *Brinn v. Russell Jones &* **10–286** *Walker* [2003] P.N.L.R. 16. The judge held that the defendant had to plead, and had an evidential burden if they wished to raise the issue, of insolvency. As the defendants had satisfied this, the burden of proof rested on the claimant.

Add to NOTE 75: This was followed by Garland J. in *Hunter v. Earnshaw* **10–287** [2001] P.N.L.R. 42, who assessed damages in that case at the date the original action was struck out, and not at a later date when the action would otherwise have come to trial.

Add to NOTE 82: This was doubted, *obiter*, by the Outer House in **10–288** *Campbell v. Imray* [2004] P.N.L.R. 1, where the potential problems with the reasoning were explained.

Add to NOTE 84: Neuberger J.'s reasoning was followed, albeit not in the **10–289** context of lost litigation, in *Griffiths v. Last Cawthra Feather (a Firm)* [2002] P.N.L.R. 27, TCC. In *Browning v. Brachers (A Firm)* [2004] P.N.L.R. 28 Jack J. awarded interest at the ordinary commercial rate, broadly reflecting the cost of the claimants' borrowings.

Add: The Court of Appeal applied these principles in *Sharif v. Garrett &* **10–291** *Co. (a Firm)* [2002] 1 W.L.R. 3118. The claimants' warehouse was destroyed by fire causing a loss of £842,000, the insurance did not pay, and their claim against their broker was struck out as a fair trial was impossible. In the solicitors' negligence action, the defendants called the broker who said that the risk was uninsurable in this country, although it might be placed abroad. The judge awarded only the insurance premium on the basis that the claimants had called no evidence to support their claim. The Court of Appeal held that the starting point was that no fair trial had been possible, and the judge should therefore not attempt to try the issues himself, as he had done, although he may be assisted by evidence, including expert evidence, which would have been called in the first action. The judge should have attempted to make a realistic assessment of the claimants' prospects, and the Court of Appeal awarded £250,000 including interest to the notional trial.

Add to NOTE 87: for an illustration of the importance attached to the views of the lawyers instructed on the merits of the original action, see *Sharpe v. Addison* [2004] P.N.L.R. 23. There, two barristers had advised that the action had reasonable prospects of success, and the argument that the orginal action was of no value was dismissed in part because of the daily familiarity of barristers with valuing claims, and the fact that the allegation essentially meant that the two barristers had been negligent.

Add new NOTE 98A at end of paragraph: It may be thought that, consistent with the loss of chance approach, the cause of action accrues against a solicitor who delays prosecuting an action when there is a substantial chance that the action may be struck out. However, three possibilities have been suggested in the cases: when the claim is bound to be struck out; when it is more likely than not that the claim will be struck out; and when there is a real risk of the claim being struck out. *Kahn v. Falvey* [2002] P.N.L.R. 8 (C.A.) appears to favour the latter test, but *Hatton v. Chafes (A Firm)* [2003] P.N.L.R. 24 (C.A.) and *Luke v. Kingsley Smith & Co. (a firm)* [2004] P.N.L.R. 12 (Davies J.) appear to favour the first test

(v) *Losses on loans secured by mortgages*

10–295   Add to NOTE 1: and *Newcastle Building Society v. Paterson, Robertson & Graham* [2002] S.L.T. 177, OH.

(vi) *Loss of some other financial advantage*

10–299   Add to text. *Keep Point Development Ltd. v. Chan Chi Yim* [2003] 2 HKLRD 207 concerned a slightly different issue. The plaintiff vendors assigned their units to a purchaser in return (*inter alia*) for options to purchase new units in the building to be constructed on the site. The defendant solicitors negligently failed to register the option agreements in the Land Registry, the purchaser got into financial difficulties and sold the land to a third party, and the claimants were left without remedy save against their solicitors. But for the defendants' negligence, the sales to the vendor would not have taken place. The Hong Kong Court of Final Appeal awarded the plaintiffs: the capital value of their old units as would be assessed on the open market, taking account their development potential; the cost of removal to temporary accommodation and the rent for it; and the amount over and above the capital value of the old units required to acquire similar permanent premises when it became clear that the purchaser could not complete the construction of the new premises.

Add to note 14: see also in *Daniels v. Thomson* [2004] P.N.L.R. 33, summarised at paragraph 10–048, n. 43 above.

Add new paragraph **10–299A**:

Loss of company. Solicitors may negligently fail to advise shareholders of the risk of relying on the credit of the purchasers of their company if payment for the company is deferred, as in *Matlaszek v. Bloom Camillin (A Firm)* [2004] P.N.L.R. 17. Park J. valued the loss of a small company with a limited trading history by establishing one year's maintainable earnings, and then multiplying that sum by the appropriate price/earnings ratio, which was obtained from publicly quoted companies in the most comparable business sector heavily discounted for a small business with a limited track record. Credit was then given for the small payments which had been made for the company.   **10–299A**

NOTE 15, replace the first reference with the following: [2002] 2 A.C. 1.   **10–300**

(xi) *Physical injury, inconvenience and distress*

Add to text: Thus in *Hamilton-Jones v. David & Snape (A Firm)* [2004] 1 All E.R. 657 Neuberger J. awarded the claimant £20,000 damages for the distress occasioned by the loss of her children. She retained the defendant solicitors in a custody battle with her former husband, and they obtained orders prohibiting the removal of the children from the jurisdiction. However, they negligently failed to re-register the children with the passport agency, and the husband absconded with the children to Tunisia. A significant reason for the solicitors' retainer was to ensure that the claimant retained custody of her children for her own pleasure and peace of mind, and thus damages for mental distress were awarded.   **10–314**

Add to NOTE 52: For a discussion of this topic see Jones, Michael, and Morris, Anne: "The distressing effects of professional incompetence" [2004] 20 P.N. 118.

NOTE 61, replace the first reference with the following: [2002] 2 A.C. 1.

Add: In *Channon v. Lindley Johnstone* [2002] P.N.L.R. 41 the Court of Appeal held that damages for distress should not be awarded in a claim for ancillary relief.   **10–315**

Add to NOTE 68: Applied in *Fraser v. Gaskell* [2004] P.N.L.R. 32, where H.H. Judge Rich Q.C. awarded £750 general damages for making the client vulnerable to bankruptcy.

(e) *Mitigation of damage*

Add to NOTE 76: For a further example see *Williams v. Glyn Owen & Co.* [2004] P.N.L.R. 20. The vendor delayed the completion of a Welsh hill farm   **10–318** to the claimant, who as a result lost the profits he would have made if had been able to purchase breeding ewes in time. His solicitors, the defendants, negligently failed to serve a completion notice. The Court of Appeal held that the claimant had no duty to mitigate his loss and sue the vendor for damages, particularly as the solicitor had not recommended such a course of action.

10–320   Add to NOTE 83: In "Mistakes in wills: rectify and be damned." (2003) 62 C.L.J. 750 Kerridge, R. and Brierley, A.H.R. argue that *Walker v. Medlicott* [1999] 1 W.L.R. 727 is wrongly decided as: a rectifiable misunderstanding by the draftsman is almost inevitably negligent; the alternative remedy of a rectification action may be fraught with difficulty as it may be almost impossible to work out whether the mistake falls within the limited ambit of section 20(1) of the Administration of Justice Act 1982 and so allows for rectification; and the facts cannot easily be distinguished from *Horsfall v. Haywards* [1999] P.N.L.R. 583.

4. SHARED RESPONSIBILITY

(a) *Contributory negligence*

10–323   Add to NOTE 87: for a helpful discussion and classification of contributory negligence, see Murdoch, John, "Client negligence: A lost cause?" (2004) 20 P.N. 97.

10–324   Add: For another Australian example, see *Cadoks Pty Ltd v. Wallace Westley & Vigar Pty Ltd.* (2000) 2 V.R. 569, Victoria Sup. Ct., where the defendant solicitors negligently failed to take steps to ensure that finance was available for the purchase of a farm, but the plaintiff was 10 per cent contributorily negligent in delaying applying for finance and failing to tell the solicitors of the situation concerning finance.

NOTE 93: *Earl v. Wilhelm* is also reported at [2001] W.T.L.R. 1275.

10–327   Add to NOTE 8: For a commentary on the different views adopted on this issue in the Commonwealth, and the reasons for such positions, see Mulheron, Rachel: "Contributory negligence in equity: Should fiduciaries accept all the blame?" (2003) 19 P.N. 422.

(b) *Apportionment of liability*

10–328   Add to NOTE 12: In *Peake v. Litwiniuk* (2001) 200 D.L.R. (4th) 534, the Alberta Court of Appeal held that lawyers who failed to bring proceedings for personal injury on behalf of their client could not claim in contribution from the driver who injured the client, as the parties were not liable for the same damage.

10–329   Add to paragraph: It is likely that the damage caused by the delays of successive solicitors, or the delay of one solicitor followed by the negligent undersettlement by another, will count as the "same damage" within the meaning of the Civil Liability (Contribution) Act 1978, see and *Luke v. Kingsley Smith & Co. (a firm)* [2004] P.N.L.R. 12.

Replace last three lines by: In *Burke v. Lfot Pty Ltd.* (2002) 76 A.L.J.R. 749, **10–332** the plaintiff had purchased a small shopping complex with a financially weak tenant. The vendors, who had misdescribed the tenant as high quality, sought a contribution from the plaintiff's solicitors for failing to advise his client to investigate the financial standing of the tenants. A majority of the High Court of Australia held that there should be no contribution on the grounds that the solicitor had gained nothing from his conduct and the vendor was merely repaying a sum which had been wrongly obtained.

Add to NOTE 25: Outside the wasted costs jurisdiction, the apportionment of responsibility between solicitors and barristers is rarely litigated before the courts. For a rare example of such apportionment see *Moy v. Pettman Smith (A Firm)* [2002] P.N.L.R. 44. The Court of Appeal held that the solicitor, who failed to obtain a proper report on causation in a clinical negligence case, was 75 per cent to blame. The barrister failed to inform her client of her assessment of the chances of getting late evidence on causation accepted by the Court, as a result of which he turned down an offer of about half the value of the claim; she was found to be responsible for 25 per cent of the loss.

CHAPTER 11

BARRISTERS

1. GENERAL

(b) *Duties to the clients*

Add to NOTE 20: In *Geveran Trading Co Ltd. v. Skjevesland* [2003] 1 W.L.R. 912, the Court of Appeal held that in exceptional circumstances the court could prevent an advocate from acting even where he did not possess confidential information if satisfied that there was a real risk that his continued participation would require the order at trial to be set aside on appeal. **11–005**

(c) *Duties to third parties*

Add: In *O'Doherty v. Birrell* [2001] 3 V.R. 147, the Victoria Court of Appeal held that a barrister owed no duty of care to another barrister retained in the same case to prevent financial loss to him. **11–006**

Add to NOTE 22: In *Wakim v. HIH Casualty & General Insurance Ltd.* [2001] 182 A.L.R. 353, the Federal Court of Australia held that a barrister instructed on behalf of a trustee in bankruptcy to advise on the prospects of legal proceedings owed a duty of care to the principal creditor, because he should have been aware that the applicant was the principal and sole indemnifying creditor, and there was a coincidence of interests between the trustee and the applicant. A similar duty was owed by the barrister's instructing solicitor.

(d) *The standard of skill and care*

Replace NOTE 31 with the following: [2002] 1 A.C. 615. **11–008**

Replace NOTE 32 with the following: *ibid.* 726D–E.

Replace NOTE 33 with the following: *ibid.* 737G–H.

(e) *Immunity*

11–009   NOTE 35, replace the first reference with the following: [2002] 1 A.C. 615.

11–014   Replace NOTE 68 with the following: [2002] 1 A.C. 615.

11–016   Replace NOTE 70 with the following: [2002] 1 A.C. 615 at 681F (Lord Steyn), 684C (Lord Browne-Wilkinson), 688G–H (Lord Hoffmann), 710D–F (Lord Hope), 728D–E (Lord Hutton).

Replace NOTE 71 with the following: *ibid.* 682D.

Replace NOTE 72 with the following: *ibid.* 682D–E.

Replace the two references in NOTE 73 with the following: *ibid.* 710D–F, and 736F–G.

Replace NOTE 74 with the following: *ibid.* 724F–G.

NOTE 75, replace the two references with the following: *ibid.* 728H–729H, and 728E–H.

Replace NOTE 76 with the following: *ibid.* 745B–D.

11–017   Replace NOTE 77 with: *ibid.* at 681F (Lord Steyn), 691A–692C (Lord Hoffman).

Replace NOTE 78 with: *ibid.* 683B–F (Lord Steyn), 704C–705A (Lord Hoffman), 737A–B (Lord Hobhouse).

11–018   Replace NOTE 80 with the following: [2002] 1 A.C. 615 at 682H–683A (Lord Steyn), 704A–C (Lord Hoffman), 710B–C (Lord Hope), 736H–737A (Lord Hobhouse).

Replace NOTE 81 with the following: *ibid.* 710C.

11–019   Replace NOTE 83 with the following: See also Lord Hope at [2002] 1 A.C. 615 at 714D–F.

Replace NOTE 84 with the following: *ibid.* 678G–679A.

Replace NOTE 85 with the following: *ibid.* 696G–697A.

Replace NOTE 86 with the following: *ibid.* 739G–740C.

11–020   Replace NOTE 87 with the following: see also Lord Hope at *ibid.* 714G–715A.

Replace NOTE 88 with the following: *ibid.* 679A–C.

Replace NOTE 89 with the following: *ibid.* 697B–698F. *Cf.* Lord Hobhouse at 740H–741D.

Replace NOTE 90 with the following: *ibid.* at 679C–680A (Lord Steyn), **11–021** 684E–685C (Lord Brown-Wilkinson), 686C–G and 698G–703D (Lord Hoffman), 715B–F (Lord Hope).

Replace NOTE 91 with the following: *ibid.* 679C–D (Lord Steyn), 685A–B (Lord Browne-Wilkinson), 703D–F (Lord Hoffman), *cf.* Lord Hope in relation to criminal proceedings at 722G–723B.

Replace NOTE 93 with the following: [2002] 1 A.C. 615 at 698G–699G.

Replace NOTE 94 with the following: *ibid.* 686E–G. Lord Hobhouse **11–022** discusses this argument at 738H–739F.

Replace NOTE 95 with the following: *ibid.* 680C–F.

Replace NOTE 96 with the following: *ibid.* 690B–D. See also Lord Hutton at 728G. Lord Hobhouse rejected the analogy as the conflicting duties were only ethical, see *ibid.* at 739B.

NOTE 97, replace the three references with the following: *ibid.* 680H–681C, 695B–G and 721A–722E.

Replace NOTE 98 with the following: *ibid.* 689C–693E.

Replace the reference in NOTE 99 with the following: *ibid.* 739C–E.

NOTE 1, replace the two references with the following: *ibid.* 771A–D, **11–023** 722G–723F.

Replace NOTE 2 with the following: *ibid.* 730A–734C.

Replace NOTE 3 with the following: *ibid.* 735F–H.

Replace NOTE 4 with the following: *ibid.* 742G–743B and 750G–751F.

Replace NOTE 5 with the following: *ibid.* 745D–749G.

NOTE 6, replace the three references with the following: *ibid.* 679G–680A, 695H–696F, 753E–G (Lord Millett).

Add: It would appear that immunity survives in Scotland, see *Wright v.* **11–024** *Paton Farrell* [2003] P.N.L.R. 20, Outer House.

Add to NOTE 7: In *Lai v. Chamberlains* [2003] N.Z.L.R. 374, a two-judge High Court held that they were bound by the rules of precedent to follow *Rees v. Sinclair*, but they considered that retention of the immunity in at least civil law matters was no longer justified.

(f) *Abuse of process*

11–025   Replace NOTE 13 with the following: [2002] 1 A.C. 615.

(g) *Liability for costs*

11–027   Add to NOTE 16: In *Re Mintz (Wasted costs order)*, *The Times*, July 16, 1999, the Court of Appeal held that before deciding to make a wasted costs order a judge should consider the relevant guidance given in the textbooks on the exercise of that power, such as Archbold.

Add new paragraph **11–027A**:

11–027A   **Scope of jurisdiction**. In *Brown v. Bennett (No.2)* [2002] 1 W.L.R. 713, defendants applied for wasted costs orders against the claimant's solicitors and barristers. Neuberger J. held that on the true construction of section 51 of the Supreme Court Act 1981 a wasted costs order could be made in favour of one party against the legal representatives of another party to proceedings. Subsequently, in *Medcalf v. Mardell* [2003] 1 A.C. 120, the House of Lords rejected a submission that on the true construction of section 51 of the Supreme Court Act 1981 a wasted costs order could only be made in favour of the clients of the lawyers concerned. In *Brown v. Bennett (No.2)* [2002] 1 W.L.R. 713, the judge also held that the liability of a barrister was not limited to his conduct of the proceedings in court, but extended to his involvement in advising and drafting, which were included in the meaning of exercising a right to conduct litigation in section 51(13) of the Act. However, the judge dismissed at the show cause stage almost all of the application that the lawyers show cause why they should not pay the costs personally, which mostly related to allegedly improperly pleading dishonesty. However, in *Byrne v. Sefton Health Authority* [2002] 1 W.L.R. 775, it was alleged that solicitors had negligently failed to issue proceedings within the limitation period, where subsequent solicitors had done so and the action was then dismissed on limitation grounds. The Court of Appeal held that there was no jurisdiction to make a wasted costs order under section 51(6) as the solicitors had not conducted litigation.

11–028   Add to NOTE 22. In part because the judge who has conducted the trial will be aware of the conduct of the legal representatives, it will be very rare for the Court of Appeal to interfere with a judge's decision on a wasted costs order, particularly at the first stage, see *Persaud v. Persaud* [2003] P.N.L.R. 26 (C.A).

Add new paragraph **11–028A**:

11–028A   **Privilege**. In *Medcalf v. Mardell* [2003] 1 A.C. 120, leading and junior counsel signed a draft amended notice of appeal which made allegations of dishonesty against the claimant and his legal advisers. In relation to most of the allegations, no evidence was served supporting those allegations. The barristers submitted that there had been no waiver or privilege, that they were aware of their obligation imposed by the Bar's Code of Conduct not to draft any notice of appeal containing allegations of fraud without clear instructions to make them and reasonably credible material before them establishing a *prima facie* case of fraud, and that they would like to put material before the Court full details of what material was before them but could not do so because of privilege. The House of Lords held that the court should not make a wasted costs order where privilege is not waived and the lawyers wished to put privileged material before the court unless a number of conditions were met: full allowance must be made for the inability of the lawyers to tell the story, and the lawyers are entitled to the benefit of any doubt, both of which will rarely be possible; where a lawyer is precluded from given his account of the material before him, the court will be very slow to conclude that he had no sufficient material; and the court must be satisfied that it would be fair to make an order although the practitioner is precluded by privilege from advancing his full answer. As a result, the House of Lords reversed the wasted costs order made against the barristers by the Court of Appeal. In *Brown v. Bennett (No.3)* [2002] Lloyd's Rep. P.N. 242, Neuberger J. gave guidance as to what counsel could divulge as to what documents they had seen or known of if privilege was not waived.

Add new paragraph **11–029A**:

In *Persaud v. Persaud* [2003] P.N.L.R. 26 the Court of Appeal made it clear   **11–029A** that the legal representative had to break a duty to the court itself. Thus, the failure of a barrister to follow the Bar Council's legal aid guidelines was not itself enough. In that case, the barrister was not unreasonable in concluding that two brothers who had convictions for dishonesty would be believed when they alleged that their father had promised them various benefits including a house if they worked for his company, and that if believed other legal hurdles would be overcome. The Court of Appeal appeared to hold that where the allegation was that the legal representative had pursued a hopeless case, mere negligence was not enough. However, the Court of Appeal in *Re Madden (A Barrister)* [2004] P.N.L.R. 722 thought that this gloss was unjustified and was not intended. A similar view was taken by the Court of Appeal in *Dempsey v. Johnstone (Wasted Costs Order)* [2004] P.N.L.R 25, which considered that the observation in *Persaud* was wrong and inconsistent with *Medcalf v. Mardell* [2001] 1 A.C. 120, although the Court concluded that it was difficult to see how the question of negligence in such a context could be answered affirmatively unless the legal representative had acted unreasonably, which was akin to an abuse of process.

Replace NOTE 27 with the following: [2001] 2 A.C. 678. For a case where it was alleged that the proceedings were hopeless, but no wasted costs order was made see *Daly v. Martin Bernard Hubner* [2002] Lloyd's Rep. P.N. 461, summarised at Ch.10, paragraph 10–136.

Add: In *Wasted Costs Order (No.5 of 1997)*, *The Times*, September 7, 1999   **11–031** the Court of Appeal upheld wasted costs orders against two barristers who advised the issue of a witness summons for disclosure of social services files for the speculative purpose that useful material might come to light, when it was clearly established that a witness summons in such circumstances was not proper. In *Re Madden (A Barrister)* [2004] P.N.L.R. 722 the Court of Appeal upheld a wasted costs order against a barrister who called a witness despite indications that he would not be favourable to his client's case, which led to the jury being discharged.

Add to NOTE 37. But see now *Persaud v. Persaud* [2003] P.N.L.R. 26, noted at paragraph 11–029A above.

11–032   Delete entire paragraph.

11–034   Add to NOTE 40: In *R. v. Duffy (Michael) (Wasted Costs)* [2004] P.N.L.R. 36 the Court of Appeal held that no wasted costs order should be made against a barrister who turned up late to court as a result of attending a hearing at another court. Both matters were originally listed at the same court, and the court was notified of the potential clash, but the court relisted the cases at different courts at 4pm on the working day before the hearings. The problem was caused by the court, and it was uncertain that alternative counsel could be found at such short notice.

11–035   Replace NOTE 44 with the following: [2000] Fam 104.

2. LIABILITY FOR BREACH OF DUTY

11–037   Add: Normally a barrister has no obligation to have a command of unreported Court of Appeal decisions—see *Moy v. Pettman Smith (A Firm)* [2002] P.N.L.R. 44, CA.

Add to NOTE 49: see also *Yell Ltd. v. Garton, The Times,* February 26, 2004, C.A

11–040   NOTE 65, replace the reference with the following: [2002] 1 A.C. 615.

11–042   Add to NOTE 69: see also *Popat v. Barnes, The Times,* July 5, 2004. The claimant had been convicted of rape, and appealed unsuccessfully. Following a review by the Criminal Cases Review Commission, the Court of Appeal quashed the conviction in part on the basis that an alibi direction was not given by the judge, and the claimant was acquitted at a retrial. Buckley J. held that the claimant's barrister was not negligent in failing to raise the issue before the trial judge or on the original appeal. She reasonably believed that an alibi direction was not required and may not have been to the claimant's advantage, and it was reasonable not to take the point on appeal when there had been a deliberate decision not to take the point at trial.

11–045   Replace NOTE 78 with the following: [2001] Lloyd's Rep. P.N. 716.

11–047   Add: In *Moy v. Pettman Smith (A Firm)* [2002] P.N.L.R. 44, the Court of Appeal held that a barrister was not negligent in miscalculating the prospects of admitting crucial late evidence of causation in a clinical negligence case at the start of a trial. However, she advised the client to refuse an offer made at court without giving a proper assessment of doing better than the offer, and was found to be negligent. She was influenced by a misapprehension that she had a duty to her solicitors, and that the client would have a good claim in negligence against those solicitors, when she should have advised that such a claim might be messy and could not be guaranteed to be successful.

Add new paragraph **11–047A**:

Predicting changes in the law. In *Heydon v. NRMA Ltd* (2001) 51 N.S.W.L.R.   **11–047A**
1, leading counsel and solicitors advised in relation to proposals to demutualise or convert NRMA companies limited by guarantee to companies limited by guarantee and shares, converting rights of members to shares. They advised that special resolutions were sufficient, and a scheme of arrangement was not required. Such advice was consistent with a recent Court of Appeal case called *Gambotto v. WCP Ltd*, which was later reversed by the High Court of Australia. At first instance, the lawyers were held to be negligent in failing to advert to the grant of special leave by the High Court in *Gambotto*, failing to obtain a copy of transcript of the arguments on the application for leave, and failing to advise that if the appeal were upheld it might be on grounds which cast doubt on the validity of the proposed special resolutions. The New South Wales Court of Appeal unanimously allowed the appeal. There was nothing in the existing authorities which would have caused a competent lawyer to foresee or warn against the possibility of the High Court formulating a new principle, as in fact it did. A majority held that the suggested research was oppressive, and would effectively entail that a lawyer had a duty to identify all relevant applications for leave to appeal and examine copies of transcripts of the hearings, and pending changes in statute. Such detailed research would only be required in very exceptional cases.

NOTE 86, replace the last reference with the following: [2002] Lloyd's Rep.   **11–049**
P.N. 23.

Add to NOTE 87: A similar result was reached by the British Columbia   **11–050**
Court of Appeal in *Arbutus Bay Estates Ltd. v. Davis & Co* (2003) 8 B.C.L.R.
(4th) 73, where a majority dismissed a claim against lawyers for failing to argue certain constitutional arguments in a dispute about a roadway, because those arguments had no chance of success.

Add new paragraph **11–050A**:

McFarlane has been followed and applied in stronger circumstances in   **11–050A**
Firstcity Insurance Group Ltd. v. Orchard [2003] P.N.L.R. 9. The claimants were involved in litigation concerning their obligation to take certain premises subject to certain works being carried out and completed by December 24, 1995. The client advanced an argument that the agreement could be construed in such a way that the date of completion was after the deadline. An experienced commercial Q.C. considered this argument and rejected it. He did not plead it, and did not change his view after seeing further information from the other side which appeared to follow the client's initial argument, but which he considered had been made by mistake. The case was lost at first instance, but on appeal the Court of Appeal raised the question of how the date of completion should be calculated, and eventually allowed the appeal on the basis of the client's initial argument. Forbes J. held that counsel was

not negligent. The barrister reasonably took the view that the client's construction argument was not arguable, and he was not bound to plead or argue it for its settlement value. He had formed a considered view, and did not have to clutter up the case with other arguments. While a barrister must be prepared to review his advice, counsel could not be criticised in holding to his view when nothing of substance had occurred to cause him to change it.

11–051   Replace NOTE 88 with the following: [2002] 1 A.C. 615.

Replace NOTE 89 with the following: *ibid.* 681G–682C. Lord Steyn's speech was agreed with by Lord Bowne-Wilkinson at 685E, and Lord Millett at 752B. Lord Steyn's observations were applied in the Q.B.D. in *Prettys v. Carter* [2001] Lloyd's Rep. P.N. 832 at 836, where it was held that lack of robustness in cross-examination, especially in regard to credit, cannot normally hope to found an allegation of negligence.

Replace NOTE 15 with the following: [2002] 1 A.C. 615 at 726D–G.

Replace NOTE 16 with the following: *ibid.* 737G–H.

3. DAMAGES

11–055   Replace NOTE 1 with the following: [2002] 1 A.C. 615 at 684G. *Cf.* Lord Hoffman at 687E–F.

CHAPTER 12

MEDICAL PRACTITIONERS

1. GENERAL

Add to Note 9: The activities of these regulatory bodies are now overseen **12–004** by the Council for the Regulation of Health Care Professionals, and their decisions on disciplinary matters can be referred to the courts under section 29 of the National Health Service Reform and Health Care Professions Act 2002, if the Council considers the decision was unduly lenient, or should not have been made and that it would be desirable for the protection of members of the public for the Council to take action under this section. There have been a number of such references by the Council.

(a) *Duties to Patient*

(iii) *Common Law Duty of Care*

12–015 NOTE 36: Move to main text.

12–017 Add: An interesting extension of the scope of the doctor-patient relationship arises when the parents of children that have died give their consent to a post-mortem examination. There was sufficient proximity and the fair, just and reasonableness test for imposing a duty of care was found to have been satisfied in *A & B & Others v. Leeds Teaching Hospital NHS Trust & Others* [2004] EWHC 644 (QB). The duty of care extended to giving the parents an explanation of the purpose of the post-mortem examination and what it entailed, including alerting the parents to the possibility of organs being retained. There had been a breach of this duty, but on only one of these three cases was the risk of psychiatric injury to the parents sufficiently probable to have been forseen, resulting in a successful claim for damages for negligence. The legislative control of use of human tissue has been considered by Parliament in the Human Tissue Bill 2003, which is scheduled for a further Committee Stage of consideration in October 2004.

12–018 Add new NOTE 42A at the end of the second sentence: Lord Hoffman's example is at [1997] A.C. 191, at page 213D. And see paragraphs 9–113 and 9–114 for an analysis of this decision.

12–019 Replace NOTE 44 with the following: See NOTE 36 above.

12–023 Add: In *Farrell v. Avon Health Authority* [2001] Lloyd's Rep. Med. 458, an unemployed man with a history of drug and alcohol abuse was told on his arrival at hospital that his recently born and premature son had died an hour before. A dead baby was brought into the room and the claimant kissed it and cried over it. He was then told that a mistake had been made, and he was shown his baby son who was in fact still alive. It was held that he had suffered mild PTSD as a result of this, and that this was a foreseeable consequence of what had happened. He was awarded £10,000 in damages as a "primary victim". This is an example of a medical practitioner being held liable for the consequences of giving false information to someone who was not a patient. It is submitted that the reasoning was based on the fact that there was no other primary victim, the father was the only victim, and he was therefore a participant in the incident.

12–024 Add to NOTE 64: See also paragraph 12–274.

12–025 Add to NOTE 71: See paragraph 12–305 of the main text for the facts of this case.

Add: The cases of wrongful conception concerning the recoverability of the costs of bringing up an unwanted child have been decided on the basis that this aspect of the loss claimed is purely economic loss. See paragraph 12–290 of the mainwork for the case of *McFarlane v. Tayside Health Board* and the cases following referred to at paragraph 12–290 of this supplement. **12–027**

Add to NOTE 75: Applied by Buckley J. in *A&B v. Essex County Council* [2002] EWHC 2707, reported at [2003] PIQR P21, in finding that a duty was owed by the defendant authority to prospective adoptive parents for providing relevant information about the prospective adoptive child. The Court of Appeal has upheld this decision on appeal. See discussion of this case at paragraph 12–065 below.

(b) *Duties to Third Parties*

Add to NOTE 90: See paragraphs 12–20 to 12–21 below for discussion of *Kent v. Griffiths* [2001] Q.B. 36. **12–031**

Add new NOTE 96A at the end of the second sentence: For a summary of the categories of primary victims see Brooke L.J. in *Hunter v. British Coal* [1999] Q.B. 140. **12–035**

Add to Note 2: *Julia Ward v. Leeds Teaching Hospitals NHS Trust* [2004] EWHC 2106 (Q.B.) is an example of a case where the judge held that the mother's illness was caused by the death of her daughter (itself caused by a vascular complication to surgery for wisdom teeth removal) and not any shocking or horrifying events at the hospital or mortuary. The decision turned on the lack of supportive expert psychiatric evidence. **12–037**

Add to NOTE 5: See also *Taylorson v. Shieldness Produce Limited* [1994] PIQR P329. **12–039**

Add: In *Walters v. North Glamorgan NHS Trust* [2002] Lloyd's Rep. Med. 227; [2003] PIQR P2, the claimant was the mother of a 10-month-old boy whose acute hepatic failure the defendants had failed to diagnose and treat. She was in his room when he suffered a major and dramatic epileptic seizure, leading to a coma and catastrophic brain damage. Some 36 hours later the baby was on a life support machine and the claimant was advised that her son's brain was so severely damaged that he would have no quality of life if he survived, and the life support machine was turned off, and he died in her arms. She was not a primary victim, but it was held that the period of 36 hours following the fit was a horrifying event, and the claimant recovered £20,000 as damages for her pathological grief reaction. The decision was upheld on appeal to the Court of Appeal: [2002] EWCA Civ 1792 reported at [2003] PIQR P16; [2003] Lloyd's Rep. Med. 49: where a series of events amounts to an inexorable progression from an accident, and the appreciation of the event or series of events is sudden, and the experience can be accurately described as horrifying, damages for nervous shock may be recovered. Applied in *Atkinson v. Seghal* [2003] EWCA Civ 697 reported at [2003] Lloyd's Rep. Med. 285, the **12–040** claimant mother's visit to a mortuary two hours after a fatal road accident in which her daughter was killed was within the "immediate aftermath" of the accident. The claimant's extreme reaction to her daughter's death and her psychiatric condition was not solely due to being told of the accident, but also due to the mortuary visit when she saw and cradled her daughter's disfigured body. *Cf. Julia Ward v. Leeds Teaching Hospitals NHS Trust,* discussed at para. 12–037, above.

See also the case of *Farrell v. Avon Health Authority* [2001] Lloyd's Rep. Med. 458 (the facts of which are set out above at paragraph 12–023) for an example of a medical practitioner being held liable for the consequences of causing psychiatric injury to someone who was not a patient who was treated as a primary victim.

NOTE 8, replace reference to *Farrell v. Merton Sutton & Wandsworth Health Authority* with the following: (2001) 57 B.M.L.R. 158.

12–046   NOTE 19, replace reference to *Goodwill v. BPAS* with the following: [1996] 1 W.L.R. 1397.

12–048   NOTE 22, replace reference to *Walkin v. South Manchester Health Authority* with the following: [1995] 1 W.L.R. 1543.

12–052   Add new NOTE 33A: *Cf.* the case of *Osman v. United Kingdom* (23452/94) reported at [1999] 1. F.L.R. 193; (2000) 29 E.H.R.R. 245, where the police were held to have sufficient proximity to the victim school boy who had been identified as his prospective victim by his teacher, and who was subsequently attacked by him causing injury and killing the boy's father.

12–057   NOTE 47, replace reference to *Barrett v. Enfield LBC* with the following: [2001] A.C. 550. This analysis is now further subject to the House of Lords' decision in *Phelps v. Hillingdon LBC* [2001] 2 A.C. 619 with the result that the effect of *X v. Bedfordshire* is now limited to Lord Slynn's core proposition (in *Barratt*) that decisions by local authorities concerning whether or not to take a child into care were not reviewable by way of a claim in negligence. See also paragraph 12–065 addition to NOTE 68, below.

12–060   NOTE 55, replace reference to *Barrett v. Enfield LBC* with the following: [2001] A.C. 550.

12–061   NOTE 56, replace reference to *Barrett v. Enfield LBC* with the following: [2001] A.C. 550.

12–062   NOTE 57, replace reference to *Barrett v. Enfield LBC* with the following: [2001] A.C. 550.

12–065   NOTE 58, replace reference to *Phelps v. Hillingdon LBC* with the following: [2001] 2 A.C. 619.

NOTE 61, replace reference to *Phelps v. Hillingdon LBC* with the following: [2001] 2 A.C. 619.

Add to NOTE 68: See also the Court of Appeal's decision in the appeals from **12–065** three first instance decisions on preliminary issues in claims by parents and/or the child for damages for psychiatric harm arising from false allegations made against the parents by child welfare professionals, based on negligent diagnoses that the children were victims of abuse: *(1) JD v. East Berkshire Community Health; (2) MAK & RK v. Dewsbury Health Care NHS Trust & Kirklees Metropolitan Council; (3) RK & Another v. Oldham NHS Trust & Dr Blumenthal* [2004] QB 558: since there would always be a conflict of interest between the parent and child, where the parent was suspected of child abuse, a paediatrician could not owe a common law duty of care to the parents. Whether or not such a duty was owed to the child depended on whether it was "fair, just and reasonable" on the facts of the case to impose such a duty. The decision of the House of Lords in *X v. Bedfordshire* [1995] 2 A.C. 633, on this point was effectively superseded by *Barratt* and *Phelps*, and was contrary to the Human Rights Act 1998 in that it was no longer legitimate to rule that as a matter of law no common law duty of care was owed to a child in respect of the investigation of suspected child abuse and care proceedings. See also the decision of the Privy Council in *B & Others v. The Attorney General & Others* [2003] UKPC 61 reported at [2003] 4 All ER 833 and [2003] Lloyds Rep. Med. 527: no duty owed to the parent suspected of child abuse, applying *Attorney General v. Prince* (1998) 1 N.Z.L.R. 262: Court of Appeal declining to strike out a claim in negligence brought by the child against social workers for their failure to investigate a complaint that his adoptive parents were neglecting him. The Director General owed a common law duty of care concurrent to his statutory duty to promptly investigate such complaints. See also the decision of the Scottish Court of Sessions to the same effect in *Fairlie v. Perth & Kinross NHS Trust* [2004] Scots CS 174. In *A & B v. Essex County Council* [2003] EWCA Civ 1848 reported at [2004] 1 W.L.R. 1881, the Court of Appeal found the imposition of a duty of care on professionals involved in compiling reports for adoption agencies to not fulfil the "fair, just and reasonable" requirement, but on the same facts, did find this fulfilled in respect of the local authority's social workers who had failed to provide all relevant information about two young children to the prospective adoptive parents, A and B.

NOTE 73: incorrect case name: *"Powell v. Boldaz"* not: *"Powell v. Boladz".*

Add to NOTE 73: *Powell v. Boldaz* was distinguished in *A & B & Others v.* **12–066** *Leeds Teaching Hospital NHS Trust & Others* [2004] EWHC 644 (QB) reported at [2004] 1 W.L.R. 1881. See discussion of this case at paragraph 12–017 above.

NOTE 74, replace reference to *N. v. Agrawal* with the following: [1999] P.N.L.R. 939.

(c) *The standard of skill and care*

NOTE 7A: See *McGlinchey v. The United Kingdom* (50390/99) reported at **12–070** [2003] Lloyd's Rep. Med. 264 and (2003) 37 EHRR 41 for a case where the European Court of Human Rights found (in the absence of proceedings in negligence) there had been a violation of Article 3 and Article 13 of the

European Convention on Human Rights when a detained prisoner with a history of heroin addiction died in custody, having lost 10kg of weight in five days with symptoms of vomiting, diarrhoea and abdominal pain. The European Court noted that the prison authorities had not monitored the weight loss or the prisoner's condition and had failed to treat her condition by hospital admission or seeking expert advice to control the symptoms.

12–071   Add to NOTE 13: See also Gross. J.'s conclusion in *Reynolds v. North Tyneside Health Authority* [2002] Lloyd's Rep. Med. 459 that even if there had been a practice of not conducting a vaginal examination on admission (and there was no such practice at the material time, but the practice of conducting one was not uniform) it would not have been defensible.

12–072   This need to subject expert evidence to critical analysis was thrown into stark light by the Court of Appeal's decision to overturn Angela Cannings' conviction for the killing of her three children. The conviction was based on Professor Roy Meadow's expert evidence and his now discredited theory of Munchausen Syndrome by Proxy.

12–073   Add to NOTE 20: *C v. Cairns* [2003] Lloyd's Rep. Med. 90: GP not negligent for not referring 12 year old's allegation of sexual abuse by her stepfather to relevant authorities. At the time many responsible and caring GPs would have done the same.

12–074   Add new NOTE 20A at end of fifth sentence: In *C v. Cairns* [2003] Lloyd's Rep. Med. 90, the judge cited and relied on the description of the standard of care to be expected of the reasonable professional by Bingham L.J. (as he then was) in *Eckersley v. Binnie* 18 Con.L.R. 1, at p.80:

> "He should command the corpus of knowledge which forms part of the professional equipment of the ordinary member of his profession. He should not lag behind other ordinarily assiduous and intelligent members of his profession in knowledge of new advances, discoveries and developments in his field. He should have such awareness as an ordinarily competent practitioner should have of the deficiencies in his knowledge and the limitations on his skill. He should be alert to the hazards and risks inherent in any professional task he undertakes to the extent that any other ordinarily competent member of the profession would be alert. He must bring to any professional task he undertakes no less expertise, skill and care that other ordinarily competent members of his profession would bring but need bring no more."

12–075   Add: In *P. v. Leeds Teaching Hospitals NHS Trust* [2004] EWHC 1392, Holland J. found for the claimant on the question of breach where the defendant healthcare trust was engaged as a tertiary referral opinion following a finding on ultrasound scan of an abdominal abnormality (exomphalos – a condition where the baby has a defect in its abdominal wall which may contain abdominal contents) in the claimant's unborn baby. The judge held that the claimant came to the defendant for a scan with a focus (to establish the existence or not of a much more serious anomaly called cloacal exstrophy), not a standard anomaly scan, and that this demanded a high standard of skill and care, which was to be focussed on determining whether the latter defect was present. On applying this higher standard of care, the judge found that there had been a breach of duty.

NOTE 77, replace reference to House of Lords decision in *Barrett v. Enfield* **12–084**
LBC with the following: [2001] A.C. 550.

(d) *General and approved practice*

(i) *Acting in accordance with general and approved practice*

Add: The decision of the judge in *Glicksman* has been set aside by the **12–105**
Court of Appeal and a new trial ordered on all matters. See [2001] EWCA
Civ 1097, reported at [2002] 63 B.M.L.R. 109. See also paragraph 12–072
above.

(ii) *Departing from general and approved practice*

Add new NOTE 79A: See *Simms v. Simms* [2002] EWHC 2734, reported at **12–110**
[2003] Fam 83; [2003] 2 WLR 1465, for an instance where the lack of an
alternative treatment (for two CJD victims) led their parents to seek declarations that their children should receive an experimental and untested
treatment.

(e) *Expert Evidence*

Delete the last sentence and the reference to *Glicksman*. See paragraph **12–113**
12–105 above.

Add: See also paragraph 12–072 above.

Add to NOTE 98: The judge's decision was upheld on appeal by the Court **12–116**
of Appeal reported at [2000] Lloyd's Rep. Med. 41: The judge was entitled to
prefer the evidence of the claimants' experts as to what the slides showed.

(g) *Consent to treatment*

(iv) *Capacity to consent*

Add to NOTE 81: In *Ms B v. NHS Hospital Trust* [2002] EWHC 429 **12–135**
reported at [2002] 2 All E.R. 449, the President of the Family Division gave
guidance for the treatment of future cases concerning adult refusal of
treatment (at para.100).

Add to NOTE 92: See *The NHS Trust v. Ms T* [2004] EWHC 1279 (Fam) **12–139**
for an example of an "advance directive" by the patient that she no longer
wanted to receive blood transfusions being overridden. The patient was a
self-harmer, who believed that her own blood was evil. The court considered
she had lacked capacity when signing the advance directive, and continued to
lack capacity. The balance of competing factors came down in favour of
giving the patient treatment to save her life.

Add: In *R. (on the application of N) v. Doctor M & Others* [2003] 1 W.L.R. **12–141**
562, the Court of Appeal applied the standard of proof test from
Herczegfalvy v. Austria (A/242B), (1993) 15 EHRR 437, a decision of the

European Court of Human Rights, that it had to be "convincingly" shown that the proposed treatment (and each part of that treatment) was a medical necessity. The Court stated that its duty was to consider whether or not the proposed treatment was in a detained patient's best interests; that this should be determined by reference to this high standard of proof ("the medical necessity test"), and that the existence of a responsible body of opinion (the Bolam test) that the treatment was not in their best interests was not conclusive in favour of the patient. See *R. (on the application of PS) v. (1) Responsible Medical Officer; (2) Second Opinion Appointed Doctor* [2003] EWHC 2335, for a case confirming that forcible administration of treatment (antipsychotic drugs) to a patient detained under the Mental Health Act 1983 was not "inhuman or degrading treatment" so as to engage the patient's rights under Article 3 of the European Convention on Human Rights 1950, or that those rights were not engaged due to the evident medical and therapeutic necessity of the treatment.

Add to Note 12: The exception annunciated by Butler-Sloss L.J. in *Re MB* namely where the detained patient is "unable to use the information and weigh it in the balance as part of the process of arriving at the decision" of whether to consent to the proposed treatment or not, was applied in *An NHS Trust v. C* [2004] EWHC 1657 (Fam). The case concerned an elderly patient, C, who was mentally ill, and had been detained under section 3 of the Mental Health Act 1983. A renal carcinoma was suspected but C was refusing to consent to a CT ultrasound scan. The court found that C lacked the capacity to consent; that her mental illness led to an inability to weigh the information and arrive at a decision and that it was in C's best interests for the CT scan to go ahead.

12–142   Add to Note 16: Applied by the High Court of Hong Kong in *Hospital Authority v. C* [2003] Lloyd's Rep. Med. 130 where the mother suffered irreversible brain damage when 12 weeks pregnant. By 32 weeks' gestation her condition was deteriorating and the Hospital Authority wanted to deliver the foetus by Caesarean section and sought a declaration that the proposed surgery would be lawful. In opposition to the father's wishes the declaration was granted as being in the mother's best interests.

(i) *Hospital and health authorities*

Add new paragraph **12–147A:**

12–147A   **Guidance on when to make an application to court** In *An NHS Trust v. D* [2003] EWHC 2793, reported at [2004] Lloyd's Rep. Med. 107, a case concerning an NHS Trust's application to court for a declaration prior to termination of a pregnancy of a mentally incapacitated person suffering severe schizophrenia, the Family Division of the High Court, Coleridge J., gave the following guidance:

(i)   An application to the court was not necessary where issue of capacity and best interests were beyond doubt.

(ii)   An application should be made promptly where there was any doubt as to either issue.

(iii) Applications should ordinarily be made where:

    a. There was a realistic prospect of the patient regaining capacity during or shortly after pregnancy.

    b. There was disagreement between medical professionals as to the patient's best interests, or the patient, or her family, or the father expressed views inconsistent with termination.

    c. The procedures under section 1 of the Abortion Act 1967 had not been followed.

    d. There was some other exceptional circumstance, such as the pregnancy being the patient's last chance to bear a child.

(iv) A termination in accordance with the Abortion Act 1967 in the best interests of an incapacitated patient was a legitimate and proportionate interference with rights protected by Schedule 1, Part I, Articles 8(1) and 8(2).

In *Glass v. United Kingdom* (61827/00), reported at [2004] 39 E.H.R.R. 15, the European Court of Human Rights upheld the patient's complaint that the treating hospital's administration of diamorphine had breached his rights under Article 8 of the European Convention on Human Rights, to physical integrity. The patient was a severely physically and mentally disabled child, who suffered from severe respiratory problems which had resulted in several hospitalisations. On this admission the hospital had insisted that the child was dying and that diamorphine should be administered to relieve his obvious distress. His mother, who had on previous occasions consented to her son being treated with morphine, on this occasion disagreed, and objected to the treatment believing it would harm her son's chances of recovery. The Court held that although the hospital had acted in accordance with domestic law and had legitimately pursued the aim of protecting the patient's best interests, it had failed to explain why the High Court's approval of the treatment had not been sought. It had not been shown that such an emergency application for approval had not been feasible, and the onus was on the hospital to take the initiative to seek the court's intervention.

Following and applying this decision, Munby J. in *R. (on the application of Burke) v. General Medical Council* [2004] EWHC 1879 (Admin) held that in cases concerning the proposed withdrawal of treatment seeking prior authorisation from the court, which had previously been good practice was now a requirement in law where:

(i) There is any doubt or disagreement as to the capacity or competence of the patient.

(ii) There is a lack of unanimity amongst the medical professionals as to either the patient's condition, prognosis, best interests, the likely outcome of withdrawal or otherwise as to whether or not the treatment should be withdrawn.

(iii) There is evidence that the patient, when competent, would have wanted the treatment to continue in the relevant circumstances.

(iv) There is evidence that the patient (even if a child or incompetent) disputes or resists the proposed withdrawal of treatment.

(v) There are persons who, having a reasonable claim to have their views or evidence taken into account, such as parents, partners, close friends or long term carers, assert that withdrawal of treatment is contrary to the patient's wishes or not in the patient's best interests.

In this case the claimant, who was a competent patient, had sought a declaration that the GMC's guidance to doctors entitled: *"Withholding and Withdrawing Life-prolonging Treatments: Good Practice in Decision-making"* was unlawful. The claimant was suffering from a progressive, degenerative neuropathy that would eventually result in an inability to swallow, and a need for feeding by tube. As he deteriorated he would retain full cognitive faculties until very shortly before death, and would therefore be fully aware of the pain and distress of dehydration and malnutrition if such feeding was withdrawn. He also sought declarations that such withdrawal of treatment would violate his rights under the European Convention on Human Rights under Articles 2, 3, 8, and 14. The court found for the claimant granting him the declarations sought and indicating that withdrawal of treatment may breach rights under Articles 3 and 8. Once a patient is admitted the hospital owed a duty of care to provide and continue to provide treatment that was in the best interests of the patient, where the touchstone of "best interests" in the context of life-prolonging treatment was whether the treatment, whilst of some benefit to the patient, was from the patient's point of view, intolerable. The arbiter of the patient's "best interests" was the competent patient, not the doctor. Such a competent patient's wishes were determinative (and this would include advance directives by formerly competent patients). If the doctor disagreed with the patient's wishes, then nevertheless the patient's wishes must prevail, and the doctor cannot simply decline to give that treatment unless it would offend his conscience. Even in those circumstances the doctor would be under a duty to find someone to take over responsibility for the patient. Thus the doctor's duty to the patient is to choose a form of treatment that meets the requirements of the *Bolam* test, in that it is acceptable to a responsible body of medical opinion, but also meets this "best interests" requirement. The GMC's guidance stated that it was the doctor's responsibility to decide on the withdrawal of treatment taking account of the patient's views. This was criticised as it failed to acknowledge the heavy presumption in favour of life-prolonging treatment, and the duty of a doctor who disagreed with the patient's wishes to continue treatment to find another doctor who would continue treatment. It also failed to detail the legal requirement for prior judicial approval before withdrawing treatment.

Add new paragraph **12–147B**:

12–147B   **Mental Capacity Bill 2004** This bill was introduced to the House of Commons on June 17, 2004. Some matters that it outlines are the definition of incapacity; the procedures to be followed in assessing capacity using a "functional" test; the ability of authorities, trusts and appointed friends and relatives to consent to medical treatment or care on behalf of those without capacity; the operation of lasting powers of attorney; the proposed new powers and role of the Court of Protection to make medical treatment decisions on behalf of incapacitated patients; advance directives and "living wills" whereby a person can pre-emptively refuse or require future medical treatment while they still have mental capacity. It is hoped that this future legislation will simplify and clarify the law protecting those lacking mental capacity, and thereby assist those who care for them.

Add new NOTE 66A at end of first sentence: This was confirmed by the **12–154** Employment Appeal Tribunal in *North Essex Health Authority v. David John*, No. EAT/0232/03/ILB.

Add to NOTE 77: In *A v. The Ministry of Defence and Guy's and St Thomas'* **12–157** *Hospital NHS Trust* [2003] Lloyd's Rep. Med. 339, the MoD had contracted the Trust to procure secondary elective healthcare for servicemen and their dependants in Germany, and admitted it owed a duty to exercise reasonable care and skill in selecting the secondary provider. The claimant (a child of a serviceman serving with the MoD in Germany) sought a declaration that the defendants owed a non-delegable duty to ensure that all reasonable skill and care was taken by the staff caring for servicemen at a designated hospital in Germany. Bell J. applying the general rule of no vicarious liability for acts or omissions of an independent contractor dismissed the claim. The MoD had discharged its obligations to the claimant by its contract with the Trust, the Trust had discharged its obligations by its exercise of reasonable care and skill in procuring the German services provider. The first instance trial judge was upheld on appeal. The Court of Appeal stated that the MoD did not owe the claimant a non-delegable duty of care; that the claimant was trying to extend the law of negligence and that the Court of Appeal found no policy grounds for so expanding the scope of tortious liability, [2004] EWCA Civ 641.

NOTE 89, replace reference to *W v. Essex County Council* with the following: **12–160** [2001] 2 A.C. 592.

Add to NOTE 92: See also the case of *Hardaker v. Newcastle Health Author-* *ity* [2001] Lloyd's Rep. Med. 521, where the court considered that it could not adjudicate on the defendant's system for dealing with emergency cases of decompression illness where allocation of its resources was in issue and *Ball* *v. Wirral Health Authority and Liverpool Health Authority* [2003] Lloyd's Rep. Med. 165, where the court (dismissing the claimant's claim) noted that under-funding of a hospital or a particular field of medicine was not necessarily a basis for a successful claim in clinical negligence even where the patient suffered the effects of underfunding.

Add: In *Watts v. Bedford Primary Care Trust* [2003] EWHC 2401, Munby J. **12–161** held that a claim by an NHS patient for reimbursement for the costs of a hip replacement operation carried out in France failed because the relevant treat-ment could, on the facts of this case, have been provided by the NHS "without undue delay". The claimant's attempt to obtain prior authorisation for the NHS to pay had been refused by the defendant primary healthcare trust on grounds that the treatment was routine and could be offered within 12 months and therefore without undue delay. The Secretary of State appealed on ques-tions of law and the Court of Appeal made a reference to the European Court of Justice on the obligations of the NHS to repay treatment costs and the reasonableness of refusal to pay due to budgetary constraints.

Add to Note 92: In *R. (on the application of L) v. Newcastle Primary Care Trust* [2003] EWHC 3252, Charles J. dismissed the claimant's application for judicial review of the defendant's refusal to fund treatment of him with recombinant Factor VIII, when he had refused treatment of his haemophilia with plasma derived Factor VIII.

2. LIABILITY FOR BREACH OF DUTY

(c) *Wrong diagnosis*

12–179   Add: In the case of *Murphy v. MOD* [2002] EWHC 452, there was a failure correctly to diagnose a sub-arachnid haemorrhage (SAH). The judge emphasised that the claimant's presentation was far from being typical of SAH. He found that the claimant had a number of non-specific symptoms, none of which pointed to SAH, and he accordingly found that the defendants had not been negligent in not considering a diagnosis of SAH and in not acting on such a diagnosis. The case emphasises the importance of establishing exactly what the individual clinician would have been faced with, and how he should have acted on the patient's presentation.

(f) *Failing to explain treatment or warn of risks*

12–201   Add to NOTE 63: And see, for example, the case of *Chester v. Afshar* [2003] Q.B. 356, where the *Bolam* test was applied. The claimant succeeded on causation though she could not prove that she would not have had the operation later. This was relevant only to the quantum of damages. The House of Lords upheld the Court of Appeal, by a 3–2 majority, with Lord Bingham and Lord Hoffmann dissenting [2004] UKHL 41. What might seem to be a major departure from the normal rules of causation (which might be summarised as a combination of "but for" test; finding the effective cause; that damage is a necessary requirement for the tort of negligence to be complete; that the failure to warn must have at least increased the risk to which the claimant was exposed the claimant), should it is submitted more simply be viewed as a decision based soundly on principles of legal public policy and caused by the court's wish to "right wrongs". Although two of the majority view (Lord Steyn and Lord Walker) did partly base their decisions on a justified extension of the "principled" or "modified" approach to causation as enunciated in *Fairchild*, it should be noted that both of the dissenting opinions came from members of the Committee of the House of Lords that had actually given the judgment in *Fairchild*. In the light of this there must be doubt as to whether this more relaxed approach to causation can properly be said to be appropriate in this case, or to any other normal clinical negligence cases. As Lord Hoffmann put it, the case failed on causation, but should there be a special rule, to vindicate the affront to the claimant's right to choose for herself. He proposed as a possible alternative a modest solatium. Such a view accords with the majority view (4–3) in *Rees v. Darlington Memorial Hospital NHS Trust* [2003] UKHL 52, reported at [2004] 1 A.C. 309, and Lord Millett's suggestion in *McFarlane* that a conventional award be made to mark the loss of the freedom to choose and in recognition of the wrong done, an approach that was rejected in *Rees* by Lord Steyn and Lord Hope.

See Kay's L.J.'s brief speech in *Wyatt v. (1) Dr Anne Curtis; (2) Central*   **12–217**
Nottinghamshire Health Authority [2003] EWCA Civ 1779, a case concerning a baby born with disabilities following maternal infection with chicken pox, on the significance of the potential emotional distress to the patient of being informed as to the level of risk. His Lordship notes that the duty to inform or warn the patient must be balanced against the distress caused by the warning. See discussion of this case at paragraph 12–218, below. Contrast also with *Deriche v. Ealing Hospital NHS Trust* [2003] EWHC 3104 (QB), where Buckley J. held that something more than temporary distress was needed before a doctor should decide that injury to the patient would result from such a discussion.

Add: Lord Woolf's statement of the law in *Pearce v. United Bristol Health-*   **12–218**
care NHS Trust, was confirmed and approved by the Court of Appeal in *Wyatt v (1) Dr Anne Curtis; (2) Central Nottinghamshire Health Authority* [2003] EWCA Civ 1779. This case concerned Part 20 proceedings brought by a GP against the health authority for a contribution towards the GP's admitted liability to the claimant mother for her failure to warn the mother of the risk of severe harm to the baby due to the mother's contracting chicken pox during pregnancy. The GP had simply warned that the worst effect on the unborn baby would be chicken pox lesions. It was held that the subsequently treating house surgeon, who was not asked about the risk caused to the baby by chicken pox, but was aware of the mother's infection, was not under a duty to ascertain what advice the claimant had received from her GP and to correct the errors in that advice. As the Court of Appeal indicated the false impression of security arising from the GP's incorrect advice was still operating at the time of the second consultation and this caused the claimant not to ask questions of the second doctor concerning the chicken pox infection. By contrast in *Deriche v. Ealing Hospital NHS Trust* [2003] EWHC 3014, (QB), Buckley J. found in very similar circumstances yet distinguishing *Wyatt*, that where a consultant had been the subsequent doctor he was not entitled to assume from the previous doctor's note that "full counselling" had been given, that the claimant had fully understood the nature of the risk involved.

NOTE 55, replace reference to White Book, Spring 2001, with the following: **12–221**
C3–014 and C3–019, 2004.

Add to NOTE 2: *Carver v. Hammersmith & Queen Charlotte's Special Health*   **12–231**
Authority [2000] WL 33201548.

(g) *Mishandling of Mentally Disturbed Patients*

Add: In *Reid v. United Kingdom* (App. No. 50272/99), reported at (2003) 37   **12–233**
E.H.R.R. 9, a mental patient's complaint that his continued detention in a mental hospital constituted a violation of his rights under Article 5(1) of the European Convention of Human Rights 1950 failed. However the proceedings had taken four years to be concluded and this long delay was unjustified and violated his rights under Article 5(4).

12–234   Add: The status of the Mental Health Act Code of Practice and the use of seclusion of detained psychiatric patients was considered in two separate appeals to the Court of Appeal, *R. (on the application of Munjaz) v. Mersey Care NHS Trust* and *R. (on the application of S) v. Airedale NHS Trust* [2003] EWCA Civ 1036, in terms of the requirements and remedies of domestic private law; Articles 3, 5 and 8 of the European Convention on Human Rights and public law. The court held that seclusion of otherwise lawfully detained psychiatric patients could amount to a violation of their rights under Articles 3 and 8, but not Article 5. Although there was no express statutory obligation on hospitals to comply with the Code, doing so would satisfy the State's obligation to avoid a contravention of a patient's Article 3 rights and would meet the requirements of legality for interference with Article 8, and accordingly all hospitals ought to comply with the Code unless there was a good reason for departing from it for a defined case or cases, and a policy of such departure could not be justified.

Add new NOTE 17A at the end of the first sentence: See *R. v. Responsible Medical Officer Broadmoor Hospital* [2002] 1 W.L.R. 419, for Court of Appeal guidance on the approach to be adopted to cases involving challenges to compulsory treatment of detained patients. See also para 12–141 above. In *R. (on the application of KB & 7 Others) v. (1) Mental Health Review Tribunal (2) Secretary of State for Health* [2004] QB 936, an unacceptable delay in determining applications to the MHRT was found to be a breach of the patients' rights under Article 5(4) of the European Convention on Human Rights 1950, and sounded in damages for distress.

12–238   NOTE 36, replace reference to *Barrett v. Enfield LBC* with the following: [2001] 2 A.C. 550;

NOTE 36, replace reference to *Phelps v. Hillingdon LBC* with the following: [2001] 2 A.C. 619.

3. DAMAGES

(a) *Remoteness*

(i) *Causation*

12–245   Add: In *Satwat Rehman v. University College London Hospitals NHS Trust*, [2004] EWHC 1361, Judge Eccles Q.C. awarded the claimant damages of £1,000 for the extra pain and suffering caused to her by reason of her discharge from hospital. Such discharge, following the claimant's complaint of ongoing pain following a laparoscopy was a breach of duty by the defendant healthcare trust, but the delay to discovery of her intra-operative bowel perforation had not affected the outcome.

Add to Note 57: *Peter Wardlaw v. Stephen Farrar* [2003] EWCA Civ 1719, reported at [2003] 4 All E.R. 1358: death from pulmonary embolism was caused by failure of anti-coagulant therapy to prevent its formation, and not the seven days of delay to the claimant's hospital admission, which delay had been caused by the defendant's breach of duty.

Add: The case of *Holtby v. Brigham & Cowan (Hull) Ltd* [2000] 3 All   **12–246**
E.R. 421 concerned a claimant who suffered asbestosis caused by tortious
exposure to asbestos dust in the course of his working life. About half of
his working life was spent with the defendants, and the balance with a number of other employers. On the basis that the exposure to the asbestos which
was the responsibility of the defendants made a material contribution, but
only a material contribution to the claimant's condition, he was awarded
damages which reflected a 25 per cent deduction to take account of the contribution to his condition that was made by the other employers who were
not before the court. The Court of Appeal held that the court had to consider all of the evidence and apply common sense in deciding whether the
claimant had proved that the defendant was responsible for the whole or a
quantifiable part of his condition, and there was ample evidence to support
the decision that the correct award was arrived at by making a 25 per cent
reduction to reflect the contribution to the claimant's condition that was the
responsibility of the other employers who were not before the court. See
however paragraph 12–250 below.

Add new NOTE 70A at end of paragraph: Considered in *Webb v. Barclays
Bank* [2001] EWCA Civ 1141, reported at [2002] PIQR P8; [2001] Lloyd's
Rep. Med. 500, a case concerning the apportionment of liability for the
claimant's above-the-knee amputation between an employer and a hospital
trust. The claimant's employer was found to be 25 per cent liable (the first
tort) and the negligent trust was found to be 75 per cent liable (the second
tort). See also *Clerk & Lindsell on Torts*, 18th ed., paragraph 2–55:
"Intervening medical treatment".

Add to NOTE 77: *Hossack v. Ministry of Defence* [2000] WL 544153 CA.   **12–247**

Add to NOTE 81: Considered in *Webb v. Barclays Bank* [2001] EWCA Civ   **12–249**
1141, reported at [2002] PIQR P8; [2001] Lloyd's Rep. Med. 500. See also
paragraph 12–246 above.

Add: This analysis is now subject to the decision of the House of Lords   **12–250**
in the case of *Fairchild v. Glenhaven Funeral Services* [2003] 1 A.C. 32. In a
series of conjoined appeals which were heard together in both the Court of
Appeal and the House of Lords, the claimants were the widows of mesothelioma sufferers, or in one case the sufferer himself. Each sufferer had been
negligently exposed to asbestos by more than one employer. It was accepted
that the mechanism that triggered the condition of mesothelioma in any
sufferer was unknown, but that it might be triggered by contact with a single asbestos fibre on a single occasion, and that once the condition had been
caused, it would not be aggravated by further exposure to asbestos. Continued exposure to asbestos would not increase the severity of the condition,
but it increased the likelihood of the condition being triggered. The Court
of Appeal held that since mesothelioma was (or might be) an indivisible disease triggered on a single occasion of exposure to asbestos fibre, where each
claimant had been exposed to asbestos by more than one employer and
could not show when the condition had been triggered, he had failed to
prove causation against any one or more of the employer defendants, and
the claims failed.

The House of Lords reversed this decision. Lord Bridge's analysis of *McGhee* in *Wilsher* (see paragraph 12–247 of the main text) and in particular the statement that *"McGhee laid down no new principle"* was disapproved by the majority, and Lord Wilberforce's reasoning was (partly) rehabilitated. The reasoning of the majority in *Fairchild* appears to be this: the elements of causation for attributing liability for an injury to a defendant are a matter of law; whether those elements are present is a matter of fact. It was held that in some circumstances it was right, as a matter of law, to adopt a test of causation that departed from the usual "but for" test, and that justice required that the employer in breach of his duty to his employee by exposing him to asbestos should be liable because he created a significant risk to his health, despite the fact that it could not be proved that the condition would not have been triggered if the exposure had not occurred. No argument as to apportionment was considered.

Lord Bingham acknowledged that it was likely that the principle behind the judgment would be the subject of incremental and analogical development, but he stated expressly that cases developing the principle had to be decided as they arose, and that he did not intend to decide more than was necessary for the disposals of the appeals in the case. See *Chester v. Afshar* [2004] UKHL 41 for an instance where this statement by Lord Bingham was relied on by Lord Steyn as justifying a departure from the normal rules of causation, despite Lord Bingham's contrary view and decision in the same case.

It was not thought that the decision in *Fairchild* would affect the test of causation in normal clinical negligence cases, and this prediction has largely been shown to be correct. The case of *Chester v. Afshar* appears to be an exception which should, it is submitted be regarded with caution since Lord Bingham and Lord Hoffmann, both of whom gave the judgment in *Fairchild*, dissented from the majority view in *Chester v Afshar*. See paragraph 12–201 ante for further discussion of this case.

In *Gregg v. Scott* [2002] EWCA Civ 1471, reported at [2003] Lloyd's Rep. Med. 105: (appeal dismissed, the GP's negligent delay in diagnosing the claimant's non-Hodgkin's lymphoma had no material outcome on the disease, see further discussion of this case at paragraph 12–258, below), Lord Justice Simon Brown stated that *Fairchild* did not invite a more relaxed approach to causation, and together with Lord Justice Mance suggested that its formulation would apply only in narrowly defined circumstances. There may be many situations where it is difficult to say which of a succession of factors in the negligent management of a patient might have caused an injury or condition, but it would be a rare case where those factors were the responsibility of different (or materially different) defendants. In his paper to the Professional Negligence Bar Association in September 2002, Adrian Whitfield Q.C. posed two possible examples: where a succession of healthcare professionals have negligently manhandled an accident victim with an unstable spine with the result that he is paralysed, but it is not possible to show which of them did the damage; and where a drug has been negligently overprescribed by a series of doctors, but it cannot be shown which prescription made the critical difference. In a paper published in the Professional Negligence Law Review in August 2003, Issue 2, Martin Spencer Q.C. proposed similar factual examples involving transfers of patients from a private to an NHS hospital, or referral from a negligent GP to a negligent hospital. These might be examples where the principle in *Fairchild* would allow a claim to be brought against one or more of the negligent professionals where causation might not have been established before. Although it is presumed that the restrictive conditions required for *Fairchild* to be satisfied are likely to limit its impact to clinical care cases, nevertheless the four factual scenarios posed above are not rare occurrences in the world of clinical care. Thus far one reported case outside the context of asbestos-related disease *Phillips v. Syndicate 992 Gunner & Others* [2003] EWHC 1084 considered the impact of *Fairchild* and rejected any suggestion of a more relaxed approach to causation, however that case did not involve the attributability of damage between two defendants.

A contrasting direct application of *Fairchild* but this time on the attributability of damage can be seen in the Court of Appeal's decision in *Rupert St Loftus-Brigham & Another v. London Borough of Ealing* [2003] EWCA Civ 1490, reported at [2004] 20 Const. L.J. 82. This was a tree roots case where the issue on appeal was whether the desiccation of the soil which had caused the subsidence of the property was shown to have been caused by the defendant's trees, when there was substantial vegetation on the claimant's property. The trial judge had found that the claimant had failed to show the subsidence was attributable to the root activity of the defendant's trees. The Court of Appeal (Lord Justice Chadwick and Lord Justice Buxton) overturned the trial judge because the incorrect test for causation had been applied (that the defendant's trees were the dominant cause), and substituted the correct test (that the defendant's trees had been an effective cause), but the court went further and stated: "The question that [the trial judge] should have asked himself was that approved by Lord Bingham in Fairchild: whether desiccation from the tree roots materially contributed to the damage".

Add: In the case of *Hardaker v. Newcastle Heath Authority* [2001] Lloyd's **12–258** Rep. Med. 512, Stanley Burnton J. considered the question of "loss of a chance". The claimant was diving near Leith and, after the dive, he realised that he was suffering from decompression illness ("DCI"). He was taken to hospital at the RVI in Newcastle, but the decompression chamber nearby was closed. However, he was seen by the registrar in A&E who confirmed that he had DCI. He was then taken to Sunderland to the back-up decompression chamber, which was also closed and unattended when he arrived. Decompression began shortly afterwards, but there were no oxygen facilities, and the claimant suffered serious and disabling injuries. His claim against the Health Authority was to the effect that there was culpable delay of about 30 minutes in treating his DCI, and that with earlier treatment there would have been a significantly better chance of a better outcome with earlier treatment. The claimant failed to establish that the Health Authority had been negligent, but the judge also considered that since the expert evidence only showed an unquantified chance of a better but unidentified outcome, the claimant had failed to prove any loss since a chance of a better recovery below 50 per cent was not recoverable damage. He doubted the decision in *Smith v. NHSLA* as being *per incuriam*. See also: *Gregg v. Scott* [2002] EWCA Civ 1471 reported at [2003] Lloyd's Rep. Med. 105: the claimant had developed non-Hodgkin's lymphoma, which was negligently misdiagnosed, which caused a delay to its treatment which led to its growing and spreading. The judge found that the delay had reduced the chances of survival by 25 per cent, but refused to award damages at 25 per cent of the full sum claimed because the chances of survival were in any event less than 50 per cent, thus on the balance of probabilities the claimant would not have recovered even without the negligent delay. The Court of Appeal dismissed the appeal by a majority, with Lathan L.J. distinguishing *Hotson*, but with Mance and Simon Brown L.J. feeling unable to do so. This decision provoked a reaction of "some disquiet" that the claimant should receive no damages for the chance that was lost from Waller L.J. (with whom Carnwath L.J. agreed) in *Coudert Brothers v. Normans Bay Ltd*. [2003] EWCA Civ 215, a solicitor's negligence case where the solicitor defendant unsuccessfully challenged the claim and finding at first instance that this was a "loss of a chance" case. Laws L.J. added (whilst noting that he understood and respected the decision of the majority on which *Hotson* had had influence): *"If a man's chance of a cure from a potentially fatal cancer has been reduced by another's negligence from 42% to 25%, would not a reasonable jury say that he had been grievously hurt by the negligence?"*. As both Waller and Laws L.J.'s concluded, the correctness or otherwise of the decision in *Gregg v Scott* was a matter for the House of Lords. The appeal was heard before the Committee of the House of Lords in May 2004, and judgment is still awaited.

12–262   Add: The claimant only has to establish that he would not have accepted that treatment at that time. The Court of Appeal in the case of *Chester v. Afshar* [2003] Q.B. 356, held that, but for a negligent failure on the part of the clinician to give a proper warning of risks associated with treatment or an operative procedure, the patient would not have had that treatment or that operation then; that the claimant does not have to show that he or she would not have had the treatment at a later stage, or that the risk which eventuated would have in any way been reduced if the procedure or operation had been undertaken at a later stage. The argument favoured by the minority in *Chappel v. Hart* (as to which see paragraph 12–266 in the main work) was rejected. The House of Lords upheld the Court of Appeal, by a 3–2 majority, with Lord Bingham and Lord Hoffmann dissenting [2004] UKHL 41. See also paragraph 12–201 for further discussion of the House of Lords' decision.

12–263   Replace NOTE 23 with the following: [2003] Q.B. 356.

Add to NOTE 24: Also cited at [1999] PIQR 167.

12–268   Add: *Chappel* has now been followed by the Court of Appeal in *Chester v. Afshar* [2003] Q.B. 356. The House of Lords upheld the Court of Appeal, by a 3–2 majority, with Lord Bingham and Lord Hoffmann dissenting [2004] UKHL 41. See also paragraph 12–201 for further discussion of the House of Lords' decision. Their Lordships also paid close attention to the decision in *Chappel*, with the majority view relying on the majority views in *Chappel,* and Lord Bingham dissenting and relying on the dissenting judgment of McHugh J. in *Chappel*.

12–271   Add to NOTE 59: See *Coudert Brothers v. Normans Bay Ltd*. [2003] EWCA Civ 215 for a case where this passage of Lord Browne Wilkinson's judgment in *Bolitho* was approved as an example of the general rule of the common law that a party may not rely on his own wrong to secure a benefit.

Add to NOTE 70, the reference for *Matthews v. East Suffolk Health Author-* **12–273**
ity: [2000] WL 191250, CA.

Add to NOTE 80: See also comment on *Fairchild* added to paragraph **12–275**
12–250 above.

Add: In *Pigeon v. Doncaster Health Authority* [2002] Lloyd's Rep. Med. **12–276**
130, the claimant underwent extensive surgery for cervical cancer in 1997. In
June 1988 a cervical smear that had been taken when the claimant was 22 was
wrongly, and negligently, reported as negative. The smear was not repeated
on the birth of the claimant's child in October 1988 because of the earlier
(false) negative report. Between 1991 and 1997 the claimant was urged on
many occasions both by her GP and by the FHSA to have further smear tests,
but she refused to do so—because she had found the test that had been carried out in 1988 both painful and embarrassing. The judge held that this conduct by the claimant was not such as to break the chain of causation, but it
did amount to substantial contributory negligence, and her damages were
reduced by two thirds accordingly.
See also the case of *Hardaker v. Newcastle Health Authority* [2001] Lloyd's
Rep. Med. 521. The judge dismissed the claim but would have found
contributory fault against the claimant for aggravating his injuries before
arriving at the hospital.

(b) *Measure of Damages*

(ii) *Aggravated damages*

Add: In the case of *A v. Bottrill* [2003] 1 A.C. 449, the Privy Council con- **12–288**
sidered the question of exemplary damages in New Zealand. It concluded by
a majority of 3:2, in reversing a decision of the Court of Appeal and restor-
ing the order of the judge permitting a new trial in a claim against a pathol-
ogist who was for many years the only doctor examining cervical smears in
the Gisborne area of New Zealand, that the power to award exemplary damages was not rigidly confined to cases where the defendant intended to cause
the harm or was consciously reckless as to the risks involved.

(iii) *Damages in wrongful birth and conception claims*

Add to NOTE 35: In respect of *McLelland v. Greater Glasgow Health Board*, **12–289**
the defendant's appeal was allowed (2001 S.L.T. 446) to the extent that the
damages representing the cost of looking after the child up to and including
the age of 18 were limited to the additional costs consequent upon the child's
disabilities. The rest of the damages award was upheld.

Add to NOTE 36: *McFarlane* was affirmed by a seven-man committee of the **12–290**
House of Lords: Lord Bingham, Lord Nicholls, Lord Millett, Lord Scott,
Lord Steyn, Lord Hope, Lord Hutton) in *Rees v. Darlington Memorial*
Hospital NHS Trust [2003] UKHL 52 and reported at [2004] 1 AC 309. The
claimant in *Rees* had invited their Lordships to reconsider *McFarlane*, and
they declined to do so. By a majority (four to three) a "gloss" was added to
McFarlane in that this majority (which included Lord Millett, who had heard

McFarlane before the Court of Appeal, and had proposed an award of £5,000 to reflect the denial of personal autonomy and right to limit one's own family size) added a conventional award (in addition to the award for the pregnancy and the birth) to recognise the fact that the claimant had been a victim of a legal wrong. The sum awarded was £15,000. Accordingly a fourth head of damages should now be added to the list in paragraph **12–289**.

12–291   Add: The House of Lords' approach in *McFarlane* was rejected by the High Court of Australia in *Cattanach v. Melchior* [2003] HCA 38 (July 16, 2003), which by a 4:3 majority held that claims for recovery of the cost of upkeep of the child born after a negligently performed sterilisation operation were allowed. As Kirby J. pointed out, since the majority approach in *McFarlane* was either implicitly or explicitly based on the three-stage test from *Caparo Industries Plc v. Dickman* [1990] 2 A.C. 605, which test had been rejected by the courts of Australia (*Sullivan v. Moody* (2001) C.L.R. 562), it is little surprise that the High Court of Australia declined to follow their Lordships' decision. The decision in *McFarlane* was unsuccessfully challenged in the appeal to the House of Lords in *Rees v. Darlington Memorial Hospital NHS Trust*. See addition to paragraphs 12–290 above and 12–298 below: **Unwanted healthy child born to a disabled mother**.

12–293   Add to NOTE 53: In respect of *McLelland v. Greater Glasgow Health Board*: reported on appeal at (2001) S.L.T. 446.

NOTE 54: *Farrell v. Merton Sutton* now reported at [2001] 57 B.M.L.R 158.

Add at the end of NOTE 54: In *Roberts v. Bro Taf HA* [2001] WL 1422837, reported at [2002] Lloyd's Rep. Med. 182, Turner J. followed *Parkinson v. St James and Seacroft University Hospital NHS Trust* [2002] Q.B. 266 in holding that a claim for the additional costs of looking after an unwanted disabled child should not be limited to what the family would have been able to afford. Following the House of Lords' decision in *Rees v Darlington Memorial Hospital NHS Trust* [2003] UKHL 52 and reported at [2004] 1 AC 309 , the status of the Court of Appeal's decision in *Parkinson* is uncertain. See addition to paragraph **12–298** below.

Add to end of paragraph: The status of the decision in *Parkinson* is uncertain following their Lordships' decision in *Rees v. Darlington Memorial Hospital NHS Trust* [2003] UKHL 52 and reported at [2004] 1 AC 309. Lord Bingham described it as "arguably anomalous", and considered his conventional award for a legal wrong should be made irrespective of the presence of disability whether in parent or child, thereby implicitly overruling *Parkinson* (which had not been under appeal). Lord Nicholls made no direct mention of *Parkinson* but approved of Lord Bingham's reasons. In support of this view, Lord Millett described it as an "illegitimate gloss on *McFarlane*", and Lord Scott expressly stated that it was inconsistent with *McFarlane*. However Lord Hope and Lord Hutton approved the decision and Lord Steyn approved *Parkinson*, as a "legitimate extension" of *McFarlane* (which had not involved considering a disabled child or parent). The majority suggests that the decision was disapproved, but it is not clear that it has been overruled.

Add: This approach and the decision in *Parkinson v. St James and Seacroft* **12–294**
University Hospital NHS Trust must now be in doubt following the House of
Lords' decision in *Rees v. Darlington Memorial Hospital NHS Trust* [2004] 1
A.C. 309: damages are not recoverable for the additional costs of bringing up
a child born to a disabled mother. See paragraph 12–298A below for further
discussion of this case.

Add to Note 55: There appears to have been no decision in the Court of
Appeal, and the case was presumably settled.

Note 56, replace reference to *Parkinson v. St James and Seacroft University
Hospital NHS Trust* with the following: [2002] Q.B. 266.

Add new Note 57A after the last sentence: Applied in *Groom v. Selby* [2001]
EWCA Civ 1522, reported at [2002] PIQR P18; [2002] Lloyd's Rep. Med. 1.

Note 63, replace reference to *N v. Warrington Health Authority* with the **12–298**
following: [2003] Lloyd's Rep. Med. 365.

Add to Note 64: In respect of *McLelland v. Greater Glasgow Health Board*,
reported on appeal at (2001) S.L.T. 446: the damages representing the cost of
looking after the child up to and including the age of 18 were limited to the
additional costs consequent upon the child's disabilities. The rest of the damages award was upheld, including a sum in respect of the cost of care after
the child reached the age of 40, modestly discounted to take account of the
chance (but not certainty) that state benefits would be available. In *Rees v.
Darlington Health Authority* [2003] UKHL 52 and reported at [2004] 1 AC
309, it appears that their Lordships (by a majority of four to three) disapproved of the Court of Appeal's decision in *Parkinson* (where the court
awarded the extra costs of raising a disabled child), which removes the possibility of recovering costs of raising a disabled child in a wrongful conception
claim. See addition to paragraph **12–298A** below.

Add new paragraph **12–198A**:

Unwanted healthy child born to a disabled mother. In the case of *Rees v. Dar-* **12–298A**
lington Memorial Hospital NHS Trust [2003] Q.B. 20, the claimant suffered
from retinitis pigmentosa. She was blind in one eye and had only limited vision
in the other, with the effect that she was severely visually handicapped. She was
sterilised in July 1995 because she felt that her eyesight would make it very difficult for her to look after a baby. The sterilisation was ineffective, and her son
was born in April 1997. Unfortunately the baby's father did not wish to be
involved with him. The claimant sought the entire cost of bringing up this
child, and the judge struck the claim out. On appeal the claim was limited to
the additional costs of bringing up the child that were attributable to her own
disability. Such costs were not identified in the Court of Appeal, and it is not
clear what they might be. By a majority the Court of Appeal allowed the
appeal with the effect that the claimant was entitled to claim such additional
costs—if she could establish any. The case is interesting: Hale L.J., in the
majority, loyally (but perhaps reluctantly) followed the House of Lords decision in *McFarlane* categorising the principle in *McFarlane* as one of "deemed

equilibrium" between the costs and benefits of bringing up a healthy child; Waller L.J. dissented, and both Waller L.J. and Robert Walker L.J. doubted the "deemed equilibrium" principle that Hale L.J. considered binding. The defendant's appeal from the Court of Appeal's decision was heard in June 2003 by a seven-man committee of the House of Lords. The respondent (claimant) sought to overturn *McFarlane*. After the oral hearing and the High Court of Australia's decision in *Cattanach v. Melchior* [2003] HCA 38 (July 16, 2003) (where the *McFarlane* approach was rejected by a 4:3 majority, and the claimant parents recovered the cost of bringing up the child), their Lordships sought written submissions from the parties dealing with that case. See also the addition to paragraph 12–291 above. A seven-man committee of the House of Lords, Lord Bingham, Lord Nicholls, Lord Millett, Lord Scott, Lord Steyn, Lord Hope, Lord Hutton all affirmed *McFarlane*, [2003] UKHL 52 and reported at [2004] 1 AC 309, and refused the claimant's appeal. By a majority a "gloss" was added to *McFarlane* in that this majority (which included Lord Millett, who had heard *McFarlane* before the Court of Appeal, and had proposed an award of £5,000 to reflect the denial of personal autonomy and right to limit one's own family size) added a conventional award (in addition to the award for the pregnancy and the birth) to recognise the fact that the claimant had been a victim of a legal wrong. The sum awarded was £15,000. However, the status of the decision in *Parkinson* is uncertain following their Lordships' decision in *Rees v. Darlington Memorial Hospital NHS Trust*. Lord Bingham described it as "arguably anomalous", and considered his conventional award for a legal wrong should be made irrespective of the presence of disability whether in parent or child, thereby implicitly overruling *Parkinson* (which had not been under appeal). Lord Nicholls made no direct mention of *Parkinson* but approved of Lord Bingham's reasons. In support of this view. Lord Millett described it as an "illegitimate gloss on *McFarlane*", and Lord Scott expressly stated that it was inconsistent with *McFarlane*. However Lord Hope and Lord Hutton approved the decision and Lord Steyn approved *Parkinson*, as a "legitimate extension" of *McFarlane* (which had not involved considering a disabled child or parent). The majority suggests that the decision was disapproved, but it is not clear that it has been overruled.

The case of *AD v. East Kent Community NHS Trust* [2002] EWHC 2256, reported at [2003] PIQR P3; [2002] Lloyd's Rep. Med. 424 concerned a mental patient who had become pregnant as a result of (allegedly) negligent supervision in a mixed psychiatric ward where she was treated, having been sectioned under section 2 of the Mental Health Act 1983. The (healthy) child was looked after by the claimant's mother. Cooke J. held that the claimant could not claim in respect of the cost of looking after the child on the basis that she could not look after the child herself, and would incur no costs. But he did say (at paragraph 13 of his judgment) that he saw no distinction as a matter of principle between unwanted children born to mothers with physical disabilities and those born to mothers with mental disabilities. The decision was affirmed by the Court of Appeal, [2002] EWCA Civ 1872, reported at [2003] 3 All E.R. 1167. The House of Lords granted permission to appeal and the appeal is expected to be heard in early 2005.

12–300   Add at end: This analysis is now subject to the decision of the House of Lords in *Rees v. Darlington Memorial Hospital NHS Trust* [2003] UKHL 52 and reported at [2004] 1 AC 309. See addition to paragraph **12–298A** above.

Add to NOTE 73: Affirmed in the Court of Appeal at [2001] EWCA Civ 1522, reported at [2002] PIQR P18; [2002] Lloyd's Rep. Med. 1.

(iv) *Impact of the Human Rights Act 1998*

Add to NOTE 77: Not considered by the Court of Appeal. **12–301**

.

CHAPTER 13

FINANCIAL PRACTITIONERS

1. GENERAL

(f) *FSMA*

(i) *General*

13–011   Add: All updates and changes to such rules and guidance are published on the FSA's website together with a definitive copy of the Handbook in force from time to time. Prior to February 2003 sourcebooks (see below) within the Handbook were updated individually. However, since February 2003 the Handbook has been updated collectively and each updated version of the Handbook has been given a single version number and release date.

(vii) *Exempt persons*

13–020   Add to NOTE 72: Schedules I, II and III of the Financial Services and Markets Act 2000 (Exemption) Order 2001 S.I. 2001 No. 1201, the Financial Services and Markets Act 2000 (Exemption) (Amendment) (No. 1) Order 2003 S.I. 2003 No. 47 and the Financial Services and Markets Act 2000 (Exemption) (Amendment) (No. 2) Order 2003 S.I. 2003 175 now identify categories of persons exempt from the general prohibition in respect of various regulated activities.

(viii) *Members of Professions*

Add to NOTE 79: Articles 4 to 8 of the Financial Services and Markets Act   **13–021**
2000 (Professions) (Non-Exempt Activities) Order 2001 S.I. 2001 No. 1227
now identify activities to which the exemption from the general prohibition
does not apply. Of particular interest is Article 7—Advising a person to
become a member of a particular Lloyd's syndicate.

2. DUTIES AND LIABILITIES

(c) *Application of the FSMA regime*

(i) *Regulated Activities*

Add to NOTE 10: The RAO has now been amended by the Financial Ser-   **13–030**
vices and Markets Act 2000 (Regulated Activities) (Amendment) Order 2001
S.I. 2001 No 3544, the Financial Services and Markets Act 2000 (Regulated
Activities)(Amendment) Order 2002 S.I. 2002 No. 682, the Financial Services
and Markets Act 2000 (Regulated Activities)(Amendment) (No. 2) Order
2002 S.I. 2002 No. 1776, the Financial Services and Markets Act 2000 (Regulated Activities)(Amendment) (No. 1) Order 2003 S.I. 2003 No. 1475 and
the Financial Services and Markets Act 2000 (Regulated Activities)(Amendment) (No. 2) Order 2003 S.I. 2003 No. 1476. These Amendment Orders
expand the categories of activity that fall within the scope of the general prohibition. It is important to note that the Orders are not retrospective; an
activity does not become a 'regulated activity' until the relevant Order has
come into force.

Add to NOTE 11: Issuing electronic money is now a specified activity within
the meaning of the RAO: see Article 4 of the Financial Services and Markets
Act 2000 (Regulated Activities)(Amendment) Order 2002 S.I. 2002 No. 682,
where electronic money is defined as, *"monetary value, as represented by a
claim on the issuer, which is (i) stored on an electronic device, (ii) issued on
receipt of funds, and (iii) accepted as a means of payment by persons other
than the issuer".*

Add to NOTE 12: The Financial Services and Markets Act 2000 (Regulated
Activities)(Amendment) (No. 2) Order 2003 S.I. 2003 No. 1476 now substantially widens the scope of insurance-related activities falling within the RAO.

Add to NOTE 24: : The Financial Services and Markets Act 2000 (Regulated Activities)(Amendment) (No. 1) Order 2003 S.I. 2003 No. 1475 (which
comes into force on various dates in 2004) substantially widens the scope of
regulated mortgage contract-related activities which fall within the RAO. In
particular, arranging and providing advice in relation to mortgage related
contracts become regulated activities.

(ii) *Financial Promotion*

Add to NOTE 30: The FPO has now been amended by the Financial   **13–032**
Services and Markets Act 2000 (Financial Promotion and Miscellaneous

Amendments) Order 2002 S.I. 2002 No 1310 and the Financial Services and Markets Act 2000 (Financial Promotion) (Amendment) Order 2003 S.I. 2003 No 1676.

(e) *Regulatory rules and the FSA Handbook*

(i) *General*

13–039   Add after the first sentence of NOTE 66 the following: All additions and amendments to rule-making instruments and sourcebooks are published on the website. They can be listed by date to enable a "snapshot" of the rules in force at a particular point in time to be taken.

13–040   Add: Within the "Business Standards" section of the Handbook, Mortgages: Conduct of Business (MCOB) and Insurance: Conduct of Business (ICOB) sourcebooks have now been published and are due to come into force on October 21, 2004, and January 14, 2005, respectively. The following additional specialist sourcebooks have also now been published: Electronic Commerce Directive (ECO), Electronic Money (ELM), Energy Market Participants (EMPS), Small Friendly Societies (FREN), Oil Market Participants (OMPS) and Service Companies (SERV). In addition, numerous amendments to the sourcebooks have been brought about by Instruments made by the FSA pursuant to the FSMA.

(iv) *The "Conduct of Business" sourcebook ("COB")*

13–046   Add: Since publication of this chapter, numerous minor amendments to the original COB have been brought about by *inter alia* the Conduct of Business Sourcebook (Amendment) Instruments Nos 1–18. Such amendments do not operate retrospectively. Care must therefore be taken to ensure that, when assessing the adequacy of the conduct of a financial practitioner, the correct version of COB is used.

Add to NOTE 97: From October 31, 2004, the Mortgage: Conduct of Business (MCOB) sourcebook will provide guidance as to the duties and obligations of bodies carrying on Regulated Mortgage Activities. Such bodies will include mortgage lenders, mortgage administrators, mortgage arrangers and mortgage advisors. Individual chapters within the sourcebook deal with conduct of business, promotion, advising and selling and disclosure at various stages of transactions to which MCOB applies. From January 14, 2005, the Insurance: Conduct of Business (ICOB) sourcebook will provide similar guidance as to the duties and obligations of insurers, insurance intermediaries and managing agents. ICOB aims to implement much of the EC Insurance Mediation, Distance Marketing, Consolidated Life, Third Non-Life and Fourth Motor Insurance Directives. Despite neither yet being implemented, various Amendment Instruments affecting both MCOB and ICOB have already been made by the FSA.

(g) *Other statutory liabilities*

(ii) *The Misrepresentation Act 1967*

Add to NOTE 58: See also *Clef Aquitaine SARL v. Laporte Materials (Bar-* **13–088**
row) Ltd [2001] Q.B. 488

Add to NOTE 59: In the Canadian case of *Avco Financial Services Realty Ltd. v. Norman* (Unreported April 16, 2003) the Ontario Court of Appeal concluded that while negligent misrepresentation and contributory negligence could co-exist at law, it would be necessary to consider in each case whether the conduct which amounted to reasonable and foreseeable reliance by a claimant on a defendant's representations was nonetheless open to sufficient criticism to justify a finding of contributory negligence on the part of that claimant.

(h) *Contractual duties*

(i) *Relevant contracts*

NOTE 61: *Brandeis (Brokers) Ltd v. Herbert Black* is now reported at [2001] **13–089**
2 Lloyd's L. Rep. 359.

(iii) *Incorporation of regulatory duties in contract*

NOTE 74: *Brandeis (Brokers) Ltd v. Herbert Black* is now reported at [2001] **13–091**
2 Lloyd's L. Rep. 359.

(v) *Appointed representatives*

Replace NOTE 98 with the following: See *Bowstead & Reynolds on Agency* **13–098**
(17th ed., 2001) at 3–018 *et seq.*

NOTE 1: After *Bowstead & Reynolds*, add (17th ed., 2001) at 8–013 *et seq.*

(i) *Tort-based duties*

(i) *Deceit or fraudulent misrepresentation*

Add to NOTE 4: See also *Clef Aquitaine SARL v. Laporte Materials (Barrow)* **13–100**
Ltd [2001] Q.B. 488.

Add to NOTE 5: In *Standard Chartered Bank v. Pakistan National Shipping Corp. (Nos 2 and 4)* [2002] UKHL 43, [2003] 1 A.C. 959 the House of Lords concluded that, since there was no common law defence of contributory negligence in the case of fraudulent misrepresentation, there was no possibility of an apportionment of liability in such a case between claimant and defendant under the Law Reform (Contributory Negligence) Act 1945. Note however that Lord Rodger preferred to leave open the question of whether or not a defence of contributory negligence might be open to a defendant in other cases of intentional harm to a claimant.

(iii) *Negligence*

13–109   Add to NOTE 24: For a critical analysis of the decision in *Gorham* see *Palmer* Tru. & E.L.J. 2001 23, 18–30 and *McMeel* L.M.C.L.Q. 2001 3, 321–327.

Add: *Gorham* was cited with approval by the Court of Appeal in *Dean v. Allin & Watts* [2001] Lloyd's L. Rep. 249 at 261, a solicitor's negligence claim. For the facts of *Dean* see 10–060 *supra*.

13–112   Add: In *Lloyds TSB General Insurance Holdings Ltd v. Lloyds Bank Group Insurance Co. Ltd* the claimants had been sued by individuals to whom they had sold personal pension plans. Each individual had alleged that the claimants' representatives had failed to give best advice at the time that the policies were entered into. The claimants sought indemnities against the claims from the defendant underwriters. An issue arose as to whether the individual claims were properly to be treated for insurance purposes as a series of individual claims resulting from poor advice or a single claim resulting from the claimants' failure to provide training to their representatives that was adequate to enable them to give proper advice to the individuals. The Court of Appeal concluded (albeit *obiter*) that, in order to for a claim to result from a circumstances, the circumstance had to be the *"proximate cause of"* or *"immediately causative of"* the claim in question. Accordingly although a lack of training might have created the antecedent state of affairs which led to the bad advice and/or been the underlying reason for the bad advice, the claims themselves resulted from the bad advice and not the lack of training provided to the claimants' representatives: [2001] EWCA Civ 1643, [2002] Lloyd's L.Rep. (PN) 211. The House of Lords ([2003] UKHL 48 [2003] 4 All E.R. 43) approved this aspect of the Court of Appeal's decision – the absence of adequate training and monitoring on the part of the claimant was irrelevant to the civil liability in issue since any such absence was not an "act or omission" from which a liability on the part of the claimants had resulted – the relevant "act or omission" had in each case been the failure of the claimants' representatives to provide best advice. However, (reversing the Court of Appeal) the House of Lords concluded that each case arose from a separate contravention of the relevant statutory framework and so should be treated as a separate claim for the purpose of the policy. The fact that each case might be of similar nature and/or arise from the same underlying cause was not sufficient to bring them within the aggregation clause.

(j) *Fiduciary duties*

13–115   Replace the penultimate sentence with the following: The source of fiduciary duties in a financial services context (as in any other context) is not the retainer itself but rather all the circumstances (including the retainer) which create a relationship of trust and confidence and from which flow obligations of loyalty and transparency. As long as that confidential relationship exists, the financial practitioner must not place himself in a position where his duty to act in the interests of the confiding party and his personal interest in acting for his own benefit may conflict. The termination of a retainer will not automatically terminate any fiduciary duties: see *Longstaff v. Birtles* [2001] EWCA Civ 1219 [2002] 1 W.L.R. 470 at 471F–G.

NOTE 51: *Brandeis (Brokers) Ltd v. Herbert Black* is now reported at [2001]   **13–116**
2 Lloyd's L. Rep. 359.

3. BREACH OF DUTY

(b) *Misleading promotion*

(ii) *Present position*

NOTE 62: *Aldrich v. Norwich Union Life Insurance Co. Ltd.* is now also   **13–119**
reported at [1999] 2 All E.R. (Comm) 707.

(d) *Advising and Selling*

Add: For a further example see *Primavera v. Allied Dunbar plc* Unre-   **13–122**
ported December 14, 2001, H.H.J. Hawkesworth Q.C. sitting as a High
Court judge. Although the Court of Appeal subsequently varied the judge's
Order on the issue of the measure of loss (see [2002] EWCA Civ 1327,
[2003] Lloyd's L. Rep. (PN) 14 and 13–165A below) the judge's findings on
liability were undisturbed.

(e) *Dealing and managing*

NOTE 82: *Brandeis (Brokers) Ltd v. Herbert Black* is now reported at [2001]   **13–128**
2 Lloyd's L. Rep. 359.

5. REMEDIES INCLUDING DAMAGES

(b) *Remedies available to regulators*

For an analysis of the regulatory and disciplinary powers available to the   **13–137**
FSA or the Secretary of State, see *R. (Davis and others) v. Financial Services
Authority* [2002] EWHC (Admin) 2997, [2003] 1 W.L.R. 1284 *per* Lightman J.

(iii) *Orders available*

Add to NOTE 61: In *Financial Services Authority v. Fitt* [2004] EWHC 1669   **13–146**
the defendant, trading by himself and through two corporate entities, had
breached a number of requirements relating to his authorisation under the
FSMA to carry on various financial businesses. In particular, money
entrusted to the defendant and his companies by investors had not been
returned. The FSA therefore sought an injunction pursuant to section 380(3)
of the FSMA freezing assets including *inter alia* bank accounts in the names
of the various investors. Lewison J. acknowledged that such an order went "*a
little further than the final jurisdiction warrants under section 380 [of the*

FSMA] which enables the court to make an order freezing 'assets **of his***', that is to say the person alleged to have contravened the requirements".* However, the judge concluded that he nonetheless had power under section 37 of the Supreme Court Act 1981 to make the order sought in circumstances where such an order was reasonably necessary to prevent the proceeds being stripped from those accounts by the defendant

13–147   Add to NOTE 65: For a recent example of a successful application for such relief under the 1986 Act see *FSA v. Fraser Lindhart & Webb* Unreported 14th November 2001 Simon Berry Q.C.

(v) *The FSA Enforcement Manual*

13–149   Add: The principles underlying the FSA's approach to the exercise of its enforcement powers are set out in chapter 1 section 1.3 of the Enforcement sourcebook. They comprise:

> "(1) The effectiveness of the regulatory regime depends to a significant extent on the maintenance of an open and cooperative relationship between the *FSA* and those whom it regulates (2) The FSA will seek to exercise its enforcement powers in a manner that is transparent, proportionate and consistent with its publicly stated policies. (3) The FSA will seek to ensure fair treatment when exercising its enforcement powers. For example, the FSA's decision making process for regulatory enforcement cases generally gives an opportunity for both written and oral representations to be made, and also provides a facility for mediation (where settlement discussions break down) in certain disciplinary cases."

(c) *Remedies available to private litigants*

(iii) *Damages or compensation*

13–165   Add: For critical analysis of *Needler* see *Swinton* S.L.G. 2002 70(2), 48–49 and *Turner "Heads I win, tails you lose"* Corp. Brief. 2001 15(9) 6–8.

NOTE 12: *Needler Financial Services v. Taber* is now reported at [2002] 3 All E.R. 501.

Add new paragraph **13–165A**:

13–165A   In *Primavera v. Allied Dunbar Assurance plc* [2002] EWCA Civ 1327, [2003] Lloyd's L. Rep. (PN) 14 the claimant had been advised by the defendant in 1987 to invest in executive retirement plan ("ERP") with the aim by 1995 of being able to draw down a tax-free sum of £500,000 from the fund to repay a loan and to purchase an annuity with the balance of the fund. However, the defendant neglected to advise the claimant that in order for the ERP to produce the necessary tax free sum to enable the loan to be repaid, the claimant would have to receive schedule E earnings of a particular level for at least 3 consecutive years during the 7 year life of the ERP. He could have arranged to receive such earnings, but due to his ignorance of any need to do so, did not in fact receive such remuneration. As a result, although by 1995 the fund value of the ERP was £792,896, the tax free lump sum available to the claimant from the ERP was only £125,875. Had he received higher schedule

E earnings, that tax free lump sum would have been approximately £101,000 greater. Between 1997 and 2000 the claimant did in fact arrange his affairs so as to receive the necessary Schedule E salary payments and by 2000 a sufficient tax free lump sum to repay the loan had become available under the ERP. In addition, by that date the value of the fund had risen to such an extent that the claimant was able to purchase a substantially larger annuity than he would have been able to purchase in 1995 had he received the necessary schedule E earnings prior to 1995. The claimant was found to be entitled to recover the additional tax free lump sum that would have been available to him in 1995 had he received the necessary Schedule E salary payments. However, an issue arose as to whether the claimant should have to give credit against that sum for increases in the value of the fund after 1995 from which he would not in fact have benefited had the ERP been used to pay off the loan in 1995. The Court of Appeal concluded that he did not. That benefit was not a consequences of the defendant's misconduct and it was wrong to characterise the claimant's conduct after 1995 as action taken in order to mitigate loss suffered by him as a result of the defendant's failings. Instead that conduct was properly to be described as the claimant's own '*speculation*', in relation to the consequences of which the defendant could have no risk or benefit. For an examination of this decision, see Gibbons' "*Breaking chains of causation in the avoidance of loss*" NLJ Vol 152 1714.

NOTE 14: *Brandeis (Brokers) Ltd v. Herbert Black* is now reported at [2001]   **13–166**
2 Lloyd's L. Rep. 359

7. THE PROCESS OF RESOLVING CLAIMS

(a) *Ombudsman*

(i) *Introduction*

Replace the last two sentences with the following: The final version of the   **13–171**
complaint-handling rules was published on October 5, 2001 under the title "Dispute Resolution: the Complaints Sourcebook" (DISP). Those rules came into force on December 1, 2001. Minor amendments have been made by Instrument subsequent to that date. For a review of the Financial Services Ombudsman system, including the extent of its coverage, the accountability regime, its decision making policies, rules of complaint handling and related procedural issues, see Jones & Morris '*A brave new world in ombudsmanry ?*' Public Law (2002) pp. 640–648.

(ii) *Compulsory and voluntary jurisdiction*

Add: The FOS anticipates the compulsory jurisdiction being extended to   **13–172**
credit unions, electronic money institutions, residential first-mortgages, residential first-mortgage intermediaries and insurance intermediaries in due course.

Replace NOTE 37 with the following: DISP 2.6.9. The FOS is currently   **13–173**
consulting on an extension of the voluntary jurisdiction to mortgage

intermediaries, insurance intermediaries and consumer credit firms not already included within the ombudsman scheme.

(v) *Complaints handling procedures of the FOS*

13–179   Note 65: "DISC 3.3" should read "DISP 3.3"

(vi) *The investigation*

13–181   Replace Note 69 with the following: DISP 3.2.11.

Add new Note 69A at the end of the paragraph: See DISP 3.8.1.

13–182   After the second sentence add: Note 70A: see *R. (Norwich & Peterborough Building Society)* [2003] EWHC 2379, [2003] 1 All E.R. (Comm) 65. In that case Ouseley J. declined to interfere with a decision of the Ombudsman that did "*not fall outside the broad scope of fairness*" and was not so unreasonable as to be legally irrational.

13–186   Replace Note 79 with the following: FSMA s.229(4); DISP 3.9.5. Note however that this figure is exclusive of interest: see DISP 3.9.2.

Add new Note 82A after the penultimate sentence: See DISP 3.9.6.

(b) *Compensation Scheme*

(iii) *Structure*

13–192   Replace the paragraph with the following: The broad structure of the compensation scheme is contained in the FSMA itself. The detail of how the scheme operates is contained in rules set out in the Compensation Sourcebook (COMP) which came into force on December 1, 2001 and has been amended subsequently by a number of Instruments. The Compensation Sourcebook also contains Funding Rules in relation to the scheme.

(iv) *Qualifying conditions for compensation*

13–195   Replace Note 7 with the following: COMP 5.2.1, 5.3–5.5. Note also COMP 14.5.

(v) *Compensation*

13–200   Add: For claims which arise under the Third Party (Rights against Insurers) Act 1930, concern a COMP Article 9 default and fall within COMP 5(1)(b) the limit is 90 per cent of the value of the claim.

CHAPTER 14

INSURANCE BROKERS

1. GENERAL

Add: An insurance broker may be an individual, a partnership or a com-   **14–002**
pany. If the broker is a company, then the claim will usually be against the
company. However, in *European International Reinsurance Co. Ltd v. Curzon
Insurance Ltd* [2003] EWCA Civ 1074, [2003] Lloyd's Rep IR 793, the Court
of Appeal held that it was arguable that a broker's employees had assumed
responsibility to the reinsured and therefore were personally liable.

Add to NOTE 4: Similarly, in appropriate circumstances other parties may
be found to have assumed the responsibility of an insurance broker. Such an
allegation against a bank succeed at first instance in *Frost v. James Finlay*

Bank [2001] Lloyd's Rep. P.N. 629, but the judge's finding was over-turned on appeal: [2002] Lloyd's Rep. P.N. 473.

14–006   Add the following text at the end of the paragraph: From January 15, 2005, the sale and administration of insurance will become a "regulated activity" under the Act. The expansion of the regulation of insurance intermediaries is necessary so that the UK complies with its obligations under the Insurance Mediation Directive (2002/92/EC) which was approved in September 2002 and which must be implemented by all Member States by January 15, 2005. The Directive has been implemented through amendments to the Financial Services and Markets Act 2000 and certain regulations made under that Act. The Directive sets minimum standards covering matters such as fitness and propriety, training and competence, and complaints handling. It also requires certain minimum pre-sale information to be given to customers.

The consequence of the amendments to the Act and regulations is that from January 2005 the FSA will be responsible for regulating insurance mediaries, who will be required to be authorised by the FSA. Further, all insurance intermediaries will be required to comply with the applicable rules in the Insurance: Conduct of Business sourcebook (the text of which can be found on the FSA's website, *www.fsa.gov.uk*). In the context of claims against insurance brokers, the most important rules are contained in chapters 4 and 5 of the sourcebook. Chapter 4 sets out minimum standards for advising and selling (in particular the requirement of "suitability"), and chapter 5 contains rules regarding product disclosure. Pursuant to section 150 of the Act, a breach of the rules by an authorised broker may give rise to a claim for breach of statutory duty by a private person (see further paragraph 14–008 below and Ch. 13 above).

(a) *Duties to client*

(i) *Contractual duties*

14–013   Add new Note 39A at the end of paragraph 14–013 as follows: "See further paragraph 14–014A below."

(ii) *Duties independent of contract*

Add new paragraph **14–014A**:

14–014A   In *European International Reinsurance Co. Ltd. v. Curzon Insurance Ltd.* [2003] EWCA Civ 1074, [2003] Lloyd's Rep. I.R. 793, the Court of Appeal stated that it was "at least arguable" that someone who holds himself out as "A Lloyd's Broker" assumes a personal responsibility to the person seeking to use his broking services, even if he makes it clear that that he is the agent of another broker or broking company.

(b) *Duties to third parties*

(i) *Duties to insurers*

14–019   Add: Further, in some circumstances non-disclosure may amount to a misrepresentation which does give rise to damages (if any loss is suffered). In

HIH v. Chase [2003] 2 Lloyd's Rep. 61, Lord Bingham stated (at 69): "Since an agent to insure is subject to an independent duty of disclosure, the deliberate withholding from the insurer of information which the agent knows or believes to be material to the risk, if done dishonestly or recklessly, may well amount to fraudulent misrepresentation." He went on to state that in such a case it would be open to the insurer to avoid the policy and recover damages from the broker.

Add to NOTE 51: See *HIH v. Chase* [2003] 2 Lloyd's Rep. 61 in which Lord Hoffmann (at 78) confirmed that "non-disclosure (whether dishonest or otherwise) does not as such give rise to a claim in damages."

(ii) *Duties to other third parties.*

Add to NOTE 65: In *European International Reinsurance Co. Ltd. v. Curzon Insurance Ltd.* [2003] EWCA Civ 1074, [2003] Lloyd's Rep. I.R. 793, the Court of Appeal held that it was arguable that a Lloyd's brokers' broking of a reinsurance risk amounted to a voluntary assumption of responsibility to the reinsured, so giving rise to a duty of care, even though the reinsured had no knowledge of the involvement of the Lloyd's broker or its personnel. **14–025**

2. LIABILITY FOR BREACH OF DUTY

Delete the first sentence and replace with the following: Instances in which it has been held that insurance brokers are, or may be, liable for breach of duty are discussed below under ten headings, (a)–(j). **14–037**

(c) *Effecting insurance which does not meet the client's requirements*

Add a new paragraph **14–046A**:

Rule 4.3.1 of the Insurance: Conduct of Business sourcebook provides that: "An insurance intermediary must take reasonable steps to ensure that, if in the course of insurance mediation activities it makes any personal recommendation to a customer to buy or sell a non-investment insurance contract, the personal recommendation is suitable for the customer's demands and needs at the time the personal recommendation is made." Breach of this rule gives rise to a cause of action at the suit of a private person (see paragraph 14–008 above). Further, rule 4.3.2 of the sourcebook imposes an obligation on the insurance intermediary to seek "such information about the customer's circumstances and objectives as might reasonably be expected to be relevant in enabling the insurance intermediary to identify the customer's requirements." **14–046A**

Add to NOTE 48: Rule 4.3.2 of the Insurance: Conduct of Business sourcebook imposes an obligation on an insurance intermediary to seek "such information about the customer's circumstances and objectives as might reasonably be expected to be relevant in enabling the insurance intermediary to identify the customer's requirements." **14–051**

Add new paragraph **14–055A**:

14–055A   In *William Jackson & Sons Ltd. v. Oughtred & Harrison (Insurance) Ltd.*
[2002] Lloyd's Rep. I.R. 230 (Morison J.), the claimant suffered a loss at a time
when its premises were greatly under-insured. The premises had been valued
by an independent firm of surveyors. That valuation was negligently low.
Thereafter the premises were developed and the level of insurance was varied
as the development progressed based on the cost of the building works. The
judge rejected the claimant's allegation that the brokers were negligent in failing to advise the claimant to have a further valuation carried out at some stage
during the development work. Nor were the brokers negligent in failing to raise
the possibility of an alternate form of insurance cover for a part of the site
which they knew was going to be demolished during the insurance year.

(f) Failure to disclose material facts to the insurers

14–060   Add to NOTE 79: "; *Assicurazioni Generali v. Arab Insurance Group* [2003]
2 Lloyd's Rep. I.R. 131 (CA)."

14–064   Add to NOTE 86: Rule 4.3.2 of the Insurance: Conduct of Business sourcebook states that: "In assessing the customer's demands and needs, the insurance intermediary must. . . explain to the customer his duty to disclose all
circumstances material to the insurance and the consequences of any failure
to make such a disclosure, both before the non-investment insurance contract
commences and throughout the duration of the contract; and take account
of the information that the customer discloses."

*(h) Failing to keep the client properly informed as to the existence
or terms of cover*

Add new paragraph **14–074A**:

14–074A   A claimant who suffers a loss while uninsured may put his case on the basis
that, had he known that he was uninsured, then he would have taken greater care
to avoid the loss which he suffered. In *Sharif v. Garrett & Co.* [2001] EWCA 1269,
[2002] Lloyd's Rep. I.R. 11 (for the facts see paragraph 14–113A below), the
Court of Appeal indicated that such a claim is unlikely to succeed. For an
insured is required to act in the same way as a prudent uninsured. Accordingly,
an insurance broker cannot be expected to foresee that someone who thinks he
is insured would take different precautions if he knew he was uninsured.

(i) Failing to give proper advice

14–082   Add: The extent of a broker's duty to advise depends on the relevant surrounding circumstances. For example, a broker acting for a large organisation
with an experienced property department will not be expected to give the
same level of advice as one acting for an individual or small company. See
William Jackson & Sons Ltd v. Oughtred & Harrison (Insurance) Ltd [2002]
Lloyd's Rep. I.R. 230 (Morison J.) (for the facts of which see paragraph
14–055A above).

Add new heading (j) and new paragraph **14–085A**:

(j) *Failing to submit a claim to the insurer*

Typically when an insured suffers a loss he will inform his broker of the **14–085A** fact, and will rely on his broker to notify his insurer as required. The broker must take care to ensure that he notifies the correct insurer, complies with any time-limits for notifications (so far as that is still possible), and complies with any other notification requirements. In *Alexander Forbes Europe Ltd v. SBJ Ltd* [2003] Lloyd's Rep. I.R. 432 (David Mackie Q.C. sitting as a deputy High Court judge), the brokers were found to have acted negligently in failing to notify circumstances to the insurer based on information received from the insured. The judge described the duties of a broker who has received information from an insured as follows:

"Brokers owe duties going beyond those of a post box. It was for the brokers to get a grip on the proposed notification, to appraise it and to ensure that the information was relayed to the right place in the correct form . . . it was the duty of [the brokers] to have a strategy in place . . . that ensured that when such information was received from clients, the broker was alive to making such notifications accurately and promptly."

3. Damages

(b) *Causation*

(i) *Intervening error or omission of the claimant*

Add new NOTE 71A at end of paragraph: In *Stowers v. GA Bonus Plc* **14–091** [2003] Lloyd's Rep. P.N. 402 (H.H.J. Knight Q.C.) the insurer successfully avoided the claimant's policy for material non-disclosure, on the ground that his proposal form was incomplete. The claimant alleged that his brokers should have noticed that the proposal form was incomplete and queried this with him. His claim against the brokers failed on the ground (among others) that even if the brokers had queried the incompleteness of the proposal form with the claimant, he would not have made any further disclosure. Thus the insurer would have been entitled to avoid the policy in any event.

(ii) *Where the claimant would not have been insured in any event*

Add new paragraph **14–098A**:

Claimant would not have complied with a policy condition. If a claimant **14–098A** alleges that a broker failed to advise him of a particular condition or warranty in a policy, then he must go on to show that, had he been properly advised, he would have complied with that condition or warranty. The claim in *Bhopal v. Sphere Drake Insurance plc* [2002] Lloyd's Rep. I.R. 413 (CA), failed on that basis. In that case the insurers denied liability on the grounds of the insured's breach of a heating warranty. The insured made a claim against his brokers in negligence alleging that they had failed to give him any explanation as to the crucial significance and effect of the warranty. The claim was summarily dismissed on the basis that, on the evidence, the inexorable conclusion was that no advice on the part of the brokers about the effect of the warranty would have led the insured to act differently.

(c) *Foreseeability*

Add new paragraph **14–113A**:

14–113A   The issue of foreseeability will arise where an uninsured claimant puts his case on the basis that, if he had been aware he was uninsured, then he would have taken greater care to avoid the loss which he suffered. In *Sharif v. Garrett & Co.* [2001] EWCA 1269, [2002] Lloyd's Rep. I.R. 11, a claim against solicitors, the Court of Appeal had to consider the claimant's prospects of success in an earlier claim against his insurance brokers which had been struck out for want of prosecution. The Court found that the claimant had negligible prospects of success in his claim against the brokers which had been put on the basis that, if he had known he was uninsured, he would have taken further precautions to avoid the loss. For an insured is required to act in the same way as a prudent uninsured. Accordingly, an insurance broker cannot be expected to foresee that someone who thinks he is insured would take different precautions if he knew he was uninsured.

(i) *Measure of damages*

14–115   Add new NOTE 16A at the end of the first sentence: In *Alexander Forbes Europe Ltd v. SBJ Ltd* [2003] Lloyd's Rep. I.R. 432, David Mackie Q.C. (sitting as a deputy High Court judge) commented on the proper approach to the assessment of damages as follows (at 443): "I am not strictly concerned with what as a matter of law a claimant was entitled to under a policy but with what, on the balance of probabilities, would have occurred had there been no breach of duty".

Add new paragraph **14–120A**:

14–120A   The central issue in *Aneco* was the scope of the duty of care owed by the brokers, *i.e.* whether it was limited to the giving of specific information, or extended to advising the client whether or not to enter into the transaction. The brokers advised on the availability of reinsurance. However, and this was the determinative point, the availability of reinsurance was indicative of the market's assessment of the risk and thus the merits of the transaction. Accordingly, the duty to advise on the availability of reinsurance encompassed a duty to advise on the merits of the transaction. If the brokers had correctly advised the client that reinsurance was not available, then the transaction would not have proceeded at all. Therefore, the brokers were liable for all the losses suffered by the client as a result of entering into the transaction.

14–124   Add: In *Sharif v. Garrett & Co.* [2001] EWCA 1269, [2002] Lloyd's Rep. I.R. 11, a claim against solicitors, the Court of Appeal had to consider the value of the claimant's earlier claim which had been struck out for want of prosecution. The earlier claim was a claim against insurance brokers for failing to obtain insurance cover. In assessing the value of that lost claim, the court held that the factors which would have affected the quantum of the claim against the brokers included the facts that the insured would almost certainly have had to pay a much larger premium to obtain cover, and that they would probably have had to pay for expensive security measures and take a share of any risk as a condition of obtaining cover.

Add new NOTE 60A at the end of the paragraph: In *GE Reinsurance Corp*   **14–127**
v. New Hampshire Insurance [2003] EWHC 302 (unreported), Langley J. considered whether the reinsured was contributorily negligent in failing to spot a problem in the wording of its reinsurance slip. He held that it was not: in a novel type of transaction the onus was on the broker "to get it right" and it would not be fair to attribute fault to the reinsured in failing to spot the problem.

Add new sub-heading (iii) and new paragraphs **14–132** and **14–133**:

(iii) *Mitigation of damages*

A claimant cannot recover damages in respect of any loss which he ought   **14–132**
reasonably to have avoided. In an insurance brokers' negligence action an issue which a claimant will often have to consider is whether or not he is obliged to commence proceedings against his insurer in an attempt to mitigate his loss. For example, if the insurer has avoided the policy as a result of a non-disclosure for which the broker is responsible, should the insured commence proceedings to challenge the insurer's entitlement to avoid?

In *Alexander Forbes Europe Ltd. v. SBJ Ltd.* [2003] Lloyd's Rep. I.R. 432,   **14–133**
David Mackie Q.C. (sitting as a deputy High Court judge) rejected the brokers' argument that the insured had failed to mitigate its loss by failing to sue its insurer. He commented (at 443) that: "While there is no invariable rule that a claimant does not have to embark on litigation as part of mitigating damage this is in practice generally the case." He went on to approve the section headed "generous treatment of the claimant" at paragraph 10–317 above.

Add new section 4, and new paragraph **14–134**:

4. CLAIMS FOR CONTRIBUTION

Claims against insurance brokers do not often give rise to claims for an   **14–134**
indemnity or contribution under the Civil Liability (Contribution) Act 1978. However, such a claim was brought in *Hurstwood Developments Ltd v. Motor & General* [2001] EWCA 1785, [2002] Lloyd's Rep. I.R. 185. In that case the claimant was a design and build contractor. On the advice of a third party, HHB, it had used a particular process for the construction of a factory. The factory suffered subsidence and remedial works had to be carried out. The claimant brought proceedings against its insurance brokers alleging that the brokers had failed to procure appropriate insurance for its work, with the result that it was obliged to carry out the remedial works at its own expense. The brokers issued Part 20 proceedings against HHB pursuant to section 1(1) of the Civil Liability (Contribution) Act 1978, alleging that any loss suffered by the claimant and claimed against them was caused by HHB's negligence and/or breach of contract in recommending an

inappropriate construction process. The judge struck out the brokers' Part 20 claim, but the Court of Appeal allowed the brokers' appeal, finding that the damage for which the brokers and HBB were liable was the same. However, in *Royal Brompton NHS Trust v. Hammond* [2002] 1 W.L.R. 1397, the House of Lords held that *Hurstwood* was wrongly decided.

CHAPTER 15

ACCOUNTANTS AND AUDITORS

1. Introduction

15–002   Add: The emerging scandals in the United States concerning Enron and WorldCom have heightened awareness within the United Kingdom of the importance of audit independence and of the role of audit committees. In January 2003 the DTI's Co-ordinating Group on Audit and Accounting Issues submitted its Final Report. The proposals made in this Report and elsewhere in the financial press include restrictions on the freedom of auditors to provide non-audit work, rotation of audit firms (or at least of partners within audit firms), a greater role for audit committees (made up of non-executive directors) in recommending auditors and dealing with them, wider powers for auditors to obtain information from directors and employees and criminal sanctions against directors and employees who do not provide information. During the same month, the Higgs Review on non-executive directors and the Smith report for the Financial Reporting Council on audit committees were also published. The DTI is currently reviewing the regulatory regime of the accountancy profession. The latest information can be found on the DTI's website: "Company Law and Investigations: Post-Enron Initiatives" (www.dti.gov.uk/cld/post_enron.htm).

15–004   Add: On July 10, 2003 the Government announced plans for reforming company law in the aftermath of Enron. Details may be found on the DTI's website: "New Companies Legislation" (www.dti.gov.uk/companiesbill/index.htm).

2. Duties

(a) *The statutory context*

(i) *Companies legislation: the company audit*

15–011   Add: In *Man Nutzfahrzeuge AG v. Freightliner Ltd*. 2004 PNLR 19, [2003] EWHC 2245 (Comm), Cooke J. focussed on one of the purposes of an audit being to give information to the shareholders as a body. Where there is only one shareholder, in practice he may be able to control the administration of the company (*e.g.* by dismissing employees). Hence it was arguable that the loss caused by the auditor's negligence extended to the shareholder's failure to take the steps which he would have taken, had he been alerted to the employee's defalcations.

15–023   Add: The time limit for objecting to an auditor's resignation statement under section 394 is mandatory: *P & P Design plc v. Price Waterhouse Coopers*, Ferris J. [2002] 2 BCLC 648; [2002] EWHC 446 (Ch).

(b) *Duties to client*

(i) *Contractual duties*

15–031   Add: In *Nederlandse Reassurantie Groep Holding BV v. Bacon & Woodrow* [1997] L.R.L.R. 678, a firm of accountants was retained to carry out a "due diligence" exercise on the take-over of a reinsurance company. Colman J. held (at 745), having regard to the factual matrix and to the purpose for which the advice was sought, that the standard of care required was "somewhat higher than that to be expected from accountants whose function was to advise a company in respect of its annual accounts or its annual setting of loss reserves". *Fawkes-Underwood v. Hamiltons* (unreported, March 24, 1997, Goudie Q.C.) is an example of a contract which imposed a higher duty on an accountant than that usually imposed on an auditor. In this case the accountant was advising on investment in a Lloyd's syndicate.

Add: One consequence of the fall-out from Enron has been the ongoing dispute between the Office of Fair Trading and the Big Four firms as to whether auditors should be permitted to limit their liability. The OFT has refused so far to countenance a cap on liability.   **15–032**

Add: An auditor auditing the accounts of a group has a duty to be satisfied with the accounts of the subsidiary companies in so far as they are relevant to the group: *ADT v. Binder Hamlyn* [1996] BCC 808 at 836.   **15–033**

(iii) *Fiduciary duties*

Add: In *Pilmer v. Duke Group Ltd* [2001] 2 BCLC 773, an accountant produced a report as required by Listing Rules for the purposes of a take-over of one company by another. The acquiring company alleged that the accountant was in breach of fiduciary duty in making his report. The High Court of Australia held (by majority) that no fiduciary duty had been owed by the accountant. Fiduciary duties are usually proscriptive rather than prescriptive. There are specific prohibitions (such as not acting for two clients with conflicting interests) rather than a positive requirement to act in the best interests of a client. Although an accountant required by Listing Rules to make a report had to be independent, the mere fact that he hoped to gain more work from a former client did not compromise his independence; there was therefore no basis for alleging breach of fiduciary duty. Kirby J. (dissenting) said that the accountant's duty to report for the purpose of Listing Rules was fiduciary (in the sense of imposing a duty of loyalty) and that he could only discharge that duty by giving a negative report or refusing to act. The case is discussed by Nolan and Prentice, (2002) 118 L.Q.R. 180.   **15–039**

One important reason why claimants may seek to allege a breach of fiduciary duty is that contributory negligence is no defence. For a recent discussion of this point, see the article by Mulheron: "Contributory Negligence in Equity: should fiduciaries accept all the blame?", 2003 P.N. 421.

Add: See also *Koch Shipping Inc v. Richards Butler*, [2003] PNLR 11 (C.A. held that the risk of an experienced solicitor committing a breach of confidentiality in acting for the other side was fanciful).   **15–044**

(c) *Duties to third parties*

(i) *Overview*

Add: Some auditors have now started to add the following words to their audit reports so to reflect the basic rule as set out in this paragraph: **15–045**

"This report is made solely to the Company's members, as a body, in accordance with Section 235 of the Companies Act 1985. Our audit work has been undertaken so that we might state to the company's members those matters we are required to state to them in an Auditor's report and for no other purpose. To the fullest extent permitted by law, we do not accept or assume responsibility to anyone other than the company and the company's members as a body, for our audit work, for this report, or for the opinions we have formed."

15–049   Add: *Customs & Excise Commissioners v. Barclays Bank plc* [2004] EWHC 122 (Comm Ct), *The Times*, February 11, 2004, was a claim, not against an auditor, but against a bank for loss caused by breach of a freezing order. Its relevance in the present context is that Colman J. considered Sir Brian Neill's three tests in *BCCI v. Price Waterhouse*. He said that the assumption of responsibility test was especially appropriate in cases of negligent misrepresentation or professional negligence causing purely economic loss where there was a need to identify the individual or group to whom the duty was owed. The incremental test was not an independent test but was a cross-check. There may be cases where the nexus between the parties is not akin to contract but is more oblique. In such cases it may be unhelpful to adopt an extended definition of assumption of responsibility in order to see whether the defendant has "crossed the line", since this was likely to be unduly constricting. *Smith v. Bush* is an example of a case which was not decided on the basis of being akin to contract, but on the basis of proximity; in such a case responsibility is not voluntarily assumed but is imposed by law. Therefore one should start by asking whether the relationship is akin to contract. If the answer is yes, one should ask whether there has been an assumption of responsibility; if the answer is no, one should ask whether the relationship is sufficiently proximate to justify imposing a duty.

15–051   NOTE 40: Add: *Man Nutzfahrzeuge v. Freightliner* (paragraph 15–011 above).

(ii) *Caparo*

15–061   Add: See *Guan Xin* and *Temseel* (paragraph 15–124 below).

(iii) *Factors which may be relevant*

15–065   Add: In *Royal Bank of Scotland plc v. Bannerman*, [2003] P.N.L.R. 6, the Court of Session held, when dismissing an application to strike out, that in order to show a duty of care owed by the auditor to the company's bankers, it was not necessary to prove that the auditor expressly intended that the accounts be relied on by the bank. It was sufficient that the audited accounts were provided to the company in the knowledge that it was likely (i) that the accounts would be passed to the bank for the purpose satisfying itself that the company was able to continue as a going concern and (ii) that the bank would place reliance on the accounts for that purpose. The court placed reliance on the fact that the auditor had not disclaimed responsibility to the bank.

(iv) *Categories of advisee*

15–080   Add: In the *Barings* litigation (*Barings v. Coopers & Lybrand* [2002] P.N.L.R. 16), Evans-Lombe J. set out a definition of the "purpose" test and held that the auditors in that case owed no duty of care to other companies in the group.

NOTE 21: Add reference to *Guan Xin* (see paragraph 15–124 below) and to **15–083**
Barings (see paragraph 15–148 below).

Add: In *Independents' Advantage Insurance Co. Ltd. v. Cook* [2004] **15–084**
P.N.L.R. 3, C.A.: the defendant audited accounts for a travel agency in the knowledge that the accounts would be submitted to ABTA and IATA and that the requisite travel bond might be provided by an insurer such as IAIC. Although there was no allegation that the defendant had the particular insurer in mind, the law was still in a transitional state and therefore it would be wrong to strike out without knowing all the facts.

Add: *Law Society v. Sephton* [2004] P.N.L.R. 25; [2003] EWHC 544, is **15–085**
another case in which the Law Society sued a reporting accountant. Briggs Q.C. held that in principle the Law Society might suffer loss before it made the decision to pay out any money from the Compensation Fund. On the facts, he held that time ran (in respect of most of the claims) from the date when the Law Society relied on the report by not taking steps to intervene in the firm's practice.

Add: *Hughes v. Colin Richards & Co.* [2004] EWCA Civ 266; [2004] **15–086**
P.N.L.R. 35, the Court of Appeal held that it was strongly arguable that an accountant instructed by parents as trustees of a trust to advise on investments owes a duty to the trustees and not the beneficiaries, but court was not prepared to strike out claim on the particular facts.

(vi) *The Contracts (Rights against Third Parties) Act 1999*

As to whether a third party who relies on audited accounts is able to take **15–088**
the benefit of the 1999 Act, see articles by Burbidge, [2002] P.N. 40 at 59, and Arnull, *ibid.* 146 at 153.

(vii) *The Human Rights Act 1998*

Add: In *Hands v. Coopers & Lybrand* [2001] Lloyds Rep. P.N. 732, it was **15–089**
held that the restrictions on the duty of care embodied in *Caparo* did not breach the claimant's right to a fair hearing under Article 6.
See article by P. Burbridge, "Liability of statutory auditors to third parties—is the European writing on the wall for *Caparo v. Dickman*?" (2002) P.N. 40.
In *Matthews v. Ministry of Defence* [2003] 2 W.L.R. 435, [2003] UKHL 4, the House of Lords considered *Z v. United Kingdom* and held that Crown immunity was a substantive, not a procedural, bar with the result that there was no breach of Article 6.

(d) *The standard of skill and care*

(ii) *Auditing*

For a recent application of the Singapore equivalent of the SASs to a claim **15–093**
against an auditor, see *Barings*, noted at paragraph 15–148 below.

(e) *Limitation of liability*

15–100   See paragraph 15–002 above. See also by Arnull: "Professional advisers and limitations on liability", [2003] P.N. 536

3. LIABILITY FOR BREACH OF DUTY

(a) *Auditing*

15–102   *et seq.* See article by Hemraj: "Audit failure due to negligent audit: lessons from DTI investigations" in (2003) Comp. Law. 45.

(i) *Planning, control and recording*

15–103   NOTE 4, replace the reference to SAS 200 with the following: SAS 220.

(b) *Other breaches of duty*

15–117   Add: In *Goldstein v. Levy Gee* [2003] PNLR 35, Lewison J. held that negligence in the process of valuation is irrelevant, as long as the end result is within the range of reasonable values. He applied *Arab Bank v. John D. Wood* (see paragraph 9–059 of the main work). (For a discussion of *Goldstein*, see article by Dugdale, [2004] P.N. 21.)

15–119   Add: *Wade v. Poppleton & Appleby* [2004] 1 BCLC 674, is an example of the duty of care owed by an insolvency practitioner to the company and its shareholders.

Add new paragraph **15–119A**:

15–119A   An auditor's working papers belong to the auditor: *Chantrey Martin v. Martin* [1953] 2 Q.B. 286. The same goes for an accountant's working papers. However, the Professional Negligence Pre-Action Protocol (White Book Vol. 1 section C7–001) imposes duties on both sides to co-operate in an early exchange of information. If the auditor or accountant refuses to give early disclosure of working papers and the claimant can demonstrate a need for such disclosure in order to be able to plead his case, he may make an application for pre-action disclosure under CPR, rule 31.16. In *Bermuda International Securities Ltd. v. KPMG* [2001] Lloyds Rep. P.N. 392, the Court of Appeal refused to lay down guidelines for early disclosure but said that it may be appropriate in a vast range of cases. See also *Medisys plc v. Arthur Andersen* [2002] P.N.L.R. 538 and *Moresfield Ltd v. Banners*, July 3, 2003, [2003] EWHC 1602 (Ch).

4. DAMAGES

(a) *Remoteness*

(i) *Causation*

The penultimate word in the fourth line should read "as".   **15–124**

Add: in his seminal lecture to the Chancery Bar Association in 1999 entitled "Common sense and causing loss", Lord Hoffmann suggested that there may be policy reasons why an auditor should not be liable for loss caused where his negligence results in the company going into liquidation, since this would be a back-door method of imposing a duty of care upon auditors for the benefit of creditors. This suggestion has been considered by the courts in two cases where they have said that they can see the force of it but are not prepared to decide the point on a strike-out application: *Man Nutzfahrzeuge v. Freightliner* (see paragraph 15–011 above) and *Guang Xin*.

In *Guang Xin Enterprises Ltd v. Kwan Wong Tan* [2002] 2 H.K.L.R.D. 319, a Hong Kong judge of first instance said that the judge in *Sew Hoy* had wrongly applied a "but for" test and had asked the wrong question ("Did the decision to continue trading cause the loss?"). He should have asked: "Was the loss the kind of loss which it was the auditors' duty to guard against?" The H.K. judge took account of the policy argument that indemnity insurance would become prohibitively expensive if he followed the "but for" approach which he said was to be found in *Sew Hoy*. He also said that, since the creditors have no direct cause of action, it would be wrong to give them a claim via the liquidator. He thought that there was a strong argument for saying that, since the auditors' duty is to protect the interests of shareholders as a class, the extent of that liability should be coterminous with their interests, *i.e.* liability should be limited to the value of the shares. On appeal ([2003] 3 HKLRD 527) the judgment was upheld without discussing the critique of *Sew Hoy*.

In *Temseel Holdings Ltd v. Beaumonts Chartered Accountants* [2003] P.N.L.R. 27, [2002] EWHC 2642 (Comm), an auditor applied to strike out a claim. The judge held that it was arguable that he owed two duties: a duty to protect the company itself from the consequences of its own undetected errors, as well as a duty to provide shareholders with information to which they were entitled by statute. He said that *Galoo* does not prevent all trading losses from being recoverable but only those which were not caused by reliance on the negligent audit. The judge cited *Sew Hoy* with approval. (This and other recent cases are discussed in an article by Dugdale: "Auditor's liability to the client: ups and downs", [2003] P.N. 536.)

After *Environment Agency v. Empress Engineering*, add a reference to   **15–125**
Barings (see paragraph 15–148 below).

Add: In *Equitable Life Assurance Society v. Ernst & Young* [2003] P.N.L.R.   **15–126**
23, [2002] EWHC 112 and [2003] EWHC 804, the troubled insurance company brought a claim against its former auditors for negligence in having failed to make provision for the enormous potential liabilities arising from policies with guaranteed annuity rates, and also for having failed to draw the

board's attention to these potential liabilities. The company claimed that, if properly advised, (i) it would (or might) have sold its business before the business became worthless and (ii) it would not have declared bonuses. Langley J., applying *SAAMCO*, struck out the first claim on the ground that the fall in the value of the company's assets was outside the scope of the auditor's responsibility; however he permitted an amendment to allow the claim for bonuses. The C.A. (*The Times*, September 10, 2003, [2003] EWCA Civ 1114) has now allowed an appeal against the striking-out, saying that in an area of developing jurisprudence the claim ought to be permitted to proceed to trial (*cf.* paragraph 15–051 above). C.A. thought it arguable that the "loss of a chance" principles in *Allied Maples* applied.

In *Man Nutzfahrzeuge AG v. Freightliner* (paragraph 15–011 above), the alleged breach of duty was the failure to detect the fraud of a company officer. Cooke J. refused to strike out the claim, saying that it was arguable that the loss caused by further fraud was the very thing from which the auditor should have saved the company, as in *Sasea*.

15–130   Add: In *Sayers v. Clarke Walker* [2002] 2 BCLC 16, an accountant gave advice within his general field of competence but suggested that the client seek a second opinion from a specialist. C.A. held that the client did not break the chain of causation by ignoring this suggestion.

An auditor may be liable for loss which continues after he has retired and a new auditor has been appointed. The question is whether it is the old auditor or the new one who is the effective cause of the loss: see *Barings*, noted at paragraph 15–148 (point 4) below and also *Sasea Finance Ltd. v. KPMG* [2000] 1 All E.R. 676.

(b) *Measure of damages*

15–133   Add: For a recent example of "loss of a chance" applied to auditors, see *Equitable Life*, noted at paragraph 15–126 above.

15–134   Add: *Hanif v. Middleweeks* is reported at [2000] Lloyd's Rep. P.N. 920.

(c) *Heads of damage*

(ii) *Overpayment*

15–137   Add: In *Pilmer v. Duke Group Ltd.* [2001] 2 BCLC 773, a company ("KO") took over another company ("Western") by acquiring the shares in Western in exchange for shares in KO plus cash. KO sued Western's auditor for negligent misstatement in relation to Western's value. H. Ct of Aus. (on appeal from the S. Ct of S. Aus.) held that the measure of damages was limited to the loss suffered by the claimant, KO, rather than by its shareholders. Since KO was not permitted to trade in its own shares which it had allotted to Western's shareholders, its loss extended to the cash which it had paid (less the value received) but did not extend to the value of the shares allotted.

(iii) *Moneys wrongly paid out*

NOTE 37: At the end of the final sentence, add a reference to *Barings* (see **15–138** paragraph 15–148 below). *Segenhoe Ltd v. Akins* is now reported at [2002] Lloyds Rep. P.N. 434.

(vi) *Avoidance of double recovery*

Add: See also *Shaker v. Al-Bedrawi* [2003] Ch. 350, [2002] EWCA Civ 1452, **15–141** which considers whether a claim may be brought by a shareholder as beneficiary of a trust.

Add: *Giles v. Rhind* has been reversed on appeal ([2003] Ch. 618, [2002] **15–142** EWCA Civ 1428). C.A. held that, on the facts of that case, the shareholder's loss was not merely reflective of the company's loss and that the company was not the alter ego of the shareholder. But, even if the loss had been reflective, C.A. held that it was arguable that the shareholder should be entitled to sue if the wrongdoer had made it commercially impossible for the company to sue.

(vii) *Tax advice and returns*

Add: *Slattery v. Moore Stephens*, [2004] PNLR 14, [2003] EWHC 1869 **15–143** (Ch), is a recent example of negligence in relation to alerting a claimant to the tax benefits of receiving payment off-shore. Damages were reduced by 50 per cent for contributory negligence in failing to query a tax refund which would have revealed his mistake in assuming that he was being paid abroad.

In *Grimm v. Newman* [2002] STC 1388, the C.A. held (allowing the accountants' appeal) that although a tax scheme upon which the accountants advised would not have worked, the claimant had failed to establish that any other scheme would have worked and had therefore suffered no loss.

(d) *Contributory negligence and contribution proceedings*

Add: *Eastgate Group Ltd. v. Lindsey Morden Group Inc.* is now reported at **15–147** [2002] 1 W.L.R. 642.

Add: The long-running *Barings* litigation includes a claim by a Singapore **15–148** subsidiary of Barings against its auditors for losses arising from the Leeson fraud. On the application for summary judgment (*Barings v. Coopers & Lybrand* [2002] 2 BCLC 410, [2002] EWHC 461 (Ch)), Evans-Lombe J. held that there was a triable issue as to whether management representations were made with an honest belief in their truthfulness. He went on to say (*obiter*) that, if he had been satisfied that the representations were made without an honest belief in their truthfulness, they would have been made recklessly and hence fraudulently and that this would have been a complete answer to the company's claim against the auditor for negligence. The basis of this argument is as follows: the company has a claim against the auditor for negligence; the auditor has a counterclaim against the company which is vicariously liable for the fraud of its employees; the auditor's negligence is no defence to that claim for fraud; and accordingly the company's vicarious liability for fraud "trumps" the auditor's liability for negligence.

At the trial of the proceedings ([2003] PNLR 34, [2003] EWHC 1319 (Ch)) Evans-Lombe J., held *inter alia* as follows:

1. The auditors were not negligent, either in failing to see this as a high-risk audit or in failing to devise procedures for the specific purpose of detecting unauthorised trading. However, they were negligent in failing to detect that a significant payment had been credited to the first day of the new year instead of the last day of the previous year and also in failing to detect that a large sum on the balance sheet was incorrect. If these matters had been detected, this should have led to a train of inquiry which should have uncovered the fraud.

2. In the context of a contract, the question of vicarious liability depends upon whether the employee has acted within the scope of his authority. In the context of a tort claim, the question depends upon whether the employee has acted within the scope of his employment. There needs to be some connection between the wrongful act and the employment but this was satisfied in this case, since Leeson's duties as manager extended to the provision of information to the auditors. The judge declined to follow *Dairy Containers* (see paragraph 15–150 in the main work), where Thomas J. had held that the company was not vicariously liable for the actions of employees in concealing the frauds of other employees, since this was "dramatically and deliberately hostile to the employer's interest". He also declined to fashion a special rule of attribution that reflected the special status of the auditor (see Note 68 to paragraph 15–151): instead he adopted the reasoning in his earlier judgment.

3. As stated above, the judge had held on the application for summary judgment that, if an employee for whom the company was vicariously liable made fraudulent representations which were a cause of the loss, the company was not allowed to say that the auditor's negligence was also a cause. However, it was alleged at trial that the auditor owed an additional duty to the company to investigate the *bona fides* of the representations and was negligent in failing to realise that they were fraudulent. The judge held that this additional allegation brought the matter within the principle in *Environment Agency v. Empress Engineering* (see paragraph 15–125 in the main work) and *Reeves v. Commissioner of Police of the Metropolis* [2000] 1 A.C. 360. In other words, answers to questions of causation will differ according to the purpose for which the question is asked; this in turn depends on the purpose and scope of the rule by which responsibility is being attributed. If the auditor was himself under a duty to investigate the *bona fides* of the dishonest answers being given by the company's employee, then the company *is* allowed to say that the auditor's negligence was also a cause of the loss.

    [We think it likely that this will not be the last word on the subject. The approach taken on the application for summary judgment has serious implications for claimants wishing to pursue auditors. It would mean that the auditor would wholly escape liability by reason of the fraud of the very employees concerning whose frauds he had a duty to warn the company. The extra twist added in this judgment redresses the balance to some extent by providing a mechanism for the loss to be shared.]

4. The auditor may be liable for losses which continue after the audit engagement is at an end. However, subsequent negligence by the company's officers or employees may break the chain of causation. The board is responsible for the negligence of its delegates, which may include other companies in the group.

5. The judge did not follow the approach of McHugh J. in *Esanda* (paragraph 15–083, NOTE 21), who had said that there were policy reasons for limiting the kind of loss which falls within the scope of the duty. This would narrow "scope of duty" further than *Caparo*.

6. The extent of the reduction for contributory negligence will depend on the nature of the auditor's duty: the question is whether it was reasonable for the company to rely on him to protect it from the damage in question. On the facts the judge made a deduction of 50 per cent for the company's failure to have a proper system of checks and balances, rising to 80 per cent for other specific failings.

7. If the negligence of other companies in the Group is taken into account as contributory negligence, the same cannot also found a claim for contribution.

8. The company did not have to give credit for profits made as a result of Leeson's activities by other companies in the group. The principle in *McAlpine v. Panatown* [2001] 1 A.C. 518 (whereby a company is permitted in certain circumstances to sue for losses suffered by other companies in the group) does not apply in reverse. Even if it did, since the claimant company did not itself benefit in this case.

9. Where the company has sued auditor X for overlapping loss and has compromised that claim, may it appropriate X's payment to losses which do not overlap with its claim against auditor Y? The court applied the ordinary contractual principles of appropriation: as long as it is made in good faith, the court will accept it.

10. For the purpose of section 727 of the Companies Act, it is possible to have acted reasonably even though the auditor was negligent, *e.g.* if the negligence was minor or technical. In this case there were numerous allegations of breach which were not proved. The proven breaches were lapses in an otherwise proper audit; hence section 727 applies. In exercising the discretion under section 727, it is relevant to consider the financial consequences of the damages. This enables the court to give credit for gains made by other companies in the group.

Add: In *Pilmer v. Duke Group Ltd* [2001] 2 BCLC 713, the High Court of **15–151** Australia allowed an appeal from *Duke Group Ltd v. Pilmer* on two issues (noted at paragraphs 15–039 and 15–137 above).

(f) *Statutory relief*

15–153   See *Barings* (noted at paragraph 15–148 above).

Add: In *Re MDA Investment Management Ltd.* [2004] 1 BCLC 217, Park J. confirmed that the test under section 727 as to whether the officer had acted reasonably was an objective one.

CHAPTER 16

MEMBERS' AND MANAGING AGENTS AT LLOYD'S

1. GENERAL

(b) Duties to Client

(ii) Duties independent of contract

Add: Where the members' agent is a company, then in the absence of any **16–012**
assumption of personal responsibility, a director of the company will not owe
a personal duty of care. For example, in *Noel v. Poland* [2002] Lloyd's Rep.

I.R. 30 (Toulson J.), the claimant alleged that she had been misled into becoming and remaining a name by the defendants, directors of the members' agent. Her claim was summarily dismissed on the basis that any arguable case which she might have lay against the company and could not be brought against the defendants personally.

(iii) *Fiduciary duties*

16–015　　Add new NOTE 44A at the end of the first sentence: In *Sphere Drake Insurance Ltd. v. Euro International Underwriting Ltd. (The Times*, August 11, 2003) Thomas J. held that there was a fiduciary relationship between the members of Lloyd's syndicates and the active underwriters of those syndicates.

CHAPTER 17

INFORMATION TECHNOLOGY PROFESSIONALS

2. DUTIES

(a) *Duties to client*

(iv) *Implementation and testing*

Add new paragraph **17–037A:**

17–037A   What constitutes a "reasonable time" within which to complete implementation was considered by Seymour QC in *Astea (UK) Ltd. v. Timegroup Ltd.*[86a] The claimant was a supplier of software packages for use in call centres, which could be used independently or linked to other software systems. The defendant ran a call centre and wished to replace its existing computer system with a number of software packages including a package supplied by the claimant. The claimant and defendant entered into a licence and support agreement whereby the claimant granted the defendant a licence to use the software and agreed to provide implementation services, including configuring the software and integrating it with the other software packages. At trial it was agreed that the claimant's obligation was to complete that implementation within a reasonable time. After some months of implementation the defendant declined to pay the claimant's invoices and alleged that the claimant's delay in completing implementation constituted a repudiatory breach of contract. The claimant sued for its outstanding fees and the defendant counterclaimed for damages for repudiatory breach. Judge Seymour held that it was necessary to take a broad consideration of what in all the circumstances was a reasonable time for performance, and that the following factors should be taken into account:

(1)   any estimate given by the performing party of how long it would take it to perform;

(2)   whether any estimate had been exceeded, and if so in what circumstances;

(3)   whether the party for whose benefit the relevant obligation was to be performed needed to participate in the performance or not at all;

(4)   whether it was necessary for third parties to collaborate with the performing party in order to enable it to perform;

(5)   what exactly was the cause, or what were the causes, of the delay to performance.

[86a] Masons Computer Law Reports [2004] 1–17, [2003] EWHC 725.

On the particular facts in *Astea (UK) Ltd. v. Timegroup Ltd.* Judge Seymour held that at the time when the defendant purported to accept the claimant's repudiation a reasonable time for performance had not passed. He was particularly influenced by the fact that the defendant itself was late in preparing to receive the software, and that the claimant had been willing and helpful throughout the testing period. Judge Seymour went on to conclude (*obiter*) that even if a reasonable time for performance had passed, the delay did not deprive the defendant of substantially the whole benefit of the contract, and, since the claimant intended to complete the implementation, and was applying appropriate resources, it would not have represented a repudiatory breach of contract.

(v) *The importance of co-operation between the parties*

In the 2nd cumulative supplement reference was made under this para-   **17–043**
graph 17–043, and also under paragraphs 17–088 and 17–111, to the decision of *H.H.J. Seymour QC in Co-operative Group (CWS) Ltd. v. International Computers Ltd.* [2003] EWHC 1 (TCC). In December 2003 the Court of Appeal overturned that decision and ordered a re-trial. Accordingly in this 3rd supplement references to that decision have been deleted, although the approach taken by Judge Seymour, particularly in relation to "bugs" and "bedding in" (referred to under paragraph 17–088 of the 2nd supplement, and probably not affected by the appeal) may be of interest to readers pending any such re-trial.

(vi) *Duties of support*

Add new paragraph **17–044A**:

Problems can arise post implementation where the client's contractual enti-   **17–044A**
tlement, and in particular the precise deliverables under the contract, are not precisely defined. An example arose in *Psychometric Services Ltd. v. Merant International Ltd*,[98a] in which the dispute concerned whether the claimant was entitled to access to software source code. The claimant provided psychometric testing services for companies interested in assessing job applicants. The defendant agreed to develop websites for the claimant which would enable it to offer companies the opportunity to test candidates on their own home computers via the internet. The claimant secured a number of lucrative clients for the service, but the defendant was unable to overcome defects in the software. The claimant wished to approach a third party to remedy the defects, but needed access to the source code to do so, which the defendant declined to provide. The claimant therefore sought an interim injunction requiring delivery up of the source code, relying on a number of provisions of the software agreement including (a) its entitlement to the "software deliverables" and (b) the provisions in relation to ownership of the source code. Granting the injunction, Laddie J. held that the claimant had an arguable claim to access to the source code under (b) but not under (a), since, in a normal software development context, the term "software deliverables" would include the object code, but not the source code.

[98a] Masons Computer Law Reports [2003] 23–24; [2002] F.S.R. 8.

(vii) *Staff training*

17–045   Add new Note 98A: An example of a supplier being criticised for breach of its duty to train the purchaser's employees in the use of the software is *SAM Business Systems Ltd. v. Hedley & Co.* (TCC, H.H.J. Bowsher QC, December 19, 2002, unreported), at paragraph 83 of the judgment. The case also offers an example of a representation made by the supplier during the pre-contractual phase that the system was going to be operable by people who were not technically qualified (paragraph 21 of the judgment). Both of these factors were invoked to defeat the supplier's contention that the system was not working properly because of the purchaser's defective operation of the system.

3. Standard of Care and Breach

(b) *"Bugs" and "bedding in"—inevitable defects and software*

17–088   Add to Note 48: The attitude of the courts in relation to standard software has recently been demonstrated in the decision of H.H.J. Bowsher Q.C. in *SAM Business Systems Ltd v. Hedley & Co.* (TCC, December 19, 2002, unreported). In that case the software in question was called InterSet and was described by the judge as:

> "not as simple as going into a shop and buying a shrink wrapped package, but it is not a bespoke system. The customer can make choices between certain modules and certain services, but it is sold as a developed system." (paragraph 8 of judgment)

In relation to the acceptability of bugs within the software the judge said this:

> " . . . InterSet was sold as a developed system allegedly already working well in other places. This is a much stronger case than St Albans against toleration of bugs. I am in no doubt that if a software system is sold as a tried and tested system it should not have any bugs in it and if there are any bugs they should be regarded as defects. Of course, if the defects are speedily remedied without charge, it may be that there will be no consequential damage." (paragraph 20 of judgment)

4. Causation

17–095   Add: An additional causation question and one related to the implied duty of co-operation upon the purchaser (see paragraphs 17–038 to 17–043) is whether or not the purchaser would in any event have been ready to implement the new system at the contractually agreed date. In the *CWS* case (see addition to paragraph 17–088, above), the judge found (at paragraphs 239 and 266 of the judgment) that the purchaser would have been unable to implement the new system in time owing to deficiencies in its own understanding of and preparation for the new system.

Add new NOTE 55A at the end of penultimate sentence: However, these   **17–097**
problems were given short shrift by H.H.J. Bowsher Q.C. in the case of
Horace Holman Group Ltd v. Sherwood International Group Ltd (TCC,
November 7, 2001, unreported), in which damages were awarded for various
"aspirational" heads of loss. See discussion of this case in paragraph 17–104,
below. The same judge adopted a similar approach in *SAM Business Systems
Ltd v. Hedley & Co.* (discussed further at paragraph 17–088, above).

5. REMEDIES

(d) *Time of the essence?*

Add: It seems however that the difficulties in proving such losses are far   **17–104**
from insuperable. In *Horace Holman Group Ltd. v. Sherwood International
Group Ltd.* (TCC, November 7, 2001, unreported), H.H.J. Bowsher Q.C.
awarded the claimant more than £2.6 million in damages, under heads of
loss such as "predicted in-house savings", "audit savings not made", and
"staff not made redundant earlier". Under this last head of damage the
claimant was awarded over £1.7 million in relation to staff costs they would
have saved had the system in question worked as it was supposed to. The
claimants also recovered a significant amount under the head of loss "Time
wasted by Directors and Staff". The judge considered the leading case of
Tate & Lyle v. GLC [1982] 1 W.L.R. 149 (which held that a court could not
award damages under this head in the absence of good evidence on the
point), but distinguished the case thus:

> "the case before me differs from the case before Forbes J in that while he had no evi-
> dence of the amount of time spent, there is before me evidence in the form of a
> reconstruction from memory of events from the past. I cannot and do not say, in
> the absence of records there is to be no recovery." (paragraph 73)

The arguments of the parties were rehearsed in paragraphs 74 to 77 of the
judgment, before the judge concluded that:

> "I do not accept the distinction that [D's expert] seeks to make between short and
> long periods of wasted time nor his distinction between senior and less senior
> posts. In all cases, the claimants were paying for time which was to be a benefit to
> them and they lost the benefit of that time . . . it is unrealistic to try to distinguish
> between profit makers and non-profit makers as the defendants have sought to
> do." (paragraph 78 of judgment—Damages of £135,567.95 awarded under this
> head).

Accordingly it would seem that the courts are evincing a willingness to
recognise the "aspirational" nature of software contracts and to award aspirational or expectation damages more readily in this area of law. The application of the defendant for permission to appeal *Holman* was rejected by
Dyson L.J. on February 7, 2002—see [2002] EWCA Civ 170. H.H.J. Bowsher
Q.C. reiterated his commitment to the approach in *Holman* when assessing
(*obiter*) damages in the *SAM v. Hedley* case.

6. EXCLUSION AND LIMITATION OF LIABILITY

Add new paragraph **17–123A**:

17–123A   The recent Court of Appeal decision in *Watford Electronics Ltd. v. Sanderson CFL Ltd.* [2001] 1 All E.R. (Comm) 696 has set out guidance on the approach to be taken in considering whether exclusion and entire agreement clauses are reasonable as between commercial entities. In *SAM Business Systems Ltd v. Hedley & Co.* (TCC, H.H.J. Bowsher Q.C., December 19, 2002) counsel for the claimant expressed the view that the *Watford* case was decided *per incuriam*. Judge Bowsher dealt with the matter thus:

"Unlike the agreement in *Watford Electronics Limited v Sanderson CFL Limited*, the Licence agreement in this case did not include an agreement 'that no statement or representations made by either party have been relied upon by the other in agreeing to enter into the contract.'" (paragraph 47).

"The clause in this case did not include an acknowledgement of non-reliance such as in the Watford case, and 'so there was no evidential estoppel of the sort put forward by Chadwick LJ in [that] case'" (paragraph 48).

"Moreover I find that the 'entire agreement clause' was waived by SAM" (paragraph 49).

" . . . I know of no ground on which it might be argued that *Watford* was decided per incuriam." (paragraph 52).

"As was made plain by Chadwick LJ in *Watford* at page 16 paragraph 50, the reasonableness of each term to which the 1977 Act applies must be considered separately even to the extent of looking to see whether each clause contains one term or more than one, 'although, of course, in considering whether that requirement is satisfied in relation to each term, the existence of the other term in the contract is relevant . . . As I understand it, the effect of [Watford] is that, by way of example, I might find that the virtually total exclusion of liability for breach of warranties is unreasonable but at the same time find that the limitation of the amount of liability to getting one's money back is reasonable.'" (paragraph 62).

In the event the judge found that:

"If SAM had not offered [the] 'standard money back guarantee on licence', I would have regarded the exclusion of liability and entire agreement clauses as quite unreasonable though I would have regarded the limitation of liability to the amount of money paid under the licence agreement as reasonable. But on the evidence before me . . . I find that all of the terms to which objection is taken in the contract were reasonable." (paragraph 72).

On the issue of whether SAM could recover their service charges under the maintenance agreement for putting right defects in relation to which they had successfully excluded their liability, the judge was forthright in his view:

" . . . I cannot see that it is right that SAM should be paid for putting right a defect in respect of which they have excluded liability to pay damages . . . no customer would or should accept liability to pay for rectification of defects existing in goods on delivery even if there was no contractual liability on the part of the supplier to pay damages arising out of those defects . . . Exclusion clauses exclude liability for breach of contract: they do not amount to an agreement that performance has been given by providing equipment that is fit to be maintained: nor do they amount to an agreement that the purchaser should pay for any efforts made by the supplier to put right the defects." (paragraph 78).

Add new paragraph **17–123B**:

It does not appear that the *Watford Electronics* decision has been chal-   **17–123B** lenged in any other reported cases. Whilst the applicability of the decision to exclusion and entire agreement clauses generally has not yet been tested in a reported decision (there does not appear to be any reason for the decision not to be of general application), it certainly remains authoritative in the sphere of computer contracts. The relevant guidance given by Chadwick L.J. was as follows:

"**[31]** In order to decide whether the relevant contract term was a fair and reasonable one to be included having regard to the circumstances which were, or ought reasonably to have been, known to or in the contemplation of the parties when the contract was made it is necessary, as it seems to me, to determine, first, the scope and effect of that term as a matter of construction. In particular, it is necessary to identify the nature of the liability which the term is seeking to exclude or restrict. Whether or not a contract term satisfies the 'requirement of reasonableness' within the meaning of s 11 of the 1977 Act does not fall to be determined in isolation. It falls to be determined where a person is seeking to rely upon the term in order to exclude or restrict his liability in some context to which the earlier provisions of the 1977 Act (or the provisions of s 3 of the 1967 Act) apply.

[54] It seems to me that the starting point in an enquiry whether, in the present case, the term excluding indirect loss was a fair and reasonable one to include in the contract which these parties made is to recognise (i) that there is a significant risk that a non-standard software product, 'customised' to meet the particular marketing, accounting or record-keeping needs of a substantial and relatively complex business (such as that carried on by Watford), may not perform to the customer's satisfaction, (ii) that, if it does not do so, there is a significant risk that the customer may not make the profits or savings which it had hoped to make (and may incur consequential losses arising from the product's failure to perform), (iii) that those risks were, or ought reasonably to have been, known to or in the contemplation of both Sanderson and Watford at the time when the contract was made, (iv) that Sanderson was in the better position to assess the risk that the product would fail to perform but (v) that Watford was in the better position to assess the amount of the potential loss if the product failed to perform, (vi) that the risk of loss was likely to be capable of being covered by insurance, but at a cost, and (vii) that both Sanderson and Watford would have known, or ought reasonably to have known, at the time when the contract was made, that the identity of the party who was to bear the risk of loss (or to bear the cost of insurance) was a factor which would be taken into account in determining the price at which the supplier was willing to supply the product and the price at which the customer was willing to purchase. With those considerations in mind, it is reasonable to expect that the contract will make provision for the risk of indirect or consequential loss to fall on one party or the other. In circumstances in which parties of equal bargaining power negotiate a price for the supply of product under an agreement which provides for the person on whom the risk of loss will fall, it seems to me that the court should be very cautious before reaching the conclusion that the agreement which they have reached is not a fair and reasonable one.

[55] Where experienced businessmen representing substantial companies of equal bargaining power negotiate an agreement, they may be taken to have had regard to the matters known to them. They should, in my view, be taken to be the best judge of the commercial fairness of the agreement which they have made; including the fairness of each of the terms in that agreement. They should be taken to be the best judge on the question whether the terms of the agreement are reasonable. The court should not assume that either is likely to commit his company to an agreement which he thinks is unfair, or which he thinks includes unreasonable terms. Unless satisfied that one party has, in effect, taken unfair advantage of the other—or that a term is so unreasonable that it cannot properly have been understood or considered—the court should not interfere."